BASIC
PERSONAL
COUNSELLING

A Training Manual for Counsellors

Third edition

DAVENPO

I would like to thank my wife, Kathryn (Kitty) Geldard, for her assistance in the preparation of this edition. Her continual support and encouragement, and professional input and advice were invaluable. Additionally, I wish to thank her for drawing the sketches used to illustrate the text.

The work of Ms Julie Clarke, who reviewed the second edition and recommended many detailed changes, improvements, and additions, has helped to significantly enhance the quality of the book. Her meticulous attention to detail and useful suggestions made the work of revision easier and are greatly appreciated.

BASIC
PERSONAL
COUNSELLING

A Training Manual for Counsellors

Third edition

David Geldard

FREE ASSOCIATION BOOKS / LONDON

First published in Great Britain in 1999 by
FREE ASSOCIATION BOOKS
57 Warren Street, London W1P 5PA

A CIP catalogue record for this book is available
from the British Library

ISBN 1 85343 454 X

Printed in the EC by TJ International, Padstow

Contents

Part I
Counselling—an overview

1 What is counselling?

As I sat in front of my computer ready to revise *Basic Personal Counselling*, I remembered why, as a counsellor, I decided to write a book. It seemed to me that there was an absence of a readable textbook for people who wanted to learn basic counselling skills, so I decided to write one. In revising this book, I tried to remember my original goals. By doing this I hope to avoid the use of unnecessary jargon and to succeed in retaining the conversational style of the second edition.

Counselling involves a relationship

Counselling involves a one-to-one relationship between the counsellor and the person seeking help. Sometimes this relationship is conducted face-to-face and sometimes by phone. In this book, I try to parallel some of the qualities of the counselling relationship by remembering that you, the reader, and I, the author, are engaging in a relationship with a purpose. We are both people with our own unique personalities so inevitably we will think sometimes similarly and sometimes differently.

People receiving help from counsellors like to know something about the person who is helping them so that they can have confidence in the help being offered. It is often sufficient for them to know that the counsellor concerned works for a reputable agency. However, I am not writing as a member of a particular association, so I will begin by introducing myself in much the same way as I would when working as a private practice counsellor.

I started my counselling work as a volunteer telephone counsellor for Lifeline in Australia. I later trained as a face-to-face counsellor and graduated in psychology. As a counsellor, I moved from focussing on personal counselling to working with couples and families. More recently, I began to specialise in counselling children, and have co-authored a textbook *Counselling Children*, with my wife Kathryn (Kitty). I find that counselling encourages me to be creative and to use myself as a person. Generally it is stimulating and satisfying, but at times it is stressful and can be exhausting.

Style of writing

I believe in sexual equality and am aware, as I write this book, that I am a male, and that however hard I try, what I write will inevitably be written from a male perspective. Please allow for this if you find that for you, what I have written does not always fit. There are clients and counsellors of both sexes, and alternative ways of writing would be to use combined personal pronouns such as "she/he" or to be ungrammatical and use plural words such as "they" as singular words. However, I do not like either of these approaches because they are not consistent with our spoken language and spoil the flow of the written word. I will therefore sometimes use the female gender (she, her), and at other times use the male gender (he, his).

Why do you want to be a counsellor?

I hope you will enjoy reading this book and find it useful. Because you are reading it, I assume that you are intending to train as a counsellor and as I write I remember how I felt when I first started my training. My feelings and attitudes then were very different from those I have now. However, it was those feelings and attitudes which motivated me to go ahead. I wonder how you feel as you think about your decision to train as a counsellor. What are your motivations? Stop for a minute and think. Ask yourself the question, "Why do I want to be a counsellor?" and, if you have the energy, write your answer on a sheet of paper so that you can refer to it later.

Your answer is, of course, individually yours, but it is quite probable that it fits into one of two possible moulds. It could be that you wrote a statement about your *own* needs. Maybe you have the idea that being a counsellor will give you status, power or satisfaction. Perhaps you think that counselling will add a new quality and richness to your life. It may be, though, that when you wrote your answer you were not thinking about your own needs at all. You may have decided to become a counsellor so that you can satisfy the needs of other people. You may have written down something like: "I want to be a counsellor because I care about others and want to help them." Most counsellors are very caring people and helping others is an important part of their motivation. However it's important for you to remember that even if you become a counsellor with the primary goal of satisfying other people's needs, you will *also* be satisfying some of your *own* needs. You will, for example, get satisfaction for yourself out of caring for others. This discussion may not seem important to you right now, but it is, because, if you are not careful, your motivation for becoming a counsellor will heavily influence the way in which you will function as a counsellor. While it probably doesn't matter greatly what your motivation is, it is important that you are aware of your motivation and of what needs of your own you hope to satisfy. With this awareness you will be better able to avoid letting the satisfaction of your own needs interfere with the counselling process, and with your ability to meet the needs of clients.

Purposes and goals of counselling

To be able to meet the needs of clients a counsellor must have an under-standing of the purposes and goals of the counselling process. If I am to become an effective counsellor, I need to have some idea of what it means to be effective. Judging the effectiveness of counselling is usually subjective and there are clearly two different perspectives—the client's and the counsellor's. It may be that the client will perceive effectiveness in a different way from the counsellor, so I am asking you, the reader, to spend a few minutes looking first at the client's expectations and then at the counsellor's.

To understand the client's perspective, it is probably useful to look at the reasons why clients seek counselling. For most people it is not easy to make an appointment and then go to see a counsellor. Our society's value system holds that it's a sign of weakness if people are able to handle their problems only if they have outside help. This tends to make it difficult for those with heavy work responsibilities to come for counselling. Such people often believe that, if they admitted to seeking help from a counsellor, their colleagues would think that they were inadequate and not capable of taking responsibility. Consequently, many people are reluctant to seek counselling unless they are in such a disturbed emotional state that their ability to carry out their normal daily tasks is significantly impaired, and they are no longer able to hide their pain and emotional distress from others.

Problems with giving advice

Often, a client will go to a counsellor with very unrealistic expectations of what is likely to happen in the counselling session. Frequently a client will expect that the counsellor will give her direct advice, and tell her exactly what to do, so that at the end of the session she can go away having solved her problems. Most counsellors would agree that they are not prepared to meet such client expectations. Moreover, there are real disadvantages to the client if the counsellor does try to give advice and provide solutions to problems.

There are several dangers inherent in giving advice. First, human beings are remarkably resistant to advice. In fact, some counsellors have become so impressed by the way that clients resist advice that in advanced counselling sessions paradoxical methods are sometimes used and a client is advised to do exactly the reverse of what the counsellor really wants her to do! Other counsellors do give direct advice but this may be counterproductive even if the client follows the advice. If the advice turns out to be inappropriate, then quite clearly the counsellor has done the client a disservice and she will not be impressed. On the other hand, if the advice has positive consequences for the client then unfortunately there may still be negative consequences in the long term. Instead of working things out for herself, the client has accepted the counsellor's advice and may now regard the counsellor as a superior expert who needs to be consulted whenever major decisions are to be made.

Encouraging self-reliance

Perceiving the counsellor as a superior expert is clearly undesirable because the client becomes disempowered instead of learning self-reliant ways of behaving. Thus, an important goal for a counsellor may be to teach or encourage the client to become self-reliant and to feel confident about her own ability to make decisions. In the long term it is not helpful for a client to become dependent on a counsellor's advice. It is far better for the client to become self-reliant, and capable of making and trusting her own decisions.

Most counsellors don't give advice, don't "problem solve" for clients and don't seek to produce quick short-term solutions without long-term gain. Instead they do help clients sort out their own confusion, and by doing this enable them to discover for themselves solutions to their problems which fit them. This is a process which is empowering for clients. Sometimes the counsellor may think that the client's solutions are not the most sensible or appropriate ones. However, it is important for a client to make decisions that are right for her. She can then test her decisions and learn from her own experiences, rather than learning to rely on the "wisdom" of the counsellor.

The counsellor's goals

If I am to be an effective counsellor, I need to have a clear idea of my goals. One of my own primary goals is to help the client to feel better, or at least to feel more comfortable, particularly in the long term. It is also my aim to help a client learn how to become more self-sufficient, and how to deal with ongoing and future life situations in a constructive way without requiring continual help. It is very much in both the client's and the counsellor's interests to promote enduring long-term change, rather than to engage in short-term problem solving. A counsellor is clearly going to feel very frustrated if clients keep returning for counselling each time new problems are encountered. It is important, if the counsellor is to feel a sense of satisfaction in her work, that clients change and grow in such a way that they learn to cope, as much as is realistically possible, on their own.

Another desirable counselling goal may be to bring about change in a client as quickly as is possible. Clearly a counsellor might be seen to be more effective if change is produced more quickly. However, be aware of the danger of producing short-term transitory change which is not sustainable, and which fails to enable the client to cope more effectively with future crises.

Contracting with the client

As discussed above, there may often be a mismatch between a client's expectations and the counsellor's goals. There are a number of ways of dealing with this mismatch. One way, of course, would be to ignore it and just to allow the counselling process to proceed. Some counsellors do this. However, an alternative approach is to discuss expectations openly with the client and to formalise a counselling contract that is mutually acceptable to both.

LEARNING SUMMARY

- A central feature of counselling is the relationship.

- Counsellors need to be aware of their motivation because this will influence their effectiveness.

- Client expectations may be at variance with counsellor goals.

- Clients often ask for direct advice and solutions to their problems.

- Counsellors generally try to empower clients so that they can be self-sufficient and discover their own solutions rather than be dependent on someone else's advice.

FURTHER READING

Brammer, L. M., *The Helping Relationship: Processes and Skills,* 6th edn. Boston: Allyn & Bacon, 1996

Feltham, C., *What is Counselling? The Promise and Problems of the Talking Therapies.* London: Sage, 1995

Kennedy, E. and Charles, S. C., *On Becoming a Counsellor: A Basic Guide for Non-Professional Counsellors.* Melbourne: Collins Dove, 1990

McLeod, J., *An Introduction to Counselling.* Buckingham: Open University Press, 1993

2 The counselling relationship

For me, learning to become an effective counsellor was a long process during which I discovered and absorbed ideas about counselling from my own practical experience, and through contact with my supervisors, other counsellors, clients and friends. It is those ideas that I am sharing with you. Some of what you will read here has been learnt by me from my own reading. However, much has been learnt through my personal experiences as a client myself, as a trainee and then a counsellor, and through talking with people who are counsellors or who have been counselled. I believe that I have learnt more by experience than by reading. I hope that you too will put a higher value on your own personal experience than on what you read.

A good introduction to counselling is to learn methods which were developed by Carl Rogers who wrote a book called *Client-Centered Therapy* in 1955. Later, Rogers preferred to call his approach *Person* Centred Counselling because he placed a very strong emphasis on the need for counsellors to think of their clients as people rather than impersonal entities. He saw the client–counsellor relationship as a person-to-person relationship where the person seeking help was respected and valued. Many of Rogers' ideas are still relevant today. His concept of the counselling relationship is both powerful and useful, and needs to be understood by the trainee counsellor. If you initially adopt a Rogerian counselling style, you can later learn skills from other counselling approaches and integrate these into the Rogerian base so that you have a style which suits you personally. A range of other counselling approaches will be discussed in the next chapter.

Desirable qualities of the counselling relationship

What is good and what is not so good in this picture?

Rogers identified three basic qualities that are highly desirable for a counsellor, if counselling is to be effective. These qualities are *congruence, empathy,* and *unconditional positive regard.* I will describe them in the following paragraphs.

CONGRUENCE
To be congruent the counsellor must be genuinely himself, a complete, integrated and whole person. Everything about him must ring true. Let me use myself as an example. There is only one

David Geldard, even though I have a variety of roles. I am a husband, a grandfather, a father, a counsellor, a friend, a brother, a patient, a customer, etc. It is clearly true that there are differences in the way that I behave in each of these roles, and in different situations. While I'm playing with a child I am happy to romp around on the floor, and when I'm attending a professional meeting of psychologists I prefer to dress more formally and sit upright on a chair. However, in both situations I have a choice. If I choose, I can be an actor playing a role or I can in the fullest sense really be me. I can either stay fully in contact with myself as a person and be genuine, without the need to change myself, or if I choose I can disown myself, wear a mask, and pretend to be different from the real me. As a counsellor I could, for example, pretend to be an expert who has all the answers and no vulnerabilities, or I can throw away my "counsellor mask" and just be me, the real person complete with all my strengths and weaknesses. When a client comes to see me in my counsellor role, then two people meet. It is a person-to-person relationship. For the client to feel valued, I, the counsellor, need to be congruently myself, genuine in all regards. If this happens, then the relationship will be enhanced and the counselling process is likely to be more effective.

Each time I enter a counselling relationship I bring with me that part of me which is a parent, that part of me which is a professional psychologist, that part of me which is childlike and likes to have fun and play jokes on people, and the serious side of me. I also bring with me some spiritual beliefs and some doubts about those spiritual beliefs. I am very much me and not just part of me. I am, within my own limitations, genuinely me and do not pretend to be different from the real me. Naturally, when working as a counsellor I make use of those parts of me which are most relevant in the counselling relationship, and other parts of me may remain out of sight. These are not deliberately concealed from the client, but are available only if they can be appropriately used.

I ran a group some time ago, and in that group were two of my personal friends. These two people had never seen me as a counsellor but had known me only as a friend. After the group, one of them said to me, "I was really surprised because in the group you were the counsellor, but all I saw was the person that I had always known, and I expected to find someone different". A similar situation occurred when a lecturer friend of mine at our local university was teaching counselling skills. One of the students, early on in the course, said to the lecturer, "How about you show us how you counsel by giving us a demonstration. You've been teaching us counselling micro-skills, but you've never actually sat down in front of us and demonstrated how to counsel". The lecturer readily agreed, sat down and, as counsellor, helped a young student client to resolve a difficult and painful issue. After the session was over, the student who'd asked the lecturer to give the demonstration seemed to be amazed and delighted. She said to the lecturer: "You know, I really can't believe it. It was just as though you were being yourself, and Irene [invented name] and you were talking together like friends." Yes, that's how it was; the lecturer was being totally congruent and was relating to Irene as she related to other people in her daily life, as a real person. Of course, it wasn't quite the same, because in daily life we generally behave as though our own needs are equally as important as other people's needs, whereas in a counselling relationship the counsellor will generally focus on the client's needs rather than his own. After all, the counselling situation is not the appropriate place for a counsellor to work through his own problems; rather it's the place where the central focus is the client.

EMPATHY

When a client is talking I imagine that he is walking along a path. Sometimes he meanders away from the path, goes into the woods, trips over, climbs over rocks, wanders through valleys, crosses streams and generally explores. Sometimes he goes right around in a circle and comes back to the same point again. As a counsellor I am neither a follower nor a leader most of the time, although at times I will follow and at times I will lead. Most of the time, what I try to do is to walk alongside the client—to go where he chooses to go, to explore those things that he chooses to explore, and to be warm, open, friendly, concerned, caring, real and genuine. This way trust develops between the client and myself and I experience the world in almost the same way that he experiences it. I try to think and feel the way the client does, so that I can share with him what he is discovering about himself. I go on a journey with him, listening to everything he says, matching his every move, being right beside him. This is what is meant by empathy. Being empathic means having a togetherness with the client, and as a consequence creating a trusting environment in which he feels cared for and safe. In such an environment the client can talk about his darkest secrets, his innermost feelings, and the things that seem to him to be so terrible, or so personal that he has not yet dared to talk to others about them.

UNCONDITIONAL POSITIVE REGARD

The third counsellor characteristic essential for effective counselling is unconditional positive regard. Unconditional positive regard involves accepting the client completely, in a non-judgmental way, as the person that he is, with all his frailties and weaknesses, and with all his strengths and positive qualities. Having unconditional positive regard doesn't mean that I agree with or accept the values of the client for myself, but it does mean that I accept the client as he is now, value him as a person, am non-judgmental of his behaviour, and do not try to put my values onto him. I consequently enable him to feel free to be open in exploring his inner processes without censoring them for fear of criticism. This gives him the best opportunity for increased personal awareness and consequent personal growth.

Unconditional positive regard isn't always easy to achieve. The first step in attempting to achieve it is to try to see the world through the eyes of the client. By doing this I am better able to understand the client's motivations for his behaviour and to be more accepting of that behaviour. The longer I've been a counsellor, the more convinced I have become that even the most terrible behaviour is often understandable if I first understand the world that the client lives in and has lived in. I try to take the view that inside every person, behind the facade that the world sees, there is somebody who has the potential to be a good, creative, loving person. I am rarely disappointed by this expectation.

By caring for each person who talks with me in the same way that I care for myself, I am better able to be accepting and non-judgmental. I'm not going to pretend that this is easy, because it often isn't, and sometimes in a counselling room I hear things that seem at first to be quite outrageous and terrible. At these times, it is really hard for me to be non-judgmental, but it is a goal that I strive for. Only by being non-judgmental can I expect to earn the total trust of the client and really see the world in the way he does. Only then am I able to facilitate change effectively.

Clearly, being non-judgmental and accepting clients with unconditional positive regard is not easily achieved. Moreover it will be very difficult for me to create the relationship I need to have with a client and to be non-judgmental unless first I am very clear about who I am and what my own values are. If I have not sorted out my own value conflicts, then there is a risk that my own confusion will interfere with my ability to focus on the client's confusion, and I may inadvertently end up using the counselling session to resolve my own conflicts rather than the client's. To get a better understanding of my own values I have had to explore them, to scrutinise them and to question them. I have needed to carefully consider different values from my own and to understand where my feelings about those different values come from. This is an ongoing process which will never be finished. I have found that when I have had extremely polarised views, this has often been because I have been afraid to look at the opposite point of view and to seek to understand it. Through sorting out my own value system, understanding myself better, and consequently being less threatened by views diametrically opposed to mine, I am better able to take a non-judgmental attitude towards clients who have very different value systems from mine.

Importance of the counselling relationship

In this chapter I have discussed the counselling relationship, and have explained how that relationship is important in providing a trusting, caring environment in which the client will feel free to share with the counsellor in the most open way possible. The attributes of congruence, genuineness, warmth, empathy and unconditional positive regard are extremely important if a counsellor is to be fully effective. A counsellor needs to walk alongside the client and to be with him in a very real sense so that the client experiences a togetherness. The precise words the counsellor uses are less important than his ability to form a meaningful relationship with the client and to listen intently to what his client is saying. An effective counsellor listens more than he talks, and what he does say confirms for the client that he is being heard and understood. The counsellor's role involves helping the client to explore his world and so to sort out his confusion. It is not the counsellor's role to choose the direction in which the client moves, but rather to provide the environment in which the client can best decide where to go. The counsellor then accompanies him on his journey of exploration. As a counsellor, allow your client to go where his current energy is taking him rather than trying to lead him in a particular direction. When the client has learnt to trust you, and to know that you will listen to what may appear trivial, then he will feel safe enough to venture towards the real source of his pain. In other words, if you stay with what may appear trivial the important will emerge.

You may by now have come to the conclusion that counselling is a terribly serious process. It often is. It is also a process which can give a great deal of satisfaction to the counsellor, and there are even times when counselling can be fun. Is there any fun in you? There certainly is in me, and I enjoy bringing my sense of humour into the therapeutic environment when that is appropriate. Don't fall into the trap of thinking that counselling is always a deadpan, heavy and serious process. It may not be. I am a real person and I need to be congruent. I need to be able to bring all of me into the counselling relationship, and to use those parts of my personality that can add richness to the therapeutic encounter whenever possible.

LEARNING SUMMARY

- Three important qualities in a counsellor are congruence, empathy and unconditional positive regard.

- Congruence means being genuine, integrated, and a whole person.

- Being empathic means joining with the client so that there is a feeling of togetherness.

- Unconditional positive regard involves accepting the client non-judgmentally as a person of value, regardless of strengths and weaknesses.

- Counselling is usually a serious process but can legitimately involve humour.

FURTHER READING

Hackney, H. and Cormier, L. S., *The Professional Counselor: a Process Guide to Helping*. Boston: Allyn & Bacon, 1995
Mearns, D., *Developing Person-Centred Counselling*. London: Sage, 1994
Rogers, C. R., *Client-Centered Therapy*. Boston: Houghton Mifflin, 1955
Thorne, B., *Carl Rogers*. London: Sage, 1992

3 Various approaches to counselling

There are many different styles of counselling in use today. Many counsellors draw on ideas from a number of different counselling frameworks. They use what some writers (eg Culley, 1991) call an "integrated" approach because it involves integrating skills from different theoretical and practical sources.

In this book we will start by using as a base the non-directive counselling style originated by Carl Rogers, and will then build on that Rogerian foundation to incorporate techniques from other more active counselling methods.

The counselling style which you eventually adopt yourself will probably be one which suits your personality best. You may be surprised to know that it doesn't matter much what that style is, because most counsellors agree that the key to helping clients work effectively through their problems lies in the client–counsellor relationship. What is important is that the relationship between the client and counsellor is appropriate for producing therapeutic change.

In this chapter we will take a brief look at a selected number of the differing counselling philosophies and methods which many counsellors find useful. We will begin by going back in history to look at the work of Sigmund Freud who developed psychoanalysis in the 1930s. We will then consider the work of some other major contributors who have developed new styles of counselling since then.

Important contributors to counselling theory and practice

Listed below are a few of the important contributors to counselling theory and practice:

PSYCHOANALYTIC PSYCHOTHERAPY
- Sigmund Freud

HUMANISTIC/EXISTENTIALIST COUNSELLING
- Carl Rogers
- Frederick (Fritz) Perls
- Richard Bandler and John Grinder

COGNITIVE BEHAVIOURAL COUNSELLING
- Albert Ellis

There are many other important contributors to counselling theory. However, this book is an introductory book and predominantly uses ideas which were originated and developed by the people listed above. It should be remembered that this is an introductory book which deals only with individual counselling for adults who are emotionally distressed. Readers who wish to work with children, rather than adults, might like to read *Counselling Children* written by Kathryn Geldard (my wife) and myself. For readers who want to counsel families there are many books available on Family Therapy.

Many counsellors believe that working with individual adults is the best way to learn basic counselling skills. Once basic counselling skills have been mastered readers can, if they wish, build on these by learning additional skills for working with couples, families and children.

I will now briefly discuss the work of each of the people listed previously, starting with Freud. In each case I will consider only aspects of the person's work which, in some way, relate to the counselling methods discussed in this book. Readers who wish to learn more about the work of these major contributors may choose to peruse the suggested further readings list at the end of this chapter.

Psychoanalytic psychotherapy

Sigmund Freud was the originator of psychoanalytic psychotherapy. Most contemporary counsellors do not use the psychoanalytic approach. However, many of Freud's theories have significantly influenced more contemporary approaches to counselling. It is therefore useful for a new counsellor to have some understanding of Freud's ideas.

SIGMUND FREUD

Sigmund Freud made a major and profound contribution to the understanding of human personality. Although some of his ideas are contentious he was a radical thinker whose individual contribution to psychology has been of great significance in shaping the way modern counsellors think about people and understand the underlying origins of their problems. Additionally, Freud originated and developed the theory and methods of psychoanalysis. Although only a minority of counsellors work psychoanalytically nowadays, many contemporary counsellors use psychodynamic concepts to underpin their work.

Freud was a psychiatrist who saw his work as psychotherapy. Interestingly, Rogers later saw psychotherapy and counselling as synonymous. Freud made a major contribution to the recognition that counselling (or psychotherapy) was a valid and necessary process if we are to help people to overcome emotional problems. Films and TV programs often lampoon the Freudian psychoanalyst's couch on which the patient lies to talk about current and past anxieties while the psychiatrist listens. Although many people find such a situation amusing, this underlying concept is a forerunner to modern counselling methods where the counsellor gives undivided attention to the client while the client talks about troubling issues.

Freud introduced the idea of the "unconscious" and proposed that our disturbed behaviours have their origins in unconscious processes which occur within the individual. As counsellors today, we need to be aware of the reality that often a person's attitudes, beliefs, thoughts, emotions, and behaviours have their origins in unconscious processes which are suppressed.

Freud believed in what he called "free association" where one idea triggers off another. He believed that by allowing the client to talk freely, free association would occur and the client would inevitably reveal ideas which were suppressed into the subconscious. Similarly, as contemporary counsellors we need to recognise the need to allow the client to travel without interruption along her own path, so that we do not interfere unnecessarily with a process which may result in the client dealing with the underlying source of painful current and past experiences.

Freud placed a great emphasis on the influence of past and childhood experiences. Frequently in counselling we find that a person's current problems have their origin in some earlier experience. Freud also identified a number of what he called "defence mechanisms". These defence mechanisms provide some protection for a person against current pain but block the person from dealing with underlying causes of distress. He described the way that the therapist (counsellor) would meet with what he called "resistance" as the person avoided, deflected away, or suppressed painful material during psychotherapy (counselling).

Another of Freud's ideas which is important for the modern counsellor are the ideas of "transference" and "counter-transference" which will be discussed in Chapter 25. Freud had many other useful ideas, including his definitions of id, ego, and super-ego. As this is not a book about Freud's work, readers who are interested may wish to read Burton and Davey (1996).

If Freud had so many good ideas you may be wondering why we don't teach all counsellors to use the psychoanalytic method. Well, there are several very important reasons, two of which are as follows:

1. Psychoanalysis, as originated by Freud, is a very slow process. Some psychoanalysts work with their clients over a period of several years in order to help the clients to gain insight into the underlying causes of their behaviour. Psychoanalysts themselves undergo lengthy training. As counsellors today we need to be able to provide people with brief interventions which will quickly enable them to overcome emotional pain and function adaptively.

2. Freud believed that the psychoanalyst was an expert who could help the client gain insight by interpreting for the client the material disclosed by him. Many, if not most, modern counsellors do not see themselves as experts who are able to interpret what is meaningful for another person. Rather, they try to encourage and facilitate the client's own personal interpretation of their inner processes and outward behaviours. As discussed in Chapter 1, the contemporary counsellor's goals include helping the client to feel more self-sufficient rather than dependent on the counsellor.

Around Freud's time counselling theory was influenced by the psychological theories of people such as Adler and Jung. However, major advances in counselling methods did not occur until the 1950s when the existential humanistic counselling methods emerged.

Existential humanistic counselling

Two of the major contributors to existential humanistic counselling were Carl Rogers and Fritz Perls. They believed that each individual had within himself the natural ability and resources to achieve personal growth. The counsellor, therefore, did not need to be an expert but merely a facilitator to enable the client to access his own resources to bring about change. Ideas developed by Richard Bandler and John Grinder can also be usefully incorporated into existential humanistic counselling.

CARL ROGERS

Rogers originated and developed *Client-Centred Counselling* which he later renamed *Person-Centred Counselling*. In Chapter 2 we discussed some of Roger's ideas. He radically differed from the psychoanalytic approach by suggesting that people have the ability within themselves to solve their own problems. He saw the counsellor as a facilitator who listened to the client with empathy and without judgment, and thus enabled her to work through her issues. His ideas are respectful of people. He did not see himself as a superior expert but as another person, different from his client, but of equal value.

Rogers placed great emphasis on the counselling skills of reflection. He reflected back to the client what she was feeling emotionally. Also, he reflected back the content of what the client had said, but in the counsellor's own words. The skills of reflection will be discussed in Chapters 11, 12, and 13.

Roger's ideas are extremely useful to the modern counsellor, especially during the early parts of the counselling process where relationship building is paramount. Some counsellors still predominantly use a Rogerian approach. However, the problem with doing this is that the Rogerian approach, although very effective with some clients, tends to be slow in achieving results by comparison with other methods of counselling which are less time consuming. I believe that integrating the Rogerian approach with other methods, as described in this book, is most effective.

FREDERICK (FRITZ) PERLS

Fritz Perls was initially trained as a psychoanalyst but moved away from psychoanalysis to develop Gestalt Therapy. Gestalt Therapy makes use of, or modifies, many psychoanalytic ideas. In contrast to psychoanalysis which placed emphasis on the client's past experiences, Perls placed strong emphasis on the present "here and now" experience of the client. Perls encouraged clients to take personal responsibility for their current experience rather than blaming either the past or others.

Perls concentrated on raising the client's awareness of current bodily sensations, emotional feelings and related thoughts. By encouraging clients to become fully aware of their current experience in the here and now, he believed that he could enable them to work through "unfinished business", sort out their emotional confusion, achieve what he called a "gestalt", or "Ah ha" experience, and thus feel more integrated.

Fritz Perls' counselling style was quite different from Carl Rogers' warm and caring style. Perls challenged and frustrated the client during the counselling process in order to move the client into a clearer understanding of troubling issues, thoughts, emotions and behaviours. At times, when counselling some clients, and at particular stages in the counselling process, it can be very advantageous to use Gestalt Therapy techniques. However, I personally believe that, even when using Gestalt Therapy techniques, the counselling relationship should retain the qualities suggested by Rogers so that clients are not threatened by the process.

Gestalt Therapy counselling techniques include:

- giving the client immediate feedback about non-verbal behaviour as it is observed during the counselling process. This is particularly useful in drawing the client's attention to feelings which are being suppressed;
- inviting the client to get in touch with and describe bodily sensations and relate these to emotional feelings and thoughts;
- encouraging clients to make "I" statements and to take responsibility for their actions;
- challenging and confronting what the counsellor sees as "neurotic" behaviour, for example, confronting the client when he deflects away from talking about troubling issues;
- encouraging clients to role play different parts of themselves and to create a dialogue between those parts;
- encouraging clients to role play both themselves and someone else with whom they have a problem and to create a dialogue between themselves and the other person.

Ideas from Gestalt Therapy are particularly useful when helping a client to explore options, and to move forward to take action. Examples of the use of Gestalt Therapy will be given in a number of chapters but particularly in Chapters 21, 22, and 25. Readers who would like to learn more about Gestalt Therapy might like to read Clarkson (1989).

RICHARD BANDLER AND JOHN GRINDER
Richard Bandler and John Grinder were the originators of Neuro-linguistic Programming, commonly known as NLP. Readers who would like to learn about this method of helping people might like to read Bandler (1985). In this book we will make use of two very useful concepts from NLP. These are:

1. the need for a counsellor to match the way people relate to their world through the use of differing senses such as seeing, hearing, feeling etc.;
2. the concept of reframing.

These concepts will be discussed in Chapters 14 and 17.

Cognitive behavioural counselling

Starting in the 1960s Albert Ellis and other workers moved away from the humanistic existentialist approaches which gave priority to dealing with emotional feelings in the counselling process. As a consequence, what are now referred to as *cognitive behavioural* counselling methods were developed. These methods are now very popular for a number of reasons including the following:

1. They are believed to be useful in changing undesirable behaviours (particularly in adolescents).
2. Secondly, they are less stressful for the counsellor who does not encourage clients to express strong emotions. Cognitive behavioural counsellors target the client's thinking (cognitive) processes and his behaviours rather than his emotions. They believe that a person's emotional feelings depend on the way he thinks and behaves. Consequently, they believe that the best way to help someone to feel better emotionally is by helping him to change his thoughts and behaviours.

ALBERT ELLIS

Albert Ellis developed Rational Emotive Therapy which is now known as Rational Emotive Behaviour Therapy. A central idea in Rational Emotive Therapy is that emotionally disturbed people are disturbed because they are making assumptions which are based on irrational beliefs. Ellis believed that the counsellor's job was to identify and challenge these irrational beliefs and to encourage the client to replace them by what he saw as rational beliefs. In Chapter 19 we will make use of Ellis's ideas to look at ways to help clients to challenge what I call "self-destructive beliefs".

Ellis' counselling style was different again from both Rogers and Perls. Ellis did not place emphasis on joining with the client but used questions to identify irrational beliefs. He then worked enthusiastically to convince the client that these irrational beliefs were causing the problem and needed to be replaced by other beliefs. When I watched a video tape of his work, he seemed to me in some ways to be more like an educator or a salesman than a counsellor. However, his ideas are very useful for helping people to feel better. Further, I believe that it is possible to use his ideas and still retain the important qualities of the counselling relationship described in Chapter 2.

Readers who would like to learn more about Rational Emotive Therapy may wish to read Dryden (1995).

An eclectic approach

As discussed at the beginning of this chapter the counselling style described in this book is eclectic, drawing ideas from the counselling methods described in this chapter. The method relies on Rogerian ideas for relationship building and enabling the client to talk freely. It recognises the importance of understanding the psychodynamic approach as described previously. Additionally it draws on Gestalt Therapy philosophy and techniques and on ideas from both Rational Emotive Therapy and Neuro-linguistic Programming.

LEARNING SUMMARY

- Most counsellors use an eclectic or integrative approach, drawing ideas from various therapies to suit their own personalities.

- It doesn't matter much what style of counselling is used because the client–counsellor relationship is the key to producing therapeutic change.

- Freud encouraged the client to talk freely while he gave his undivided attention. He placed great emphasis on the past and on childhood experiences. The counsellor (or psychoanalyst) was the expert who interpreted for the client (patient) so that the client could gain insight and thus change.

- Existentialist humanistic counsellors such as Rogers and Perls believe that the client has the potential to solve her own problems. The counsellor (therapist) is a facilitator of change. The client is the expert.

- Rogers in Client-Centred Counselling placed emphasis on the relationship and on reflecting back to the client what the client had said.

- Perls' goal in Gestalt Therapy was to bring about increased client awareness through helping the client to integrate information from bodily sensations, thoughts and emotional feelings. He placed great emphasis on encouraging the client to take personal responsibility by using "I" statements and staying in the "here and now".

- Bandler and Grinder in Neuro-linguistic Programming recognised the need for a counsellor to match the client's way of experiencing the world through the use of particular senses. They also introduced the concept of reframing.

- Cognitive behavioural counsellors believe that our thoughts and behaviours control our emotions. Consequently they focus on changing thoughts and behaviours in order to help people to feel better and behave more adaptively.

- Albert Ellis originated Rational Emotive Behaviour Therapy. He believed that people became emotionally distressed because of irrational beliefs and that the counsellor should convince the client that she should replace these beliefs with rational beliefs.

FURTHER READING

REGARDING HISTORICAL PERSPECTIVES

Dryden, W. *Developments in Psychotherapy: Historical Perspectives*. London: Sage, 1996

REGARDING AN INTEGRATED APPROACH TO COUNSELLING

Culley, S., *Integrative Counselling Skills in Action*. London: Sage, 1991

ON PSYCHODYNAMIC COUNSELLING

Burton, M. and Davey, T., "The Psychodynamic Paradigm". In Woolfe, R., and Dryden, W. (eds), *Handbook of Counselling Psychology*. London: Sage, 1996

Jacobs, M., *Psychodynamic Counselling in Action*. London: Sage, 1988

ON PERSON-CENTRED COUNSELLING (ROGERS)

Mearns, D., *Developing Person-Centred Counselling*. London: Sage, 1994

Rogers, C. R., *Client-Centered Therapy*. Boston: Houghton Mifflin, 1955

Thorne, B., *Carl Rogers*. London: Sage, 1992

ON GESTALT THERAPY (PERLS)

Clarkson, P., *Gestalt Counselling in Action*. London: Sage, 1989

Clarkson, P., and Mackewn, J., *Fritz Perls*. London: Sage, 1993

O'Leary, E., *Gestalt Therapy, Theory, Practice and Research*. London: Chapman & Hall, 1992

ON NEURO-LINGUISTIC PROGRAMMING (BANDLER AND GRINDER)

Bandler, R., *Using your brain for a CHANGE—Neuro-linguistic Programming*. Moab: Real People Press, 1985

Bandler, R. and Grinder, J., *Reframing*. Moab: Real People Press, 1982

ON RATIONAL EMOTIVE THERAPY (ELLIS)

Dryden, W., *Brief Rational Emotive Behaviour Therapy*. London: Wiley, 1995

Ellis, A., *Better, Deeper, and More Enduring Brief Therapy: The Rational Emotive Behavior Therapy Approach*. New York: Bruner/Mazel, 1996

ON COUNSELLING CHILDREN

Geldard, K. and Geldard, D., *Counselling Children: a Practical Introduction*. London: Sage, 1997

4 ▶ Influence of the counsellor's values and beliefs

In Chapter 2 we discussed the need for counsellors to try to be non-judgmental. Can you imagine what it would be like if you were a client who was talking to a counsellor and as you were talking you formed the impression that the counsellor was disapproving of you, or of what you were saying? I suspect that in such a situation you might feel inhibited and might decide that it was not wise to talk openly to this counsellor. Alternatively can you imagine what it would be like for you if the counsellor seemed to be troubled by what you were saying and was questioning whether your values and beliefs were acceptable? Once again, I suspect that you might feel uncertain about continuing disclosing information. Clearly, there is a risk that the counselling process will be compromised if the counsellor appears to be judgmental.

Sometimes it is very hard not to be judgmental. I have found that it is especially hard when I am confused or not clear about my own values or beliefs. When I am not clear, I find that I get distracted and can easily either show disapproval or spend time thinking about my own values and beliefs instead of attending to the client. It is therefore important for counsellors to know where they stand with regard to their own personal values and beliefs.

Sometimes a counsellor's values and beliefs will match those of the client, but often they will not. If I am to be able to help a client with different values from mine, then I need to understand her world in the context of her value system and not mine. If I am not able to do this, then I will not be able to join with her empathically and what I say to her will be likely to jar, confuse, or create a barrier between us. At worst, I might get into an argument about values instead of helping my client to sort out her confusion!

I have no right to try to impose my values on a client. However, I believe that there are times when it is appropriate for me to be open with a client about my values in order for me to be congruent.

If I have a clear understanding of my own values, I have an inner strength. I will not need to be defensive in trying to justify my values; they are mine and they will stand in their own right without the need for justification.

If I don't understand and know my own values, I may well be trapped into trying to discover what they are during a counselling session with someone else. Instead of being able to concentrate on seeing the world through my client's eyes, I may be distracted by trying to sort out the confusion in my own head. Questions such as, "Is this morally right or wrong?", may trouble me and prevent me from joining the client in her own struggle to work out what is right for her.

People change as they understand themselves better

The more I work as a counsellor with people, the more I believe that most people are naturally well-intentioned, caring of others, socially responsible, and capable of giving and receiving love. When I meet someone who seems to be nasty, I almost always, as I get to know him better, recognise the damage that has been done to him by past life experiences. As counselling proceeds I notice changes occurring as that person comes to terms with past experiences. It is as though a plant that looked like a thistle is growing into a rose. With this belief I do not need to try to convince others to accept my values; I just need to understand them better and to help them to understand themselves better.

I remember a friend, who trained as a priest, telling me that while at university an agnostic lecturer told him that arguments from strongly evangelical Christian students never threatened, or made him question, his agnostic beliefs. However, he found that my friend made him think about his agnosticism. Rather than confront him with a different point of view, my friend respected him enough to accept him as he was and tried to see the world through his eyes when he talked with him. My friend knew clearly what he himself believed and openly owned his beliefs but did not push them on his lecturer or attack his lecturer's position. As a consequence, he was able to join this lecturer in a way which allowed the lecturer to explore different ways of thinking with safety and without feeling pressured. The opportunity for change was maximised.

Being non-judgmental isn't easy

As children, our values and beliefs are initially those of our parents and significant others such as teachers. As we grow up our values and beliefs will change as we accept some of our earlier values and beliefs but modify others in the light of our own personal experiences. Clearly though, our values and beliefs are likely to be influenced by both the cultural background in which we grew up as children and by the contemporary culture of the societal group within which we live. As counsellors we are therefore likely, at times, to work with clients who may have quite different values from ours.

Being non-judgmental is not so easy at times. Counsellors are sometimes faced with situations where client values strongly conflict with their own. When this happens, it is as though a button is pushed within the counsellor who immediately becomes emotionally aroused by the fear of threat to her own value system.

The first step in dealing with a values conflict between yourself and a client is to recognise it. You will probably be able to do this fairly easily if you remember that the warning sign of a values conflict is likely to be emotional arousal in yourself. If you feel your body tensing, or other bodily symptoms of arousal, then stop and think. Ask yourself, "What is happening?" Check out whether your values are being challenged. Similarly, if you find that you are starting to disagree with a client and to argue with her, then stop and think, to check out whether or not you are involved in a values conflict.

Owning your own value system

It is not going to be helpful to the client, from a counselling perspective, if you try to change her point of view. As has been emphasised, effective counsellors join with their clients and try to see the world as their clients see it. When you sense that you are encountering a values conflict, then you need to make a choice by asking yourself: "Can I put my own values to one side in order to join with this client or not?" If the answer is "Yes", then counselling can proceed. If it is "No", then to be fair to the client you will need to tell her that while you respect her and her right to have a different point of view, you have different values with regard to the issue in question. If you feel able to do so, it will be useful for you to explain to the client that you are not saying that your values are better or worse than her values; they are just different because you are two different people. You can then offer the client the option of continuing to talk with you if she wishes, or of talking with someone else. If she wants to talk with someone else, then refer her to someone who may be able to meet with her on her own value-ground.

Sometimes you will recognise an important values difference between your client and yourself, but will feel able to put your own values to one side while counselling and suspend judgment. When this happens you may need to continually remind yourself to imagine you are the client, with her world view. When your own values start intruding on the counselling process, recognise this, and once again focus on the client's perspective. If you are able to stay fully tuned in to her thoughts and feelings, your counselling will be more likely to be effective. Moreover, you will be more likely to be successful in putting your own values to one side so that they remain intact as part of you.

The need for supervision

Whenever a values conflict interferes with your work with a client, it is important for you to talk with your supervisor about the issues involved. By doing this you will minimise the possibility of future situations where the effectiveness of your counselling might be adversely affected by the particular value in question. Hopefully, if you fully explore the relevant issues, you will be able to work with clients with very different points of view from yourself without your own values influencing the appropriateness of your counselling responses.

As discussed previously, it is very important for counsellors to know, as clearly as possible, what their values are.

Knowing your values

How can you, as a new counsellor, know what your values are? There are so many areas in life where values are important that it is impossible in training to cover all value-laden situations. Inevitably some of these will emerge during counselling sessions. Counsellors have to continually address new issues. Even so, it is possible in training to examine some commonly encountered situations or beliefs where values are of importance.

A values clarification exercise

As an aid to counsellor training I suggest the following exercise in values clarification. This exercise is best done in a group where discussion of differing values can occur. A good way to carry out the exercise is to label one end of the training room "agree" and the other end "disagree". Trainees, as a group, can then be asked to respond to each statement below by positioning themselves in the room somewhere on the agree–disagree continuum along the length of the room. Once trainees have positioned themselves in response to a statement, the facilitator can invite comment and promote discussion with regard to their positions in the room.

If you are not in a group, then you may wish to think about each of the statements below to try to work out where you stand with regard to each. Do you agree or disagree with the statement, or stand somewhere between the agree–disagree position?

Please notice that many of the statements below are statements of belief rather than value statements. However, our values are determined by our beliefs, so in determining our values, it's important to also consider beliefs.

Statements for values clarification exercise

WARNING: *Some of these statements are intentionally provocative and may offend.*

- Unemployment benefits should be terminated after three months.
- People of other nationalities should be treated with suspicion.
- Termination of pregnancy is a woman's right.
- Men are always to blame for domestic violence.
- Women and men are equal.
- Guns don't kill; the people who fire them do.
- Gun laws are for the benefit of the community as a whole.
- With modern contraceptive methods sexual fidelity is no longer necessary.
- Censorship is socially desirable.
- Homosexuality is a normal condition.
- Delinquency is due to parents being too permissive with their children.
- Counsellors wouldn't be needed if people would turn to God.
- Usually one partner is mostly to blame when a marriage breaks up.
- Marijuana should be legalised.
- The Aboriginal people deserve to have land rights.
- Welfare benefits are too high.
- Couples should stay together for the sake of their children.
- Children in two-parent families are happier than children in single-parent families.
- If a person has an affair their spouse should leave them.
- Contraception is wrong.
- People who have had psychiatric treatment are not suitable for leadership positions.
- Lying is sometimes justifiable.
- Charities deserve regular donations.
- Good people should avoid immoral people.
- Anyone can get a job if they try hard enough.

- Life is to be enjoyed.
- Striving for wealth is wrong.
- Handouts do not help people.
- People can be too honest.
- Sex is overrated.
- Smoking should be banned in public places.
- Love and forgiveness are more important than punishment.
- Alcohol more frequently gives pleasure than it creates problems.
- Alternative medicine is as useful as conventional medicine.
- I don't want to change other people so that they have the same values as I do.
- It's OK for a father to bath his young daughter.
- Chemicals are harmful.
- It's a good idea to build large concrete dams.
- Masturbating is enjoyable and acceptable.
- People should not be allowed to spoil rainforests by tramping through them.
- Sex offenders are nasty people.
- Too much closeness in a family is a bad thing.
- Adult needs should take precedence over children's needs.
- Killing people is wrong.
- The use of four-letter words is offensive.
- The developed countries should feed the developing countries.
- I believe in heaven.
- Oral sex is enjoyable and acceptable.
- Divorce is wrong.
- De facto relationships are moral and acceptable.
- Children who receive sex education are more likely to be promiscuous than those who don't.
- The Bible tells us what is right and what is wrong.
- Single parents shouldn't have sexual relationships with special friends.
- Single parents who have sexual relationships with special friends should be open about what they are doing and should tell their children.
- Hospital births are better for babies than home births.
- Things are either right or wrong; there are no in-betweens.
- Smacking children is unnecessary.
- Only married people should have sexual intercourse.
- It's OK for a 16-year-old to have sexual intercourse.
- You can tell what a person is really like from their appearance.
- It is good to strive for material possessions.
- Money doesn't bring happiness.
- Children should be breastfed until they want to stop.
- Families should have clear rules.
- Children should be allowed to make their own decisions.
- Children are better off in childcare than with their mothers.
- We need fewer laws and more freedom.
- Most people are intrinsically good.

When considering your position with regard to the above statements, please remember that we are all unique individuals and different from each other. Consequently, in some ways, your values will probably be similar to mine, and in some ways they will be different. I am comfortable with that. Are you?

LEARNING SUMMARY

- Counsellors need to know their own beliefs and values so that they are not distracted during counselling sessions by trying to sort them out and so that they can respect their clients' value systems.

- Counsellors have no right to try to impose their own beliefs or values on clients.

- Whenever a values conflict interferes with your work, consult your supervisor.

FURTHER READING

Corey, M. S., and Corey, G., *Becoming a Helper.* Pacific Grove: Brooks/Cole, 1993

McFadden, J., *Transcultural Counseling: Bilateral and International Perspectives.* Alexandria, VA: American Counselling Association, 1993

Ridley, C. R., *Overcoming Unintentional Racism in Counseling and Therapy: A Practitioner's Guide to Intentional Intervention.* Thousand Oaks: Sage, 1995

Worthington, E. (ed.), *Psychotherapy and Religious Values.* Grand Rapids: Baker, 1993

5 The need for supervision

Clients are people with real needs. They need to be valued and given the best available help. It is therefore not ethical for a client to be seen by a new counsellor unless that counsellor is being adequately supervised.

My belief is that all counsellors, new and experienced, should have ongoing supervision. There are several important and quite different reasons for this including the following:

- to enable the counsellor to work through her own personal issues;
- to enable counsellors to upgrade their skills;
- to provide an external review of the counselling process for particular clients;
- to address issues concerning dependency and professional boundaries.

We will now consider each of the above.

To enable the counsellor to work through personal issues

You may be surprised at the suggestion that supervision is required to enable the counsellor to work through her own personal issues. You may be asking, "If counselling is for the benefit of the client and not the counsellor, why should the counsellor be using her counselling work in order to deal with her own issues?" The answer is simple: unless a counsellor owns and deals with her own issues, these issues are quite likely to interfere with the counselling process to the detriment of the client.

Frequently, a counsellor will feel emotional pain when her client discusses issues similar to unresolved emotional issues of her own. Consequently, when issues which are painful for the counsellor herself are discussed, she may consciously or unconsciously avoid her own pain in a number of ways:

- The counsellor might deflect away from the painful issue by encouraging the client to talk about something else.
- The counsellor might try to comfort the client rather than to help the client to deal with the issue.
- The counsellor might attempt to encourage the client to pursue a course of action that in some way satisfies the counsellor's own needs. The counsellor may wish, for example, that she had taken a particular course of action in her own life and may encourage the client to take a similar course.
- The counsellor may avoid facing both her own issue and the client's by failing to recognise the issues and subconsciously suppressing them.

A perceptive supervisor will spot counsellor behaviour that demonstrates avoidance of painful issues and will ask the supervisee to explore whatever was happening emotionally within her when the avoidance occurred. This means that counsellors need to be prepared to own and explore their own issues on an ongoing basis. Otherwise these issues are likely to diminish the effectiveness of counselling.

Most people don't look closely at their own emotional problems unless they are causing them considerable distress. It is a natural human defence to suppress uncomfortable feelings and not to delve into them without good reason. However, a counsellor must delve into uncomfortable feelings, because if I as a counsellor have a problem that I can't face, then it will be quite impossible for me to help a client with a similar problem. As counsellors, therefore, we need to explore and deal with all of our own painful issues as they come into our awareness. The spin-off for us is that our personal growth is enhanced when we do this.

To enable counsellors to upgrade their skills

Although I am an experienced counsellor I believe that it is always valuable for me to learn from other counsellors. We all have a different range of skills and use differing styles when counselling. During my counselling career I have discovered that my own style has continued to change. This has enabled me to integrate new skills into my work and to continue to take a fresh approach to my counselling work rather than sinking into a rut and becoming stale.

I find that it is sometimes useful for me to receive input from counsellors who use quite a different framework from mine. By doing this I usually find that I discover some new ideas for enhancing my own work.

Although didactic learning can be useful for counsellors, it seems to me that the experience of personal supervision is more powerful for professional development. Learning through supervision can integrate skill training with personal growth. Additionally, the counsellor is reminded in supervision of how it is to be a client. This can be helpful in enabling a counsellor to continually meet with the client as a person of equal value.

To provide an external review of the counselling process for particular clients

Often clients can't see what is obvious to the counsellor because they are personally and deeply involved in their situation. In comparison a counsellor, after joining with the client and trying to see the world in the way the client does, can stand back to take a more objective view, and thus see more clearly. A parallel process happens when a counsellor is being supervised. The supervisor is able to view the counselling process and the case details in a different way from the counsellor herself. The supervisor may recognise processes which are occurring for the client or the counsellor which have been unrecognised. Thus a supervisor is able to provide useful input on ways of working with particular clients. Additionally, supervisors hopefully have considerable experience which can be a source of useful information for a new counsellor.

To address issues concerning dependency and professional boundaries

As discussed in the previous paragraph a supervisor may recognise processes which have not been recognised by the counsellor. Of specific importance are issues of dependency and respect for professional boundaries.

It can sometimes be hard for new counsellors to recognise when the time for terminating a series of counselling sessions has been reached. This may be partly due to issues of dependence which inevitably will develop in some counselling relationships (see Chapter 23). Sometimes it is hard for a counsellor to recognise whether the client really does have a need for further counselling or whether dependency is occurring either on the part of the client or herself. Dependent clients sometimes produce new material for discussion when the counselling process is moving towards closure. This may be as a consequence of a subconscious or conscious desire to prolong the counselling relationship. By discussing cases in supervision, a supervisor may be able to recognise when dependency is interfering with appropriate termination processes. Additionally a supervisor may be able to help a counsellor devise suitable strategies for managing dependency issues.

Some counsellors have difficulty in recognising when their own personal feelings towards a client could result in behaviours which would inappropriately transgress professional boundaries and consequently interfere with the counselling process. Additionally, new counsellors sometimes have difficulty in knowing how to respond to direct and/or indirect client invitations for friendship and closeness. Once again, supervision can help a counsellor to recognise inappropriate processes which are occurring and to develop appropriate strategies to deal with these processes.

What does supervision involve?

There are a number of ways in which supervision can occur:

1. by direct observation with the supervisor in the counselling room
2. by direct observation through a one-way mirror
3. by observation using a closed circuit TV
4. by use of an audio- or video-recording and analysis
5. by direct observation together with audio- or video-recording and analysis
6. by means of a verbatim report

These methods will be discussed in turn.

1. DIRECT OBSERVATION WITH THE SUPERVISOR IN THE COUNSELLING ROOM

Trainee counsellors are usually apprehensive about seeing their first few clients. A good way to help them adjust to the counselling environment is for trainees to sit in on counselling sessions conducted by their supervisors. Naturally, the permission of the client is required. Student counsellors who are allowed to do this need to understand what their supervisor expects of them. Initially, I prefer my students to take a low profile and to sit quietly out of the line of vision of the client. This reduces the necessity for the client to feel the need to interact with two counsellors simultaneously, leaves me free to conduct the session in the way that I choose, and enables the trainee to observe without feeling pressured to participate. As the trainee's level of comfort increases, some participation by her can occur. Adopting this approach allows her to observe me as a model, and to feel at ease with a client and myself in the room. The method allows the trainee gradually to make the transition from being a passive observer to being an active counsellor under supervision.

The process just described is excellent for raw beginners who have had no previous counselling experience but there are problems connected with having both the trainee and supervisor in the room together. Obviously, some of the intimacy of the counselling relationship is lost, and as a consequence the client may find it difficult to deal openly with sensitive issues.

2. DIRECT OBSERVATION THROUGH A ONE-WAY MIRROR

The one-way mirror system as shown in Figure 5.1 provides a better alternative. Many counselling centres have a pair of adjacent rooms set up like this for training purposes, and for family therapy. The one-way mirror allows a person in the observation room to watch what is happening in the counselling room without being seen. A microphone, amplifier and speaker system provide sound for the observer, so that she is able to see and hear what is happening. Ethically, it is imperative that a client who is being observed from behind a one-way mirror is informed in advance about the presence of the observer, or observers, and that consent is obtained for the session to proceed in this way.

The one-way mirror system can initially be used to enable a trainee or trainees to watch an experienced counsellor at work. Later the trainee can work as a counsellor while being observed by her supervisor, and possibly by other trainees also. The system has the advantage that the supervisor is not present in the counselling room and therefore does not intrude on the counselling process. However, she is available to take over from the trainee if that becomes necessary, and she can give objective feedback after the session is completed.

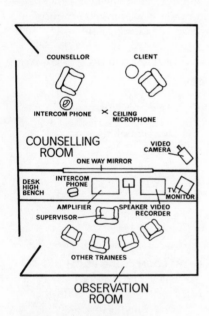

FIGURE 5.1 Counselling and observation rooms

3. OBSERVATION BY CLOSED CIRCUIT TV

A similar method to the one-way mirror system is to have a video camera in the counselling room connected to a TV monitor in another room. However, this method doesn't provide as much visual detail as is obtained with the one-way mirror system. It is often difficult to see facial expressions if the camera has a wide-angled lens to enable most of the room to be in the picture.

One of the best methods of supervision is by use of video-recordings. Audio-recordings can also be used although their usefulness is more limited because non-verbal behaviour cannot be observed. Video-recordings of counselling sessions are a rich source of information. Not only may selected segments of a session be viewed repeatedly, but it is also possible to freeze the picture so that non-verbals may be studied.

Whenever an audio- or video-recording is made it is essential to obtain the prior written consent of the client, and to tell him who will have access to the recording and when it is to be erased. Many agencies have standard consent forms for clients to sign. It is sensible to have such forms checked for their legal validity.

4. USE OF AUDIO- OR VIDEO-RECORDING AND ANALYSIS

Sometimes counsellors audio- or videotape sessions without their supervisor observing at the time. Such tapes provide an excellent opportunity for supervision. The supervisor and counsellor can then review and analyse parts of the tape. Often it can be useful for the counsellor to review additional tapes on his own in order to recognise unsatisfactory processes and to improve his counselling techniques.

5. DIRECT OBSERVATION TOGETHER WITH AUDIO- OR VIDEO-RECORDING AND ANALYSIS

A combination of a one-way mirror system together with audio- or video-recording is a very powerful arrangement for counsellor training. Trainees can be directly observed during practice sessions, and may later process their work in detail with their supervisors by analysing and reviewing the audio- or video-recordings.

6. USE OF A VERBATIM REPORT

Another method of supervision is by use of the verbatim report. A verbatim report is a written report which records, word for word, the client's statements and the counsellor's responses. It may be produced from memory, or as a transcript of an audio recording. Here is an example of a verbatim report. Note that this example is invented and does not relate to a real client or counsellor.

Structure of the verbatim report

As you will see from the above example of a verbatim report, the report begins with background information about the client, his problems and his emotional state. The first part of the report may also summarise the process and outcome of previous counselling sessions.

Verbatim report

NAME OF COUNSELLOR Fiona Smith

NAME OF CLIENT Simon Anonymous

DATE OF COUNSELLING SESSION 19.8.98

BACKGROUND INFORMATION ABOUT THE CLIENT Simon is 36 years old, has been married twice and has two children. These are a girl, 12, and a boy, 10. Both children are in the custody of Simon's second wife. He lives alone.

This was Simon's second visit to see me. He came a week ago feeling tense and depressed. He told me that he was worried about his inability to build relationships with women, and he couldn't understand why.

MY FEELINGS AND ATTITUDES PRIOR TO THE SESSION I was feeling good myself and was looking forward to working with this client again. I believed that I had built a good relationship with him during the previous session and that this would enable him to talk freely with me.

WHAT OCCURRED PRIOR TO THE RESPONSES GIVEN BELOW When Simon arrived for this session he looked pale and was very subdued. During the first 15 minutes of our time together his body looked tense and he seemed reluctant to talk. After a few minutes of silence, I felt as though he had put a barrier between us and I spoke.

F1 Seems like there's a barrier between us. (Said quietly.)

S1 Ah what ... what da ya mean? (He sounded defensive to me.)

F2 Like we're separated by a barrier. (I used my hands to suggest a barrier.)

S2 Separated? (Said with non-verbals that suggested disbelief and questioning. I felt very shut out from Simon now.)

F3 Yes, I feel shut out by an invisible barrier. Sometimes you open it up a ... (Simon interrupted heatedly.)

S3 No, no, it's a double brick wall with a door in it. The door is usually closed and that's because it keeps me safe.

F4 That brick wall's important to you!

S4 It sure is!

F5 It protects you. (Simon started to talk freely and easily after this.)

S5 Yes, it does ... (He went on to explain how vulnerable he would feel without the wall, and then started to cry. I waited.) ... You see, I've been hurt too much in the past, and I'm scared that if I'm me, if I'm really me, and open up, then I'll be rejected again.

F6 The barrier protects you from the pain of rejection. (Long pause.)

S6 It also prevents me from getting into a relationship and I'm not sure that I like that. (Said carefully, slowly, and firmly.)

✓ F7 You don't sound sure about whether you want the barrier or not.

S7 Well, it would be hard to tear it down. I'm so used to it now. You know I realise that the barrier's been there for a long time now. Goodness knows what might happen if I didn't have it there.

✓ F8 It would be risky to tear it down.

S8 It would. (He paused to think for what seemed a long time. I had difficulty staying silent because I wanted to tell him what he was discovering for himself.) ... You know, I would get hurt for sure, and what's worse, I'd have to take responsibility for the ways I hurt the women I get close to. (He laughed.) That's worse. That's worse! I can't bear it when I hurt someone I love.

✓ F9 Getting close involves lots of hurt. (He interrupted, fortunately, before I was able to take him off track by suggesting getting close could also involve pleasure. I was bursting to tell him!)

S9 Yes, it seems like that to me ... (He then told me in detail about his pain at losing his second wife. He couldn't understand how he hurt so much when he had left her.) ... It's not over yet. How can I still be hurting after so long?

✓F10 I get the impression that you're still grieving.

S10 I should be over her by now! (Said despairingly.)

✓ F11 It takes time to grieve. Can you give yourself time?

From here on the process flowed naturally as he dealt with his grief. I got the strong feeling that his barrier would gradually disintegrate as he worked through his grief.

MY FEELINGS AFTER THE SESSION I felt good because Simon had moved forwards to a fuller awareness of himself and his behaviour. I felt I had been infected by some of his sadness though.

WHAT I HAVE LEARNT FROM THE SESSION (OR THINGS I WOULD DO DIFFERENTLY ANOTHER TIME) I learnt that it was helpful for the client when I shared with him my own feelings (of separation, see F1, F2 and F3). Because he interrupted (F9 and S9), I discovered that it was better to follow his path. If I had brought the focus on to the pleasure associated with closeness then I would have made it more difficult for him to address the underlying issue of his grief. I learnt that my desire "to make the client feel good" could have been counterproductive. I'm pleased he interrupted and prevented me from doing this.

Fiona Smith

The next section of the report concerns the counsellor's own feelings and attitudes prior to the counselling session. This information is required because a counsellor's behaviour and performance is often influenced by her mood, feelings generally and feelings towards the client, and her preconceived ideas and attitudes concerning the client and the client's behaviour.

A central component of the verbatim report is the section containing client statements and counsellor responses. This section usually contains only about 10 to 20 responses from each person. It would be very laborious to write out a transcript of a substantial part of a counselling interaction and this is unnecessary. Preferably the trainee counsellor will select a portion of the session that demonstrates some important learning, or highlights some difficulties. Often a new counsellor will find that a part of the interaction seems to "go wrong" inexplicably. Such a segment provides ideal material for a verbatim report and subsequent discussion in supervision. Notice that responses are numbered and identified by the initial letter of the person's name. For example, statement F7 is Fiona's seventh in the report. After each statement other significant information is recorded, in parentheses, including non-verbal behaviour, silences and the feelings and thoughts of the counsellor.

Immediately before the verbatim client and counsellor statements is a description of what occurred in the session prior to them, and immediately after them is a brief description of what occurred in the remaining part of the session. These descriptions are required so that the statements that are recorded verbatim are seen in the context of the whole session.

The verbatim report concludes with sections that describe the counsellor's feelings after the session and her learnings for the future. It is then signed.

The value of verbatim reports

Verbatim reports enable a supervisor to tap into trainee issues that might have blocked her from satisfactorily helping the client to work through his issues. Such reports also enable the supervisor to identify unsatisfactory processes and inappropriate counsellor responses and to help the trainee discover better ones.

Confidentiality

Audio-recordings, video-recordings and verbatim reports require the same level of protection as client records in order to ensure that confidentiality is preserved (see Chapters 7 and 26). It is essential that tapes and reports are not left in places where they might fall into the hands of unauthorised persons.

In conclusion

By using any of the methods described in this chapter, a supervisor can help a new counsellor to improve her skills and to understand the process that occurred during a particular counselling session. This chapter has discussed ways in which you may be supervised as a new counsellor. Your initial training is just the beginning, and there is no end to the ongoing need for further training. A good counsellor never stops learning from her own experiences and from what others can teach her. In order to improve, it is advantageous to continue in supervision, even when an experienced counsellor.

The counselling strategies described in this book are the basic ones. Once you have mastered them, you may wish to continue to learn from experienced counsellors who have advanced skills or who are skilled in specialised counselling techniques. I believe that ongoing training can best be carried out through experiential training in workshops and seminars, together with hands-on experience under the supervision of a qualified and experienced practitioner.

LEARNING SUMMARY

- It is not ethical for a new counsellor to see clients without adequate supervision.

- A counsellor's own unresolved issues will adversely affect the counselling process.

- Common supervision methods involve direct observation, observation using a closed circuit TV, audio- or video-recording and analysis, and then use of verbatim reports.

FURTHER READING

Carroll, M., *Counselling Supervision: Theory, Skills and Practice*. London: Cassell, 1996

Feltham, C. and Dryden, W., *Developing Counsellor Supervision*. London: Sage, 1994

6 Exploring the hidden parts of self

I will state the obvious by saying that the human personality is incredibly complex. However, in order to help us understand the ways in which people behave, it is useful to describe human personality in terms of easily understandable models. Any model we use is certain to be a gross over-simplification, but even so it may help us to understand better what happens in ourselves and in our clients. In this chapter we will consider two models to help in our understanding of the way in which clients coming to counselling have a natural tendency to hide parts of themselves. These models are useful to us in enabling us to help our clients to change and feel more comfortable. The two models are:

1. the Johari window
2. the iceberg model

The Johari window

The Johari window, as devised by Joseph Luft and Harry Ingham at a workshop in 1955 (see Luft, 1969), is shown in Figure 6.1. According to Luft the name "Johari" is pronounced as if it were Joe and Harry, which is where the name comes from: Joe–Harry. The window has four panes as shown. Each pane in the window contains information about the person represented by the window.

The two panes on the left-hand side contain information which is known to the person herself, whereas the two panes on the right-hand side contain information which is unknown to the person. The two panes at the top contain information which is known to others and the two panes at the bottom contain information which is unknown to others.

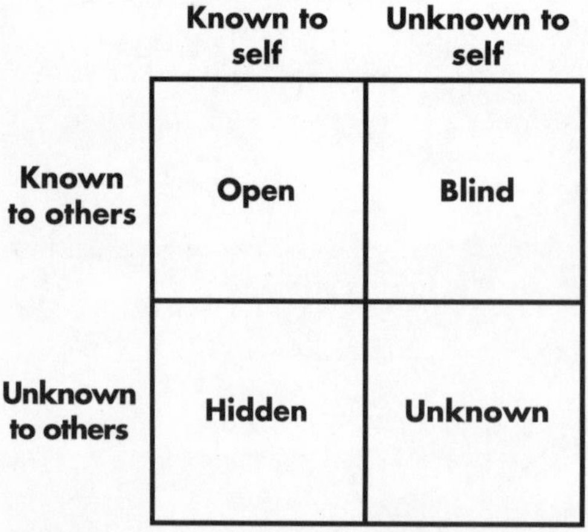

	Known to self	**Unknown to self**
Known to others	**Open**	**Blind**
Unknown to others	**Hidden**	**Unknown**

FIGURE 6.1 The Johari window
(From: *Group Processes: An Introduction to Group Dynamics*, 3rd edn., by Joseph Luft © 1984, 1970, 1963. Reprinted by permission of Mayfield Publishing Company.)

Information in the top left-hand pane (the *open* pane) is openly recognised by the person himself and by other people. If I use my own personal window as an example, I know that I get satisfaction from writing textbooks and other people are aware of this information. Consequently this information is in my *open* pane. Information in the bottom left-hand pane, labelled *hidden*, is known to me and unknown to others. I can think of some characteristics and beliefs of mine which fit into that pane, but I won't let you know what they are or they would no longer be in that pane. Information in the top right-hand pane labelled *blind* is known to others but not to me. For example, other people may know that I am arrogant but I may not recognise this. Information in the bottom right-hand pane labelled *unknown* is totally unseen and is locked in my subconscious.

THE INFLUENCE OF COUNSELLING ON THE JOHARI WINDOW

The likely influence of successful counselling on the Johari window is shown in Figure 6.2. When a person comes to talk with a counsellor it is quite likely that at first he will talk about information in the *open* pane. However, if a trusting relationship develops the person may take the counsellor into his confidence and self-disclose information from the *hidden* pane, thus enlarging the open pane. Additionally, as counselling proceeds the counsellor may give the client feedback concerning information which is unknown to the client but recognisable by the counsellor and once again the open pane is enlarged. As a consequence of the counselling process the client may gain in insight (to use a psychodynamic term) or in awareness (to use a Gestalt Therapy term). As shown in Figure 6.2 the person's self-knowledge is likely to increase during an effective counselling process, allowing for personal growth and change to occur.

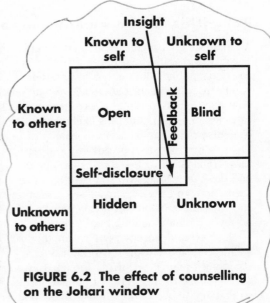

FIGURE 6.2 The effect of counselling on the Johari window

The iceberg model

I think that a good model for human personality is the iceberg as illustrated in Figure 6.3. An iceberg floats so that most of it is below the waterline and cannot be seen. Human beings are a bit like that. As you get to know a person, you will see parts of her personality. You will see those parts that are, metaphorically speaking, above the waterline. There are other parts of that person's personality too, but you do not see these as they are submerged below the waterline. Even the person herself will not be fully aware of all those parts

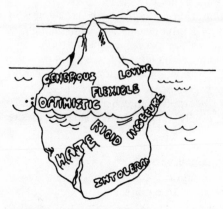

FIGURE 6.3 The iceberg model of human personality

of herself which are below the waterline. Icebergs have a tendency to roll over from time to time and as they roll over, some parts of the iceberg that had previously been submerged come into sight. From time to time, hidden parts of a person's personality come unexpectedly into view, rather like those parts of the iceberg that show when it rolls over. Sometimes it is other people who are surprised by what they see when this happens, and sometimes the person herself gets a surprise too.

Polarities in the human personality

An interesting characteristic of human personality has been described in Gestalt Therapy and is the existence of polarities or opposites (see Chapter 3). The most commonly talked about polarities are "love" and "hate". How often have you heard someone talk about a love/hate relationship? You may be aware from your own experience that a love/hate relationship can exist. If I have a strong capacity for loving, then it is likely that I also have the potential to hate. I may of course deny my capacity to hate. Just imagine the iceberg with the word "love" sitting on the top, out in the open for everyone to see, and the word "hate" right down below the sea, and hidden from view. The danger exists that one day the iceberg will roll over and the "hate" side will be all that will be seen. Time and time again we see a relationship where a couple falls in love, and then the relationship breaks up, and the love that was there is replaced, not by something neutral, but by hate.

Hostility and acceptance are another set of polarities. Sometimes if I'm feeling very angry with somebody, my hostility prevents me from forgiving and accepting them. It seems as though forgiveness and acceptance are on the opposite side of the iceberg to anger and hostility. If the iceberg rolls around so that my anger is uppermost, then forgiveness is buried beneath the sea. However, in my experience, it's only by fully accepting my anger, by experiencing it totally, and by allowing it to surface fully, that I am able to allow the iceberg to roll over again and reveal forgiveness.

ACCEPTANCE OF THE HIDDEN PARTS OF ME

It's important for me to recognise and own that opposites exist within me, because if I want to strengthen a particular quality, I need to accept and deal with its opposite. I'm capable of loving and hating. I'm capable of anger and I'm capable of being forgiving. I'm capable of being tolerant and capable of being intolerant. I'm capable of being generous and miserly, I'm capable of being optimistic and of being pessimistic, of being fun-loving and of being a kill-joy, of being light-hearted and of being serious, of being religious and of having doubts about my religious values and beliefs. In order to feel integrated and comfortable within myself, I need to accept all the parts of me, and not just those parts that are socially acceptable and consistent with my being a "nice" person.

Clients often come to counselling because they are unable to accept parts of themselves. It seems as if parts of themselves have become submerged beneath the sea, never to be seen, and never to be owned. The submerged parts are continually wanting to surface, and there is an inner struggle to prevent the iceberg from rolling over. Naturally clients feel great discomfort when they try to keep parts of themselves submerged and try to deny parts of themselves that really want to be expressed.

A common example of client distress caused by suppressing a part of self is the depression caused by repressed anger. I have found that many clients who are depressed are unable to express their anger. Often, when I suggest to them that maybe they feel angry with a person who has wronged them, I'll be met with a denial. "No I'm not angry, I'm just sad", they will say. Gradually, however, as the counselling relationship builds up, they will begin to express themselves more fully. After a while, as the depression starts to lift, anger will emerge. At first the anger will be barely expressed and will be described in very mild terms, but gradually it will build up. The more this happens, the more the depression recedes.

DENIAL OF "NEGATIVE" EMOTIONS
Many of us are taught from childhood to deny what our parents, teachers and other significant persons regard as negative emotions. Parents often put anger into this category and tell their children not to be angry but to calm down. As a result, many children learn to think of anger as a negative emotion and start to disown it, saying, "No, I'm not really angry", when they are really very angry indeed.

Paradoxically, if I fully accept and own my anger, then I may be able to deal with it constructively rather than by expressing it destructively. If I do this, it will often disappear spontaneously and in its place I will experience a more comfortable emotion. It is important for me, however, to recognise that I have a potential for anger and to allow that potential to exist rather than suppressing it.

USEFULNESS OF THE POLARITIES MODEL
The polarities model can be useful for helping clients to feel OK about accepting and owning what they initially believe are undesirable or negative qualities or emotions. I tell my clients that for every so-called positive or desirable emotion or quality, normal human beings may also have the opposite emotion or quality. This is normal and therefore OK. Such thinking frees clients to deal with all their emotions, personal qualities, traits and attributes. They are then able to strengthen those parts of themselves that they would like to

strengthen, and can grow as people accordingly. In Gestalt Therapy terms the process involves integrating the polarities so that two opposite polarities are seen as ends of a continuum rather than as separate and discrete. This allows the client to recognise the two opposite extremes and to feel free to move to a more comfortable position on the continuum.

LEARNING SUMMARY

- Human beings naturally have information about themselves, some of which is hidden from others and/or some of which is hidden from themselves as described by the Johari window.

- Human beings have polarities or opposites in their personalities.

- Generally we try to show the more acceptable polarities but sometimes the opposite polarities emerge.

- If I can accept the hidden parts of myself, then I will be better able to deal with them and to strengthen their opposites, if that is what I want.

- The counselling process is likely to increase insight or self-awareness, resulting in personal growth and enabling the client to change and feel better.

FURTHER READING

Clarkson, P., *Gestalt Counselling in Action*. London: Sage, 1989
Luft, J., *Of Human Interaction*. California: Mayfield, 1969
O'Leary, E., *Gestalt Therapy, Theory, Practice and Research*. London: Chapman & Hall, 1992

7 Confidentiality and other ethical issues

The first part of this chapter will be devoted exclusively to confidentiality, because it is one of the most important ethical issues for a counsellor. Other aspects of professional ethics will be considered in the second part of the chapter.

Confidentiality

For counselling to be maximally effective, the client must feel secure in the knowledge that what he tells the counsellor is to be treated with a high degree of confidentiality. Ideally, a client would be offered total confidentiality, so that he would feel free to openly explore with the counsellor the darkest recesses of his mind, and to discuss the most intimate details of his thoughts. As a new counsellor I naively believed that I could at all times give my clients an assurance that what was said in the counselling session was between them and me and would not be discussed with others. I very soon learnt that this was an idealistic belief and found that in practice it is generally not possible, advisable, or ethical to offer total confidentiality.

As a counsellor you may at times be troubled by some personal difficulties regarding confidentiality and may need to talk with your supervisor about these. Counsellors are faced with a dilemma with regard to confidentiality. Unless we give our clients an assurance that what they tell us will be in confidence, they are unlikely to be open with us. However, there are limits to the level of confidentiality which we can offer and we need to be clear with clients about these limits. Most importantly, you yourself need to be aware of the limits to the confidentiality which you are offering.

Many experienced counsellors would agree with Woolfe and Dryden who in the *Handbook of Counselling Psychology* (1996) go so far as to say that promising total confidentiality is unethical. It is certainly true that confidentiality is compromised by the following:

- the need to keep records;
- the requirements of the counsellor's own supervision;
- where others need to be protected;
- when working in conjunction with other professionals;
- when participating in educational training programs, conferences, workshops and seminars;
- in cases where the law requires disclosure of information.

The above list will now be discussed in detail.

THE NEED TO KEEP RECORDS

As explained in Chapter 26 there are compelling reasons for keeping good records. Counsellors who work in agencies frequently use computerised systems or centralised filing systems for such records. This may make it possible for other counsellors and non-counselling staff such as receptionists and filing clerks to have access to confidential records. Some counsellors omit to note certain categories of sensitive material on their record cards as a way of protecting clients. However, there are obvious consequences if this policy is adopted, as important information may be overlooked or forgotten during subsequent counselling sessions. Clearly, for the protection of clients, computerised records need to be protected by adequate security systems. Similarly, hard-copy records should not be left lying around in places where they can be read by unauthorised people, and should be stored in lockable filing cabinets or in a secure filing room.

THE REQUIREMENTS OF THE COUNSELLOR'S OWN SUPERVISION
The requirements of professional supervision, as described in Chapter 5, demand that counsellors be free to fully disclose client material to their supervisors. This is essential if clients are to receive the best possible service, and is also necessary for the well-being of counsellors themselves. Some counsellors openly talk with their clients about the requirements of professional supervision and sometimes it can be reassuring for a client to know that his counsellor is receiving supervision.

WHERE OTHERS NEED TO BE PROTECTED
Experienced counsellors sometimes work with dangerous clients, or with clients who have committed serious offences against other people and may possibly repeat such behaviour. Clearly, counsellors have responsibilities not only to their clients, but also to the community. There may be instances where a counsellor needs to divulge information to protect a third party. For example, if a counsellor knows that his client possesses a gun and intends to kill someone, then it would be unethical and irresponsible if the person at risk, the police and/or the psychiatric authorities were not informed. Where there is doubt about the desirability of informing others, the counsellor needs to consult his supervisor.

WORKING IN CONJUNCTION WITH OTHER PROFESSIONALS
Professionals such as psychiatrists, medical practitioners, psychologists, social workers, clergy and welfare workers frequently phone counsellors to talk with them about mutual clients. It is sometimes important for the welfare of such clients that other professionals are appropriately informed about their situations. It is also desirable for counsellors to maintain good working relationships with other helping professionals. Sensible judgments need to be made about what information is disclosed and what is withheld. If you believe that it is desirable that sensitive material be disclosed, then obtain the client's permission first, unless there are unusual and compelling reasons for not doing so. Obtaining the client's permission involves informing the client about what you wish to do and why. Thus the client is able to give *informed consent*. This informed consent should be verified in writing so there can be no misunderstanding. Many agencies have a standard consent form which can be used when

information is to be shared. This form is discussed with the client and then signed by both the client and the counsellor.

To some new counsellors it may seem undesirable and unnecessary to ever allow the sharing of such information. However, consider the following example. Imagine that a client comes to see you and that a psychiatrist who is treating another member of the family gives you some helpful and useful information, and asks you to help

An issue of trust

him by confirming that his perception of the family situation is accurate. It may well be advantageous, in the therapeutic management of both clients, if you work cooperatively with the psychiatrist. In such an instance, it could be appropriate to obtain client permission, and to keep the client informed of ongoing contact with the psychiatrist.

Where two members of a family require counselling help, the need for Family Therapy is usually indicated. However, if Family Therapy is not available, or is considered inappropriate, then any helping professionals involved with members of the family are likely to achieve more for their clients if they consult each other, have case conferences and work together as a team.

Sometimes you may discover that a client of yours is also consulting another counselling professional. There is rarely justification for two counsellors working with the same client, and so after discussion with the client it is sensible to contact the other counsellor to decide who will take over the case. There are exceptions to most rules, and sometimes if good contact is maintained between two counsellors it may be possible for them both to remain involved provided that each sets clear boundaries and goals for their individual work.

EDUCATIONAL TRAINING PROGRAMS, CONFERENCES, WORKSHOPS AND SEMINARS
Another problem area regarding confidentiality concerns ongoing training, upgrading of skills and sharing of new techniques. Counsellors need to grow and develop as people and as counsellors. This can partly be done through personal supervision and partly through large group sharing at conferences, seminars, workshops and case conferences. Client material that is presented at such events can sometimes be disguised by changing names and other details, but often this is not possible, particularly when video-recordings of counselling sessions are used. Client material should never be used in this way without the prior written consent of the client. Moreover, there could be legal as well as ethical problems if consent is not obtained.

WHERE THE LAW REQUIRES DISCLOSURE OF INFORMATION

Remember that client confidentiality may be limited by legal intervention. Sometimes counsellors are subpoenaed to give evidence in court and in such cases withholding information may be in contempt of court. Additionally, mandatory reporting is required by counsellors from certain professions in some countries with regard to issues such as child abuse.

Respecting the client's right to privacy

Clearly, from the preceding discussion, there are many reasons why confidentiality in the counselling situation is limited. However, it is the counsellor's task to ensure that client confidentiality is preserved as far as is sensibly, legally and ethically possible. Assure your clients that you will do this to the best of your ability, because they need to feel that whatever they share with you is protected information which will not be carelessly or unnecessarily divulged to others. It is quite unethical to talk about clients or client material to any person whatsoever, except in the circumstances previously described in this chapter. What a client shares with you is his personal property and must not be shared around, so if you do have a need to talk about a client or his issues then talk with your supervisor.

You will need to make your own decisions, in consultation with your supervisor, about how best to deal with the confidentiality issue. My own policy is to be up front with clients and to explain the limits of confidentiality as they apply. For example, I do some part-time work in a government agency and when working for that agency I warn clients about the limits to confidentiality which apply there. If I need to divulge information for an ethically acceptable and professional reason, then I will obtain the client's informed consent. In a situation where a third party is in danger, I will seek the informed consent of the client but if this is not given I will be direct and open about my intentions to disclose, subject of course to my own safety. This policy ensures maximum client and community protection.

Professional ethics

The issue of confidentiality has been discussed in some detail. However, there are many other ethical issues for counsellors, and a new counsellor needs to be informed of these. Many counsellors belong to professional associations with codes of ethical conduct. These codes are readily available on request, and it is sensible for a new counsellor to read through the relevant code for her profession. Some of the more important ethical issues are included in the list below, and these will be discussed in subsequent paragraphs:

- respect for the client
- limits of the client/counsellor relationship
- responsibility of the counsellor
- counsellor competence
- referral
- termination of counselling

- legal obligations
- self-promotion

RESPECT FOR THE CLIENT

Regardless of who the client is, and regardless of her behaviour, the client has come to you for help, and deserves to be treated as a human being of worth. If you treasure your client, then, through feeling valued, she will be given the optimum conditions in which to maximise her potential as an individual. A value position shared by most helping professionals is that within each of us is the potential for good, and for that potential to be realised we need to feel OK about ourselves. Counsellors have a responsibility to help their clients to feel OK about themselves, and to increase their feelings of self-worth.

If you try to impose your own moral values on the client, then you are likely to make her feel judged and to damage her self-worth. Moreover, she is likely to reject you as a counsellor and to reject your values too. Paradoxically, if you are able to accept your clients, with whatever values they have, you may well find that as time passes they move closer to you in their beliefs. This is inevitable because, as counsellors, we are, whether we like it or not, models for our clients. We have a responsibility to be good models. In this regard, it can be useful to create opportunities for clients to give feedback about their experience of the counselling process. This will demonstrate respect for their views and their right to have some influence in the counselling relationship.

We need to remember that the client's interests must take precedence over the counsellor's during the counselling process. It is not ethical to use counselling sessions with clients to work through our own issues. The correct time for working through our issues is in supervision sessions.

Respect involves protecting the client's rights. Clients have a right to know when information about them is being recorded and if the records are on a computer system. Further, the client has the right to see records concerning himself if he wishes. This right is covered by legislation in specific situations in various countries and states.

LIMITS OF THE CLIENT/COUNSELLOR RELATIONSHIP

In all our relationships we set limits. Each of us has a boundary around us to preserve our identity as an individual. The strength of that boundary, and its nature, depends on whom the relationship is with, and on the context of the relationship. The client/counsellor relationship is a special type of relationship, established by the client for a particular purpose. The client enters into the relationship, entrusting the counsellor with her well-being, and expecting that the counsellor will, throughout the relationship, provide her with a safe environment in which she can work on her problems.

As discussed previously, the client/counsellor relationship is not an equal relationship, and inevitably, whether the counsellor wishes it or not, she is in a position of power and influence. She is often working with clients who are in highly emotional states and are consequently very vulnerable. The way in which a counsellor relates to a client is uncharacteristic human behaviour. A counsellor devotes most of her energy to listening to and understanding the client, and so the client sees only a part of the counsellor's character. In these circumstances, a client may perceive a counsellor as unrealistically caring and giving. The counsellor's power and the client's biased perception combine to make the client very vulnerable to offers of friendship or closeness.

The counsellor is also vulnerable. In the counselling relationship, the client often shares her innermost secrets, and so inevitably there may develop a real closeness between the client and counsellor. Counsellors learn to be empathic, and so they develop special relationships with their clients. If they are not careful they too become vulnerable to offers of closer relationships than are appropriate. Counsellors therefore need to be careful not to discount signposts that the counselling relationship is being compromised.

Unfortunately, it is almost always unhelpful, and often damaging to the client, when the client/counsellor relationship is allowed to extend beyond the limits of the counselling situation. If such an extension occurs, the counsellor's ability to attend to the client's needs is seriously diminished, and there may well be serious psychological consequences for the client.

As a counsellor, it may at times be hard to refuse invitations to get closer to your clients than the counselling situation allows. Remember that if you do not set appropriate boundaries you will merely be satisfying your own needs at the expense of the client. You will have abused your special position of trust as a professional, and you will have to live with that knowledge, and with any more serious consequences. When counsellors breach appropriate boundaries they may damage or diminish the usefulness of the counselling process and reduce the possibility that the client will seek further counselling help. Be aware of the danger signals when your relationship with a client is becoming too close, and bring the issue into the open by discussing it with your supervisor and with the client, if that is appropriate.

Counsellors need to exercise care if they touch a client in any way. Unwelcome touching is not only unethical but also can result in sexual harassment charges.

RESPONSIBILITY OF THE COUNSELLOR

Counsellors frequently experience a sense of conflict between their responsibilities to the client, to the employing agency and to the community. You will at times need to make your own decisions about which of these responsibilities needs to take precedence, and in my view the decision is unlikely always to be the same. If you are in doubt about any particular decision, consult your supervisor.

Clearly, the counsellor has a responsibility to the client and needs to directly address the client's request for counselling help. When a client comes to you for confidential help, you have an implied contract with her to give her that, unless you tell her something to the contrary. Clearly though, you cannot ethically fulfil the client's needs if doing so would:

- involve working in opposition to the policies of the organisation that employs you

- involve a breach of the law
- put other members of the community at risk
- be impossible for you personally

However, in these situations you need to be clear with your client about your own position, so that she understands the conditions under which she is talking to you.

Counsellors who are employed by an organisation or institution have a responsibility to that employing body. All the work they do within that organisation or institution needs to fulfil the requirements of the employing body, and to fit in with the philosophical expectations of the employing body. For example, I currently work in a part-time capacity for the Queensland Department of Health. While working for the Department of Health it is my responsibility to comply with the policies of that department. If I were not able to do that, then I would have an ethical responsibility to discuss the issue with my employers, or to resign.

Counsellors, at all times, have to be aware of their responsibilities to the community at large. As discussed earlier, this raises problems with regard to confidentiality. Whenever a member of the community is at risk, property is likely to be damaged, or other illegal actions are likely to occur, or have occurred, then you have an obligation to the community to take appropriate action. Often decisions do not involve choosing between black and white, but rather between shades of grey, and sometimes you may find it difficult to decide what is most appropriate, to serve the needs of the community in the long term. At these times the sensible approach is to talk through the ethical issues with your supervisor.

COUNSELLOR COMPETENCE

A counsellor has a responsibility to ensure that she gives the highest possible standard of service. This cannot be done without adequate training and supervision. All counsellors need to attend to their own professional development and to have supervision from another counsellor on a regular basis. Failure to do this is certain to result in the counsellor's own issues intruding into the counselling process, and this will be to the detriment of the client (see Chapter 5).

A counsellor also needs to be aware of the limits of her competence. We all have limits professionally and personally, and it is essential that as counsellors we are able to recognise our limits and to be open with our clients about those limits. The client has a right to know whether she is seeing someone who has, or does not have, the abilities necessary to give her the help she requires.

REFERRAL

When a client's needs cannot be adequately met by a counsellor, then that counsellor has a responsibility to make an appropriate referral, in consultation with the client, to another suitable professional. However, it is not appropriate for a counsellor to avoid all difficult and unenjoyable work by excessively referring clients to others. There is a responsibility on all counsellors to carry a fair load, and to be sensible about referral decisions. Such decisions are best made in consultation with a supervisor.

It may sometimes be appropriate for the counsellor to continue seeing the client, while under intensive supervision, instead of referring. If this happens, then the counsellor has a responsibility to inform the client.

Often, referral is useful where people have special needs. For example, people with particular disabilities, people from other cultures, and people who speak another language may benefit from referral to an agency (or professional) which can provide for their specific needs.

When referring clients to others, it may be useful to contact the professional to whom the referral is being made, with the client's permission, to ensure that the referral is acceptable and appropriate.

TERMINATION OF COUNSELLING
Termination of counselling needs to be carried out sensitively and with appropriate timing (see Chapter 23). It is not ethical to terminate counselling at a point where the client still needs further help. If for some unavoidable reason (such as leaving the district) you need to do this, then it is incumbent upon you to make a suitable referral to another counsellor who can continue to give the necessary support.

LEGAL OBLIGATIONS
Counsellors, like all other professionals and every other member of the community, need to operate within the law. Therefore, as a counsellor, you need to familiarise yourself with the relevant legal requirements for your profession. It is particularly important to know whether mandatory reporting of specific behaviours such as suspected child abuse is required.

SELF-PROMOTION
Most professional associations for counsellors have specific rules about advertising. There is clearly an ethical issue with regard to the way in which counsellors describe themselves and their services. It is unethical for a counsellor to make claims about herself or her services which are inaccurate or cannot be substantiated. Counsellors who do this not only put their clients at risk, but may also face the possibility of prosecution.

LEARNING SUMMARY

- For counselling to be most effective a high degree of confidentiality is required.

- Confidentiality is limited by the need to keep records, professional supervision, the law, the protection of others, participation in training, conferences, and so on and cooperation with other professionals.

- Professional ethics relate to issues such as respect for the client, limits to the relationship with the client, responsibility to the client, the employing agency and the community, competence, referral to others, termination of counselling, legal obligations and self-promotion.

FURTHER READING

Corey, G., Corey, M. S. and Callanan, P., *Issues and Ethics in the Helping Professions*, 4th edn. California: Brooks/Cole, 1993

Shillito-Clarke, C., "Ethical Issues in Counselling Psychology". In Woolfe, R. and Dryden, W. (eds), *Handbook of Counselling Psychology*. London: Sage, 1996

8 ▶ The counselling environment

In earlier chapters we have discussed the way in which counselling involves the creation of a safe, trusting relationship between the client and counsellor. In order to assist in the promotion of such a relationship it can be helpful, when counselling a client in a face-to-face situation, if the counselling environment is one which will enable the client to feel comfortable and at ease. Similarly, in a telephone counselling situation it is desirable for the telephone counsellor to work from a space which will enable the client to have some reassurance that the privacy of the call is being respected. Firstly, I will discuss the face-to-face counselling situation and then requirements for telephone counselling.

Unfortunately, it is not always possible for counsellors to have the use of a specially designed counselling room. In some situations counsellors are visitors to an agency, school, or government department and have to make the best of use of rooms which are intended for another purpose. Where this is the case it is desirable for the counsellor to do whatever is possible to protect the privacy of the client. Many adults and children don't like others to know that they are seeing a counsellor. In offices and schools the confidentiality of the counselling process may be compromised at some level by lack of privacy. Clearly, counsellors need to do their best to seek the most private facilities and arrangements as possible.

Special purpose counselling rooms for face-to-face counselling

Whenever I walk into a room, that room has an effect on me. Is it the same for you? Have you noticed that sometimes when you have entered a room you have felt comfortable and at ease, almost as though the room welcomed you? At other times you may have entered a room that felt clinical, cold and unwelcoming. A well-designed counselling room will have a warm, friendly feel about it. In addition to being warm, pleasant, welcoming and comfortable, it is an advantage if the room can be set up so that it is especially suitable for counselling.

Where a counsellor has her own personal room, that room can reflect something of her individual personality. My own room is decorated with plants and pictures. Pictures on the walls are peaceful, showing natural scenes of trees and landscapes. The colours are muted and not harsh, and these combine with comfortable furnishings to provide a welcoming, relaxed atmosphere.

Your room will be different from mine because you are different from me and have different tastes. Make your room an extension of yourself, so that you feel at ease in it, and then in all probability your clients will feel comfortable in it too.

Your furnishings will not be the same as mine, but ideally they should include comfortable chairs for yourself and your client, together with other furnishings appropriate for a professional office. You may need to write reports, draft letters, keep records and carry out some administrative duties. Hence a desk, telephone and filing cabinet will be useful, together with bookshelves for a professional library.

LAYOUT OF THE ROOM

The sketch in Figure 8.1 shows a suitable layout for a counselling room for the personal counselling of individual clients. Notice that the desk and filing cabinet are unobtrusively in a corner facing the wall, where their importance for clients is diminished. Personally, I will not usually sit at a desk when clients are in the room with me. Instead, I sit in an armchair, facing the client and at her own level. Thus, there is no furniture separating us. In this set-up the client may join with me as an equal partner in exploring her issues, and I'm not perceived as a powerful "expert" separated from my client by a desk. If I do need to sit at the desk to do some written work in a client's presence, the desk doesn't come between her and myself. I don't have a client chair and a counsellor chair, but rather two chairs that are similar. When a client enters the room she may sit where she chooses, but if she hesitates, I will direct her to a chair. This is a small point, but an important one. Remember that clients are usually anxious when they enter your room, which is your space. They may be more at ease if you make it clear what is expected of them, rather than leaving them to decide what is appropriate.

My chairs are arranged so that neither chair faces directly into the light coming from the window. Looking towards a window is unpleasant, as after a while the glare will cause eyestrain. During a counselling session, the client and counsellor will be looking at each other most of the time, so the background against which each is framed is really important for comfort. Preferably the client's and counsellor's chairs will face each other, but at a slight angle with enough space between them so that the client does not feel that her personal space is being invaded.

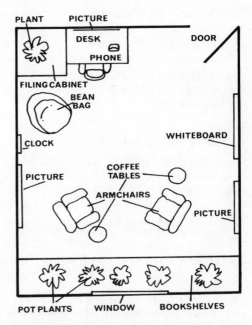

FIGURE 8.1 Counselling room arrangement

EQUIPMENT NEEDED

It is highly desirable to have a whiteboard in every counselling room. Clients who predominantly operate in the visual mode are likely to focus more clearly and gain in awareness if important statements are written on the board, and if their options are listed there. Sometimes a client's dilemma can be expressed through a sketch that metaphorically describes her situation. A whiteboard is particularly useful for helping clients to challenge irrational beliefs or to construct assertive statements. It may also be used as an aid when carrying out educational and administrative tasks which counsellors inevitably undertake as part of their duties.

Always have a box of tissues in a handy place in your counselling room. It is inevitable that some clients will cry and ready availability of tissues saves unnecessary embarrassment.

THE NEED FOR PRIVACY

As discussed in Chapter 7, confidentiality is essential when counselling. A client will not feel comfortable about disclosing intimate personal details unless she is confident that she will not be overheard. If a client can hear voices from outside the counselling room, then she may be justified in fearing that her voice can be heard by others. Counselling rooms should therefore be suitably soundproofed.

Preferably the counselling process should be uninterrupted by the intrusion of people knocking on the door, entering the room, or phoning in unnecessarily. For this reason, many counsellors have a rule that when a counselling room door is closed, no attempt is made by others to enter the room except in unusual circumstances. In many counselling agencies, when a counselling room door is shut, the procedure for contacting the counsellor when unusual circumstances make this necessary is for the receptionist to use the phone. The receptionist allows the phone to ring a few times only and if it is not answered then the counsellor is left undisturbed. This minimises the possibility that the client might be interrupted at an important stage in the counselling process. It enables the client to feel that confidentiality is assured, and allows her to let out her emotions in privacy without the risk of being observed by others.

Setting up your own room

Setting up a counselling room gives the counsellor an opportunity to be creative, and to use her own personal ideas to generate a suitable environment in which clients may feel comfortable and do useful work. You may wish to experiment with the layout and decoration of your own room so that it becomes individually yours and welcoming to others.

Suitable rooms for telephone counselling

The needs of telephone counsellors are obviously somewhat different from those of face-to-face counsellors. Sometimes telephone counselling has to be carried out in open areas where there is not much privacy. However, this is not ideal. Preferably, the counsellor should be in a quiet area where others will not intrude. Certainly, if a caller is to believe that the call has some level of confidentiality then it is essential that extraneous noises or voices are not heard by the caller. Additionally, it is unhelpful for a counsellor to be distracted by the activities of other people.

The ideal situation is for a telephone counsellor to work in a separate room so that quietness and privacy are ensured. However, many crisis counselling agencies prefer to use booths for phone counsellors. These provide some level of privacy and have the advantage that they enable the counsellor to make contact with peers and supervisors easily.

Counsellors have personal needs and it is desirable for the telephone counselling space to be an inviting place which is pleasantly decorated. It needs to have adequate lighting and air-conditioning, or other suitable cooling, heating, or ventilation.

FURNISHINGS AND EQUIPMENT

Telephone counsellors are usually most comfortable if they are seated at a desk so that they are able to make notes and to spread out resource materials. If the desk is facing a wall, information which might be useful for the counsellor can be pinned to a notice board fixed to the wall.

In crisis counselling agencies, it is sensible to provide a second phone line, so that in emergencies the counsellor can seek any help which the caller may be unable to obtain, such as an ambulance or police.

Crisis counselling agencies such as Lifeline sometimes provide beds or sofas for counsellors who are working overnight so that if there are quiet times, counsellors can rest and take turns to relieve each other.

LEARNING SUMMARY

- Counselling rooms need to be client-friendly.

- Client and counsellor chairs that are similar and have no barriers between them suit the empathic relationship.

- Looking towards a window is unpleasant.

- If chairs are too close, personal space may be invaded.

- Counselling rooms are best if soundproofed, have whiteboards, and a supply of tissues.

- Procedures to ensure that counselling sessions are not interrupted are useful.

Part II
Learning specific skills

9 An overview of skills training

How to learn counselling skills

I believe that it is possible to learn some useful counselling skills for use in everyday life just by reading about them. However, I do not believe that you can learn to be a counsellor just by reading a book. If you intend to use this manual alone, then its value will be limited. Alternatively, if you use this book in conjunction with practical training, then my hope is that you will find it really useful.

There are two components involved in learning to become a counsellor. One is understanding what counselling is about and how you are going to use counselling skills and processes. This understanding provides the theoretical framework from which you can operate. The other component is to obtain practical skills training under the supervision of a competent counsellor and trainer. I doubt whether it is possible to learn to be a counsellor in any other way. My assumption is that most readers are reading this book to gain an understanding of basic counselling principles, and are at the same time undergoing a practical course of training.

Enhancing natural counselling skills

Many people have the idea that counselling requires a great deal of skill and is something rather difficult and complicated to learn. If that is what you believe, then stop and ask yourself some questions. Have you ever comforted a child who was crying? Have you ever spent time sitting quietly with a friend who was terribly upset? Have you ever listened to somebody who was in a dilemma, and who did not know what to do? My guess is that you have done all of these things many times. If so, you have on many occasions in your life acted in a natural way as a counsellor with a friend, a relative, a child, or maybe even with someone you met casually.

What was the most important thing you did in these situations? Was it just to let the person know that you cared enough about her to listen to her problem and to be with her in her distress? If it was, then you were behaving like a counsellor. Counselling is an extension of what we all do naturally in our relationships with others when they are suffering emotional pain.

From your own experience you will know that some people are more gifted than others at counselling in a natural way. We all know people who are such good listeners that their friends frequently talk over problems with them. Such people are natural counsellors. The aim of counsellor training is to help you to improve your natural counselling skills, and so become more effective in helping others to deal with their pain.

Learning specific skills (micro-skills)

In Chapter 2 we considered the importance of the counselling relationship. Certainly the relationship is central in counselling, but also there are a number of individual skills that can be learnt which greatly enhance the quality and effectiveness of the counselling relationship. Techniques used by counsellors have been analysed and broken down into small elements of counselling behaviour known as micro-skills. Each of the micro-skills can be learnt individually. However, be warned: a trainee needs to remember that counselling competence seems initially to diminish after each input of micro-skill training. This is because the trainee inevitably concentrates on using the new skill, rather than on building and maintaining the relationship. Also, the trainee isn't able to behave naturally when using a new skill until that skill is fully mastered. Once the skill is fully mastered it becomes a natural part of the counsellor's way of relating, and counselling effectiveness is considerably increased.

Learning in triads

In the following chapters, each of the micro-skills will be explained, one by one. After reading each chapter, it will be best if you practise the relevant micro-skill in a group setting. The usual way to do this is in a triad or a group of three students. One student takes the role of counsellor, a second student takes the role of client and the third student takes the role of observer.

Here are some suggestions about how to work in triads. If you are training for face-to-face counselling, set the room up with the chairs facing each other as shown in Figure 9.1, so that the "client" faces the "counsellor" and the observer watches both.

Telephone counselling is rather different from face-to-face counselling because the telephone counsellor can't see the caller who is her client. Consequently the counsellor doesn't have any visual indication of the client's non-verbal behaviour. The chairs for triad practice for trainee telephone counsellors should therefore be set out with the "counsellor" chair and the "client" chair in a back-to-back arrangement as shown in Figure 9.2, so that the "counsellor" and "client" cannot see each other. However the observer's chair should face the other two chairs so that the observer is aware of what is happening non-verbally, and can feed this back to the other two students at the end of each practice session.

THE USE OF GENUINE PERSONAL PROBLEMS

If counsellor training is to be most effective, then the "client" in the triad needs to present a current and real personal problem of her own. Sometimes I have met students who have told me quite emphatically that they did not have such a thing as a personal problem, and I have found that difficult to believe. I doubt whether such people really exist. In my experience, whenever people have said to me that they don't have any personal problems, I have discovered later that there have been areas of their lives that they were unwilling to discuss, and that they had blocked off and were afraid to venture near. However, I can understand why many trainees worry about using real problems. There are a number of reasons for this, including the following:

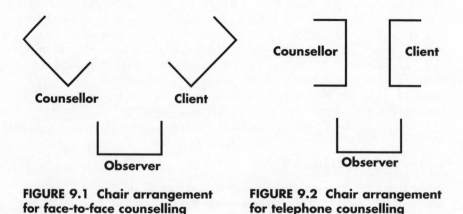

FIGURE 9.1 Chair arrangement for face-to-face counselling practice

FIGURE 9.2 Chair arrangement for telephone counselling practice

1. The worry may be related to a lack of trust in other members of the triad, leading to feelings of vulnerability associated with self-disclosure. The trainee may think, "They won't respect me if they find out about my problems".
2. Unfortunately trainee counsellors frequently believe that they will not be accepted as counsellors if they disclose problems of their own. My response to this is to say that as a counsellor trainer I prefer to work with trainees who are able to own and address their problems. I am always worried by trainees who are not able to do this, because later, when they are trained, their disowned and unresolved issues may interfere with their ability to counsel effectively.
3. Trainees may be justifiably afraid that they may become distressed if they use a real problem.
4. Trainees may fear that if they do become distressed that they may not receive adequate counselling help from the trainee "counsellor". This is understandable. However, I believe that responsible trainers will inform trainees that follow-up counselling from experienced counsellors will always be available.

Trainees have often asked me whether they can use invented problems or other people's problems, but in my view this is not very satisfactory. Most people who have been involved as trainers of counsellors would agree that it is much easier for the student counsellor to respond in a real and genuine way to what is being said if the problem is real, and not invented or borrowed from someone else. Whenever a make-believe problem is used, it is difficult for the trainee counsellor to accurately pick up the "client's" feelings and to appropriately practise counselling skills.

TASKS OF TRIAD MEMBERS
The "counsellor" in a counselling triad should listen, and practise only those micro-skills that have been taught up to that point and not use any other type of response at all. This may seem to be very limiting, but in fact it is possible to carry out an effective counselling session by using only one or two micro-skills on their own. In Chapter 11 there is a transcript of a counselling session where only minimal responses and paraphrasing are used.

The observer's role in the triad is to take notes of anything significant she observes during the counselling practice session. The observer does not make judgments about what should have been done, but rather has the task of observing, as objectively as possible and without making interpretations, what actually happens during the practice session. This information is fed back to the "counsellor" and "client" at the end of the session.

LENGTH OF TRIAD PRACTICE SESSIONS
Practice counselling sessions should typically be short, of about 10 minutes' length, and at the end of each session the observer should share his observations with the other two members of the triad. After that, the "client"

should be given the opportunity to talk about how he felt during the counselling session, and finally the "counsellor" should explore his own feelings, and share with the group how the session was for him. Preferably, in addition to the student observer there should be an experienced trainer observing the triad throughout. Unfortunately, in large group counsellor training, it frequently happens that trainers have to go from triad to triad and are able to spend only a short time with each small group.

MODELLING OF MICRO-SKILLS

Before working in a triad, the micro-skill to be practised should be modelled by a competent counsellor. There are two ways in which this can be done. Either the demonstration can be performed live, or a video-recording may be used. My favoured option is the video-recorded demonstration, because too often live demonstrations, even with competent counsellors, include segments of inappropriate modelling or long sections of client material where it is not appropriate to use the relevant micro-skill.

Ongoing training

This chapter has dealt with an overview of skills training for beginners with no previous counselling experience. Once basic skills have been learnt, the trainee counsellor needs to have ongoing training with real clients under supervision as discussed in Chapter 5.

The following chapters on micro-skills have been deliberately arranged in the most suitable sequence for training. By learning the skills in this sequence, the trainee can practise counselling by using only one or two micro-skills initially, and can then gradually incorporate additional skills into her repertoire. The sequence given is such that the most important basic skills are learnt first, with the consequence that more practice will be obtained in using these skills and the trainee counsellor will begin to rely on them as being the ones that are most appropriate for frequent use.

LEARNING SUMMARY

- Learning to be a counsellor must involve practical training and supervision as well as theoretical knowledge.

- Some people are natural counsellors; however counsellor training can improve their effectiveness.

- A micro-skill is a small element of counsellor behaviour which can be learnt and practised.

FURTHER READING

Dryden, W., Horton, I. and Mearns, D., *Issues in Professional Counsellor Training*. London: Cassell, 1995

Dryden, W. and Thorne, B. (eds), *Training and Supervision for Counselling in Action*. London: Sage, 1991

10 Joining and listening

This chapter deals with both joining and listening because these two processes are interrelated. If I am to join with a client I need to listen and attend to what she is saying. I also need to use a range of behaviours to help her to feel at ease.

The first meeting

Joining doesn't just occur at the initial meeting with the client but is an ongoing process. Throughout the counselling process the client needs to feel comfortable with his connection with the counsellor. However, the initial meeting with a client is extremely important. The client's first impressions of the counsellor will influence her willingness to share openly. First impressions can be enduring and even if they aren't, they are likely to influence the early part of the relationship. It is therefore very important that the climate of the relationship is established right from the beginning.

We need to consider two situations. One is the face-to-face counselling situation and the other is the telephone counselling situation. However, we will discuss the initial contact in telephone counselling later in Chapter 27.

GREETING THE CLIENT

Consider the face-to-face counselling situation. Imagine that I am meeting a client for the first time in my waiting room. What I do, as I move towards the client to greet her, will in some way affect her feelings towards me, and her confidence in me. It's important that the person I meet feels valued and at ease with me. As I meet her, I need to be true to myself rather than putting on an act. I like to be seen as an ordinary person, somebody who is not intimidating, neither expert nor inferior, but friendly, open and informal. You will have your own style, of course, and it may well be different from mine. However, be aware of your style, and use it to help the client to feel welcome.

Be aware of cultural considerations when greeting clients. In some cultures hand-shaking is seen as an intimate act so offering your hand may be excessively intrusive for some people.

OBSERVING THE CLIENT

As you greet the client you can, if you take notice, pick up a lot of information from her. Notice the way she is sitting or standing. Her non-verbal behaviour will tell you something about the way she feels. Look at the clothes she is wearing, and how they are worn. By doing this you will learn something about how she sees herself, and how she wants to be seen. Don't jump to unverified conclusions, but use the information gleaned from your first meeting so that you can gradually build up a picture of the client's world and of her view of that world.

PUTTING THE CLIENT AT EASE

When I meet a client for the first time, I introduce myself and usually chat to her as we walk to my counselling room. This helps her to feel at ease. When I meet her prior to subsequent interviews I am generally less chatty, and often silent. This enables the client to stay with any troubling thoughts rather than to be taken away from them. Be aware that as a client leaves the waiting room and walks to your consulting room, she may well be putting her thoughts together, and may be experiencing the beginnings of heavy emotion as she gets nearer to the issues she wants to discuss. If she is doing that, then it isn't helpful to be talking about trivia. It's better to be silent.

Notice that I have differentiated between the first and subsequent sessions. I try to help the client to feel very much at ease during the first session, and am happy to sacrifice a few minutes of time during that meeting to allow the client to feel comfortable with me, and with the room that I work in. I allow the client to sit down, to look around, and maybe to comment on my plants or some other aspect of my room or the agency. We may even talk about some other casual topic like how she travelled to the agency, and what the traffic was like, or I may share something of myself and my day with her. As a result we start to establish a relationship before moving forward into working on issues.

THE INVITATION TO TALK

Clients sometimes find it difficult to know how to start to talk about their problems. There are obviously many different ways of inviting a client to talk about her problems. Here are some suggestions:

"Would you like to tell me what made you decide to come to see me today?"

"I'm wondering what is troubling you."

"What is it that you would like to talk to me about?"

Some clients may feel pressured to respond to your invitation by talking quickly and concisely so that they don't take up too much of your time. Reassure them that it is OK to take time. Other clients may find it difficult to start to talk and may say that they don't know how to begin. When this happens, I say something like:

"Just relax and take time. Then if you can, tell me whatever it is that comes into your head even if it's unimportant."

This invitation is good for enabling a nervous client to start talking. Once the client has started to talk it is important for her to know that I am listening and attending to what she is saying.

TUNING IN

Have you ever talked about being on the same "wavelength" as someone? Maybe you have sometimes noticed that a person has really "tuned in" to what you are saying. Joining is about "tuning in", or "being on the same wavelength" as someone else. Thus, a harmonious connection is established between the person who is talking and the person who is listening. This is what we need to achieve as counsellors.

Whenever we listen to someone, we give out very subtle clues. These clues give an indication of how we are responding to what is being said, and give an indication of our feelings towards the person who is speaking. As helpers we therefore need to be careful to give out the right messages.

Listening with intent

People usually go to counsellors because they are troubled and don't know what to do to cope with their emotions. They will often expect that the counsellor will give them advice to enable them to change their situation. Because of this it is easy for new counsellors to feel pressured into trying, even early in the counselling process, to find solutions for clients. As a new counsellor, try to remember that the counsellor's primary task is to *listen to the client* and to use strategies which will enable him to find his own solutions. These solutions are likely to suit him because he discovered them. He will have also discovered that he is capable of making his own decisions.

In my experience, before looking for solutions, the first thing most people want to do when they come to see me for counselling help is to *talk about* the things that trouble them. They want to get things off their chests, to vent their feelings, and to say things which might be very difficult or maybe impossible to say to friends or family.

When you are with a client, try to remember that the client has come to talk to you and wants to feel free to unload the stuff that is troubling him. To do this he needs an invitation and opportunity to talk without unnecessary interruption. If you do a lot of talking, then you are likely to interfere with his ability to talk freely and the counselling process is likely to be less useful.

A counsellor is primarily a listener. By listening to what the client says, the counsellor is able to help him to sort through his confusion, identify his dilemmas, explore his options, and come away from the counselling session feeling that something useful has occurred. The counsellor therefore needs to attend very carefully to everything that the client is saying and to remember, as far as is possible, the details of the conversation. If you want to convince your client that you really are listening, then focus your concentration on the client and on what he is telling you. Try to remember, for example, the names of his relatives, what happened five years ago in his relationships, and those things which he briefly mentioned.

The first skill for the new counsellor to learn is to *intentionally listen* to the client. This needs to be done in such a way that the client recognises that you are intentionally focussing your attention on what he is saying, and are comprehending and understanding what he says. Intentional listening involves the use of the following:

1. minimal responses
2. brief invitations to continue

3. non-verbal behaviour
4. voice
5. silence

We will now discuss each of these.

1. USE OF MINIMAL RESPONSES

A good way of letting a client know that she has your full attention and that you are listening to what she is saying is by use of the minimal response. The minimal response is something we automatically do in our conversations when we are predominantly listening rather than talking. Minimal responses are sometimes non-verbal and include just a nod of the head. Also included among minimal responses are expressions like:

> *"'Mm', 'Mm-hmm', 'A-ha', 'I see', 'Yes', 'OK', 'Really', 'Sure', 'Right', 'Oh', and 'Really'"*

These expressions let the client know that he has been heard and also encourage him to continue talking. Some longer responses serve a similar function to the minimal response. For example, the counsellor might say:

> *"'I hear what you say', or 'I understand'"*

While the client is talking continuously, the counsellor needs from time to time to reaffirm that she is listening to what the client is saying, and this can be done by inserting minimal responses at regular intervals. Space your minimal responses appropriately. If they are given too frequently, then they will become intrusive and will be distracting. Conversely, if they are not included frequently enough the client may believe that you are not really attending to what she is saying.

Using the minimal response to convey a message
The minimal response is not just an acknowledgment that the client is being heard. It can also be a way, sometimes subtle, of communicating other messages. It may be used to signify that the counsellor agrees with the client, or to emphasise the importance of a client statement, to express surprise, or even to query what the client is saying. The way in which a minimal response is given—the tone and intensity of voice used, the accompanying nonverbal behaviour such as eye movements, facial expressions and body posture—all combine to convey a message to the client.

Counsellors need to be careful in giving out messages of agreement or disagreement. Sometimes with the best of intentions showing agreement with a client may be counter-productive. I remember being told by a woman I knew that she had discontinued going to see a counsellor because that counsellor had strongly agreed with her criticisms of her husband. I expect that the counsellor thought that by doing this she would join with the client. Unfortunately the counsellor's behaviour prevented the person concerned from talking further because she felt that by doing this she would be being disloyal to her husband. By agreeing with her, the counsellor also blocked her from talking through her own feelings of guilt about her relationship with her husband. She wanted to be heard, understood, and valued, but did not want a stranger who didn't know her husband to be critical of him.

Being empathic involves hearing, understanding, and valuing the client. Can you see how this is different from *agreeing* with the client, which may not be useful?

2. BRIEF INVITATIONS TO CONTINUE

Sometimes, a client will pause and it is important for you to allow the client time to think. However, once the client has finished thinking it may be useful to give a brief invitation to the client to continue. You could do this by using one of the following responses:

> **“‘Then …’, ‘And …’, ‘Tell me more’, ‘Can you tell me more?’, ‘Would you like to tell me more?’ or ‘Would you like to continue?’ ”**

Counselling involves the art of listening constructively so appropriate use of minimal responses and brief invitations to continue is essential.

3. USE OF NON-VERBAL BEHAVIOUR

There are a number of ways in which a counsellor can use her non-verbal behaviour to join with the client and enhance the counselling process. These include:

- matching non-verbal behaviour
- physical closeness
- the use of movement
- facial expression
- eye contact

Matching non-verbal behaviour

Along with the use of minimal responses, another way in which a counsellor can help the client to feel that he is really being listened to is to match his non-verbal behaviour. If a client is sitting on the edge of the seat, with his arms on his knees looking forward, then it may be useful for the counsellor to sit in the same way and in effect to mirror the client's posture. By doing this, the client is likely to feel as though there is some intimacy between himself and the counsellor, rather than that the counsellor is a superior expert sitting back, listening and judging what is being said. Similarly, if the client leans back in his chair with his legs crossed, and the counsellor casually matches that posture, the client may well feel more at ease. Clearly, matching needs to be done appropriately so that the counsellor is seen to be acting naturally rather than mimicking the client.

If a counsellor matches a client's non-verbal behaviour and posture for a while, then more often than not the client will match the counsellor's behaviour when the counsellor makes a change. In this way the counsellor can sometimes bring about some change in the client's emotional state. For example, a client may be so tense that he is sitting on the edge of his chair and is unable to relax into a more comfortable sitting position. If the counsellor matches his position initially and then moves back to sit more comfortably, the client is likely to follow the counsellor's example and consequently to experience a reduction in his level of tension.

Physical closeness

We all have different personal comfort levels with regard to physical closeness. Also, we need to recognise that there are major differences in comfort levels, related to physical closeness, for people from different cultures.

Think about how you would feel personally if someone you were talking to was to stand a long way from you, or was to move further away while you were talking. You might get the message that he wasn't interested in what you were saying, or that he thought that you weren't a very nice person so he didn't want to be close to you. Also, consider what it's like when someone stands too close to you for your comfort. How does that feel?

Clearly, as a counsellor, it is best to sit at an appropriate distance from the person you are helping, so that he feels comfortable. Knowing the correct distance is a matter of judgment. Remember, you need to sense what is comfortable for the other person and to be careful not to intrude on his personal space.

The use of movement

Sometimes, at significant times in the counselling process or when a client is experiencing a high level of emotional distress it can be useful for the counsellor to lean forward. This can help the client to recognise that the counsellor is joining with him in an empathic way. However, a counsellor should be careful not to move her body too quickly during a counselling session, as this can distract the client and interrupt his train of thought. The counsellor does need to feel as relaxed as possible in the situation and should feel free to move her position in a natural way whenever she wants, but this should be done slowly and not suddenly.

Facial expression

Facial expression is very important in the joining process. Our facial expression can give very obvious clues about what we are thinking, and about our attitudes. Clearly, we want to show an expression of our interest, care, and concern. Also, we want to try to avoid giving the impression that we are making negative judgments about the person, or what the person is saying.

Eye contact

Eye contact is an important way in which we human beings make contact and join with each other. Not only do we use our eyes to make contact, but we also convey subtle messages by the way in which we use our eyes. I wonder what impression you would get if somebody was looking away from you while you were talking to him? My guess is that you might believe that he wasn't interested in what you were saying. However, if he were to look at you directly, eye to eye, you might feel uncomfortable and think that his eyes were "boring into you". What is required is an appropriate level of eye contact where your eyes meet with the other person's eyes in a socially and culturally acceptable way. It is important to remember that different cultures have different social norms with regard to appropriate levels of eye contact. However, if your client is to believe that you are listening to him, then eye contact, at an appropriate level, will let him know that you are attending to, and interested in, what he is saying.

4. THE USE OF VOICE

When I speak, it is not only the words which convey a message. Additionally, a message in conveyed through the way in which I use my voice. If I am to convey to my client that I am intentionally listening to what she is saying, and if I am to create an empathic relationship, then I will need to pay attention to the following voice qualities:

- clarity and volume
- speed of speaking
- tone of voice

Over an extended period I sought counselling help from a very capable and skilled counsellor. He helped me to address many painful issues and to experience satisfaction through personal growth. I very much appreciate the help he gave me. However, he had one annoying fault. Sometimes, I couldn't hear what he was saying because he mumbled. He didn't articulate words clearly and didn't talk loudly enough. At times this interfered with the counselling process by distracting me and enabling me to deflect away from issues which I needed to address. It was also embarrassing for me to have to continually ask him to speak up.

When you are counselling, be careful to talk clearly and at a comfortable volume. Make sure that your tone of voice is one which will help to create an empathic relationship. Generally, it can be helpful if you match the speed of talking and tone of voice of your client. When she talks rapidly respond similarly, and when she slows up be more leisurely yourself. If you match, to an appropriate degree, the speed and tone of speaking and the speed of breathing of an agitated client, you will be likely to join with her. Then, if you slow down your breathing and your speaking speed, and sit back comfortably in your chair, the client may follow your example, slow down and adopt a more relaxed posture.

5. THE USE OF SILENCE

When I was a new counsellor, I remember often not focussing fully on what the client was saying because I was too concerned with trying to decide what my next counselling response would be. This was really destructive to the counselling process. It was due to my nervousness and desire to appear to be professional and competent rather than friendly and real. At that time, I was uncomfortable with silence and felt that I had a responsibility to fill gaps in the conversation. Now I am more comfortable with silence so there is little pressure on me to give a response the instant the client stops talking. Instead I feel relaxed enough to allow the client, if he wants, to think in silence. Often when a client has just finished making a very powerful and personal statement, he will need time to sit silently and process what he has said.

When a client is silent, match that silence while continuing to pay attention, so that you are seen to be intentionally listening, by using appropriate eye contact. If you observe the client's eye movements and focussing, you may be able to tell when he is thinking and needs to be left to think rather than be interrupted.

LEARNING SUMMARY

- Joining is an ongoing process.

- A counsellor's primary function is to intentionally listen.

- Intentional listening involves use of minimal responses, non-verbal behaviour, voice, silence and brief invitations to continue.

- Minimal responses can be verbal or non-verbal.

- Minimal responses let the client know that you are attending, help create an empathic relationship, and give the client messages.

- Joining with the client is enhanced by matching non-verbal behaviour such as posture, matching verbal tone and speed, and making appropriate eye contact.

- Rapid movements by a counsellor can distract a client.

- Silence is important in giving the client time to think and process what has been said.

- A client's eyes may give you an indication of when he has stopped thinking.

11 Reflection of content (paraphrasing)

As explained in the previous chapter, the primary function of the counsellor is to intentionally listen so that the client believes with confidence that she is being both heard and understood. However, it's obvious that just attending to the client by matching non-verbal behaviour and giving minimal responses is not sufficient. The counsellor also needs to respond more actively, and by doing so to draw out the really important content details of what the client is saying and to clarify those for the client. The most common and generally most effective way of doing this is by using the skill called *paraphrasing* or *reflection of content*. Using this skill the counsellor literally reflects back to the client what the client has said to the counsellor. The counsellor does not just parrot or repeat word for word what the client has said but instead paraphrases it. This means that the counsellor picks out the most important content details of what the client has said and re-expresses them in a clearer way, if that is possible, and in her own words rather than in the client's. The following are some examples of paraphrasing to help you understand how the skill is used.

Examples of paraphrasing or reflection of content

Example 1

CLIENT STATEMENT I'm fighting with my daughter, my husband's not speaking to me, at work the boss keeps picking on me, and what's more my best friend doesn't seem to understand me any more.

COUNSELLOR RESPONSE You're having a lot of relationship problems.

Example 2

CLIENT STATEMENT I spent all day Saturday cleaning up my girlfriend's yard but she was annoyed because she said I'd cut the shrubs too short, I'd over-pruned them. Then I went to a great deal of trouble repainting the back door. Once again she didn't like the colour. Finally I suggested that she might go out to eat with me and would you believe when she got to the restaurant she decided that she really didn't like that restaurant at all. I keep trying to think of things that she would like but whatever I do she never seems to be happy.

COUNSELLOR RESPONSE It seems as though you just can't please your girlfriend.

Example 3

CLIENT STATEMENT Yesterday I rushed around, I seemed to have no time to myself, I went from one place to another and it was really hard to fit everything in.

COUNSELLOR RESPONSE You had a very full day yesterday.

Do you understand what is meant by "paraphrasing" or "reflection of content" now? What the counsellor does is literally to tell the client, in a clear, brief way, in the counsellor's own words, the most important things that the client has just told the counsellor. The counsellor tries to capture the essential ingredients of what the client is saying and reflect these back. This method alone, together with minimal responses, can be used successfully throughout a complete counselling session, if it is carried out by a skilful person who is capable of accurately and clearly reflecting content.

The following transcript of a short counselling session (using invented names) demonstrates the way in which paraphrasing alone can be used to bring a client to a sense of resolution.

Transcript of a counselling session using minimal responses and paraphrasing

MARY Susan, you said that you would like to talk something over with me. Can you tell me what is troubling you? (Mary gives Susan an invitation to talk.)

SUSAN Yes. I'm worried about what's happening at work. I'm getting very stressed when I'm there.

MARY Mm-hmm.

SUSAN It seems as though I am continually at odds with some of the other workers and with my boss. I just don't seem to be on the same wavelength as them.

MARY You're not fitting in.

SUSAN No, I'm not. I don't agree with the policies which are being adopted by the top management because they don't fit in with the way I learnt to deal with customers. Over the years I've developed ways of working which I think work …

MARY Right.

SUSAN And now I'm being expected to change my whole style of working.

MARY They want you to work in a way which doesn't suit you.

SUSAN Yes they do, and I'm beginning to think that I'll either have to resign or compromise my principles. I'm just not sure what to do.

MARY You have a difficult choice to make.

SUSAN Yes, I have … (pause)

MARY (silent but attending)

SUSAN … but you know I don't see why I should resign. I need the job, it's convenient, the money's good and there aren't many other jobs I could do which would suit me. They will just have to put up with me.

MARY You sound as though you've made a decision to stay.

SUSAN Yes, I have, but I'll need to think about the implications.

MARY Mm-hmm.

SUSAN I suppose that if I continue to work in the way I think is best I'll still get the outcomes the boss wants but she'll get annoyed because I'm not following policy … Somehow, I've got to compromise so that I can satisfy the boss and still feel OK about what I'm doing myself.

MARY You'd like to please the boss and still feel OK yourself.

SUSAN Yes, I would. I would like to please the boss so that the atmosphere at work is more relaxed. I suppose I've been a bit stubborn in resisting change.

MARY Mmm.

SUSAN That's probably the issue. I don't like change. But then nobody does. I'd rather change and continue working where I am than move somewhere else.

MARY Accepting change is difficult for you.

SUSAN Yes it is. But that's what I need to do. I suppose that if I agreed to do some in-service training I'd feel more confident about the new methods but I don't like other people believing that I need further training after all these years.

MARY Ah-ha.

SUSAN I suppose that the truth is that I do need further training and it's hard for me to accept that fact.

MARY You want other people to respect you as an experienced worker.

SUSAN Yes, and at the moment they see me as a dinosaur. Out of date and inflexible.

MARY Ah-ha, they don't see you as able to adapt.

SUSAN Well, I am out of date but I'm not inflexible. I can learn new ways of working. I'll show them that an old conjurer can learn new tricks!

MARY You're going to accept the challenge.

SUSAN Yes, I am. I don't want to be seen as an old fossil, because I'm not.

MARY You seem to have reached a firm conclusion.

SUSAN Yes, I have. Thank you for listening to me.

If you look through the transcript above, you will notice that Mary has used no other responses except minimal responses and reflection of content. Once she combined a minimal response with paraphrasing by saying, "Ah-ha, they don't see you as able to adapt".

Did you notice as you read the transcript that there was a natural flow in the conversation? Each time Susan made a statement and Mary paraphrased it, her reflection of Susan's statement set off a train of thoughts for Susan so that she continued with the conversation in a natural way. Consequently, it would have seemed to Susan that Mary really was understanding what she was saying. Mary wasn't intruding on Susan's thoughts by adding in her own ideas.

By reflecting back what Susan said, Mary was able to help her think clearly about what she had said. This enabled her to continue talking about the same issue, in a constructive way. It was as though she was walking along a path, in her thoughts, with Mary walking alongside her.

You may have noticed that even though the conversation between Susan and Mary was short, Susan resolved her issue without Mary asking questions, putting in suggestions, or giving advice. All she did was to skilfully reflect back to Susan what she was saying.

It's important for you to learn how to paraphrase. In order to help you to do this I have provided some more examples of paraphrasing below. In each case I suggest that you might like to cover up the counsellor response with a sheet of paper, read the client statement and see whether you can work out a suitable counsellor response to the client's statement. Good paraphrasing doesn't intrude. It doesn't distract the client from the real issues which she is trying to resolve.

Further examples of paraphrasing

Example 1

CLIENT STATEMENT Within a week I've had a rates notice, an electricity bill, my car broke down and I've had to spend $200 having it fixed, there was a big dinner I had to attend as part of my work and it was very expensive, and in addition I've had to fork out money for my son's trip overseas and for my daughter's school fees.

COUNSELLOR RESPONSE You've had a lot of expenses to meet in a very short time.

Example 2

CLIENT STATEMENT Now that my father has died I can't help thinking about him. I think about the good times I had with him when I was young and about the way he showed so much interest in me in the early days of my marriage. I remember the way in which he played with my children, his grandchildren. He always seemed to be enjoying himself.

COUNSELLOR RESPONSE You have some good memories of your father.

Example 3

CLIENT STATEMENT The house is old and ramshackle, the rooms are very large, there isn't much in it and it needs redecorating. Parts of it are starting to fall down. Where you walk there are bare floorboards and they creak. It doesn't sound very much like home because it is such a big, open, old, barren sort of a place, but you know I really like living there.

COUNSELLOR RESPONSE Even though the house is in poor condition it's home to you.

Example 4

CLIENT STATEMENT I used to have a very bad drinking problem so I stopped drinking for a couple of years. Well last night I had a drink and now I'm just wondering how that's going to affect me in the future. I'm really surprised though because I was able to have just one drink and stop, whereas in the past I always used to carry on drinking once I'd started.

COUNSELLOR RESPONSE Although you surprised yourself, you're not too sure how you'll cope with alcohol from now on.

Example 5

CLIENT STATEMENT My daughter's a very attractive girl, she's good looking and vivacious, she dresses very nicely and she is a good-natured person. She often smiles and seems to be very happy.

COUNSELLOR RESPONSE Your daughter has many positive qualities.

Please remember that individual counsellors may paraphrase the same client statement differently. They may not pick up on the same detail as each other. The model answers which I have given above are not necessarily the best responses. I believe that I am a good counsellor, but I do not consider myself to be perfect in any of the micro-skills. I have yet to find someone who is. It's really important to remember that it doesn't matter how perfect your responses are. What does matter is that you create a real, trusting, caring, empathic relationship in which you are genuinely yourself. This may mean sometimes being a bungler, and occasionally saying something inappropriate. I have many times given an inappropriate response. Although I try not to do that, there will always be times when I do.

USING INAPPROPRIATE RESPONSES

I used to think that it was a disaster to give an inappropriate response until an artist friend of mine talked to me about pencil sketching. I told her how it was that when I tried to sketch I very often had the sketch three-quarters complete and then ruined it by putting in a dark line in an inappropriate place. My artist friend laughed and said, "You never draw lines in the wrong place, because whenever you put in a line you can use it to create something different". I learnt a lesson from what she said and applied it to my counselling. When I make an inappropriate response, I use that response. It will generate an interaction between myself and the client, and I am able to encourage the client to explore the effect that the inappropriate response had on her. By doing this I am using the immediacy of the relationship between myself and the client. This will be discussed more fully in Chapter 25.

PARROTING

Paraphrasing is not the same as parroting. Parroting involves repeating word for word what the client has said to you. Occasionally it can be useful to parrot the client's last few words to draw attention to the importance of these words, or to enable the client to continue a half-finished statement. As a general rule, paraphrasing is a much more helpful process. This is because paraphrasing picks out the most important and salient parts of the content rather than just repeating the words the client has used. Continually repeating part or all of what the client has said would be likely to annoy the client rather then create a good relationship. Skilful reflection of content in the counsellor's own words does the reverse. It makes the client feel valued, listened to, and heard, and is useful in helping the client to move forward in her exploration.

In conclusion

In this chapter you have learnt about paraphrasing or reflection of content. Paraphrasing is a very useful basic skill to use. To paraphrase you have to listen carefully and to repeat back in your own words the essence of what the client has said. By doing this the client feels that you have heard her and also becomes more fully aware of what she has said. She is then able to really savour the importance of what she herself is talking about and to sort out her confusion.

> **LEARNING SUMMARY**
>
> - Paraphrasing involves reflecting back to the client the important content of what the client has said but in a clearer way and using the counsellor's words.
>
> - Parroting involves repetition of some of the client's words.
>
> - Occasional parroting can be useful either to emphasise the importance of what the client has said or to help a client to complete a half-finished statement.
>
> - Paraphrasing, together with the use of minimal responses, helps the client to follow through on a train of thoughts and continue talking.

Examples of client statements for use by trainers in teaching paraphrasing

1. "My brother has had a serious motorbike accident and it looks as though he may be permanently crippled. He's a builder by trade and now he may never be able to walk again. I don't know how he'll be able to work."
2. "The cancer is malignant and now I only have six months to live at the most. There is so much that I want to do and I can't decide what to do first. I am certainly going to have to do things in a hurry."
3. "The law is very unjust. He discovered where I live, followed me, deliberately aimed the gun, and fired several shots directly at me to try to kill me. He even asked the police if I was dead, and then he's given a light sentence on so-called psychiatric grounds. It's not fair."
4. "I've never stayed in one place for more that a couple of years. In the last few months I've lived in five different houses. It's hardly worth unpacking when I move now because I know I'll move on again. I just can't settle."
5. "The pain starts in my head and moves down into my back. Sometimes my whole body aches. The pain never stops and is overwhelming."
6. "I think my father is a hypocrite. He's a preacher who preaches love and forgiveness and is charming to everybody except his own family. In the family he's a tyrant who bullies everyone and is unforgiving. I'm rapidly losing my respect for him."

12 Reflection of feelings

As explained in the previous chapter, one of the best ways to help a client to feel as though you are listening to him is to reflect back to him the content of what he is saying. Reflection of feelings is similarly useful. Personally, I believe that it may be the most useful micro-skill of all.

Reflection of feelings is at the same time similar to and different from paraphrasing. It is similar because it involves reflecting back to the client information provided by the client. However it is different because it deals with emotional feelings, whereas paraphrasing generally deals with the information and thoughts that make up the content of what the client is saying.

Feelings are different from thoughts?

Feelings are quite different from thoughts. Thoughts mill around in our brains. They are at a "head" level, whereas feelings are to do with emotions. Feelings are at a gut level, not a head level, and they tie into our physiological sensations. For example, a person who is feeling tense emotionally may experience the tension in his muscles, often in the neck or shoulders, and an anxious person may have sweaty palms, an increased heart-rate or the sensation of "butterflies in the stomach".

AVOIDING FEELINGS

Frequently clients try to avoid exploring their feelings because they want to avoid the pain associated with strong emotions such as sadness, despair, anger, and anxiety. I know that for me personally it's much less painful to philosophise about my problems, and to discuss them as though they were "out there" and didn't really belong to me. Unfortunately when I avoid my feelings, philosophise, and talk in a general way about my problems rather than fully experiencing the effect they have on me emotionally, I rarely feel better or reach a resolution. Instead, I tend to go around in circles and get nowhere. However, if I get in touch with my feelings, own them, and experience them fully, then I usually move forward, to feel better emotionally and maybe then to make sensible decisions for myself.

EXPERIENCING FEELINGS

It may be tempting for a new counsellor to help the client to avoid painful feelings rather than to face them. Many of us learn from childhood to comfort people by encouraging them to run away from their feelings. We are taught to say, "Don't cry, it'll be all right", when it quite probably won't be all right, and the person really needs to cry to release his emotional pain. I believe that to be an effective counsellor you will need to unlearn some of what you learnt as a child. You will generally need to encourage your clients to experience their emotions, to be sad, to cry, to be angry and to shout, to be overwhelmed, to be amused, to be frightened or whatever. By doing this you will help them to gain from emotional release and to move forward. This healing process of emotional release is called *catharsis*.

There are exceptions to this approach. Some people are so continually in touch with, and overwhelmed by their emotions, that to encourage them to do more of the same is unlikely to be useful. These people may find it more helpful to make use of their thinking processes in order to control their emotions. For them a more cognitive behavioural approach may be preferred (see Chapter 3).

DISTINGUISHING BETWEEN THOUGHTS AND FEELINGS

New counsellors often have problems in distinguishing between thoughts and feelings because people often use the word "feel" when they are describing a thought. For example if I say "I feel angry" then I am expressing a feeling, but if I say, "I feel that counsellors learn best through practical experience", I am really not expressing a feeling at all but rather a thought and I would have been more accurate if I'd said, "I think that counsellors learn best through practical experience". The words "feel that" followed by a string of words generally mean that a thought is being expressed and not a feeling. Feelings are usually expressed by one word. For example I can feel "angry", "sad", "depressed", "frustrated", "miserable", "tense", "relaxed", "happy" or "frantic". Each of these feelings is expressed by one word, whereas thoughts can only be expressed by using a string of words.

Reflecting back feelings

When a counsellor reflects back a feeling to a client he does not necessarily need to use the word "feel" at all. Here are some options for reflecting feelings:

> ❝'You're feeling angry' or 'You feel angry' or 'You're angry' ❞

> ❝'You're feeling happy' or 'You feel happy' or 'You're happy' ❞

An experienced counsellor continually identifies his client's feelings and reflects them back at the appropriate times. Sometimes a client will tell you directly how he is feeling and at other times you will need to be able to assess what he is feeling by listening to the content of what he is saying or by noting non-verbal behaviour or by listening to the tone of his voice.

FEELING WORDS

Table 12.1 provides a list of commonly used feeling words. Notice that all of the words in the table could be used as counsellor responses by prefacing them with "You're feeling ...", or, "You feel ...", or, "You're ..." In some cases we have to be careful which option to use. For example "You're grieving" sounds empathic whereas "You're feeling grief" is rather clumsy.

The words in this table have been arranged so that the words on each line relate to each other over a continuum from strong feelings to mild feelings. Some of the cells in Table 12.1 are shaded and contain question marks. You may wish to choose suitable words for insertion in these shaded cells and then look at Table 12.2 at the end of this chapter for my suggestions. Can you see how if we choose our words carefully we may be able to accurately describe the client's feelings?

With practice it becomes easier to identify feelings such as tension, distress and sadness from a person's body posture, facial expressions and movements. Tears starting to well up in your client's eyes might let you know about his sadness.

PERMISSION TO CRY

Sometimes people need permission to cry because in our culture crying, particularly by men, is often considered to be unacceptable. I sometimes say to a client "I can see the tears in your eyes" or "For me, it's OK if you cry" or just "It's OK to cry" in a gentle, accepting tone of voice, and then the tears will start to flow. Allow your client to cry. If you hand him tissues or comfort him before the emotion subsides naturally, you may well intrude on his internal processes. The client may then withdraw from fully experiencing his feelings, and the healing effects of emotional release may be diminished.

RESPONSE TO REFLECTION OF FEELINGS

Be prepared for a possible dramatic response from your client whenever you reflect feelings. For a new counsellor this is sometimes alarming, but it is often useful for the client. If you correctly say to your client "I get the impression that you are really hurting inside", then the client will get in touch with his painful feelings and may start to cry, and you will need to deal with the feelings generated in you by his crying.

Sometimes, when you reflect back anger by saying "You're angry" or perhaps "You sound very angry" the client will respond by angrily snapping back with "I'm not angry" followed by an angry tirade, often directed at the counsellor. If this happens, allow yourself to feel good, because you have enabled the client to express anger which he does not wish to own openly. He has been able to discharge some of his anger onto you, and it may be that he will feel better for that. Dealing with angry clients can have its dangers, so be careful. A full chapter has been devoted to this topic (Chapter 29).

READY TO BURST!

Human beings can be likened in some ways to party balloons. When we are functioning effectively we have sufficient emotional energy inside us to keep us motivated to live our daily lives functionally and creatively. The balloon has sufficient air inside it to be robust and float through the air. At crisis times in our lives the emotional pressure builds up until we are ready to burst. In this state our thought processes are often blocked or distorted and we are unable to cope.

Table 12.1 Some commonly used feeling words

Line	Strong feelings	Medium level feelings	Mild feelings
1	honoured cherished treasured	valued appreciated	accepted
2	powerful energetic	strong determined	positive certain
3	powerless	weak	tired
4	thrilled	very pleased	pleased
5	???	loved	liked respected
6	optimistic confident	???	uncertain
7	paranoid	suspicious	curious
8	hated	alienated	disliked
9	proud	self-satisfied	contented
10	perplexed	puzzled confused	uncertain doubtful
11	frantic agitated	???	concerned
12	relaxed	calm	indifferent
13	jealous	envious	discontented
14	???	surprised	pleased
15	terrified	???	worried anxious
16	distraught	distressed miserable	unhappy

continued ...

Table 12.1 *continued*

Line	Strong feelings	Medium level feelings	Mild feelings
17	secure	safe	OK
18	vulnerable	???	uncertain
19	appalled	dismayed	disappointed
20	humiliated ashamed	embarrassed	stupid
21	???	worn out	tired
22	intolerant	impatient	uneasy
23	betrayed	cheated	misled
24	ready to snap	tense	???
25	bewildered	puzzled	uncertain
26	horrified appalled shocked	dismayed taken aback	surprised
27	???	delighted	happy
28	devastated shattered broken-hearted	sad miserable depressed	disappointed troubled
29	grieving	shocked lost empty	alone
30	furious mad	angry resentful	???
31	abused victimised attacked	threatened	blamed

We feel out of control of ourselves. To regain control we first need to release some of the emotional pressure. This may be difficult as many of us have been taught from childhood to hold our emotions in, not to cry, and not to be angry.

An effective counsellor can help a client to fully experience his emotions and thus to feel better as a result of cathartic release. With cathartic release the pressure in the balloon drops back to normal. Rational thinking can start to take place again so that constructive decision making can occur.

Reflection of feelings is therefore, as stated previously, one of the most important, perhaps *the* most important counselling skill. The following are examples of client statements, followed by suitable reflections of feeling. Before reading the suggested counsellor response for each example, write down the response you would give.

Examples of reflection of feelings

Example 1

CLIENT STATEMENT I keep expecting my mother to show more interest in me. Time and again I've asked her to come over to see me but she never does. Yesterday it was my birthday and she did come to visit me, but do you know she didn't even remember that it was my birthday. I just don't think she cares about me at all. (Said slowly in a flat tone of voice.)

COUNSELLOR RESPONSE "You're disappointed" or "You feel hurt".

Example 2

CLIENT STATEMENT First of all, my brother broke my electric drill. He didn't bother to tell me that he'd broken it, he just left it lying there. Then what do you think he did, he borrowed my motorbike without asking me. I feel like thumping him.

COUNSELLOR RESPONSE "You're very angry" or "You're furious".

Example 3

CLIENT STATEMENT I got a new job recently. It's quite different from the old one. The boss is nice to me, I've got a good office to work in, the whole atmosphere in the firm is really positive. I can't believe that I'm so lucky.

COUNSELLOR RESPONSE "You feel really happy" or "You're really happy".

Example 4

CLIENT STATEMENT Young people nowadays aren't like they used to be in my day, dressed smartly; they're dirty, they're rude, they don't stand for you in buses, I don't know what's become of the new generation!

COUNSELLOR RESPONSE "You're disgusted".

Example 5

CLIENT STATEMENT My boyfriend just rang me from his hotel overseas. He's a reporter and is in a real trouble spot. While I was talking to him on the phone I could hear angry voices in the background, and then there was an incredible crash, and the line went dead, and I don't know what's happened to him! (Said very quickly and breathlessly.)

COUNSELLOR RESPONSE "You're terribly worried" or "You're panicking".

These examples probably gave you an idea of how difficult it is to assess the feelings underlying a client statement when non-verbal cues including facial expression and body posture are not available. When you are actively engaged in a counselling interaction with a client it will be easier for you to identify what the client is feeling because you will have the use of all your senses. If you are attending closely to your client your own feelings may start to match his. When he is hurting, at a less intense level, you may experience something of his hurt and this will be useful in helping you to reflect his feelings accurately.

With experience at reflecting feelings you will be able to use a variety of expressions so that your responses sound natural rather than stereotyped and somewhat mechanical. Sometimes a short response such as "You're hurting" is appropriate. But at other times you might use expressions such as the following:

“I get the impression that you are really hurting now.”

“From what you are saying my guess is that you are hurting deep down.”

“Right now you're hurting.”

As a general rule try to keep your counselling responses short. Remember that it is desirable for the client to do most of the talking and that your job is to listen and hear. Long counsellor responses intrude on the client's own inner processes and prevent the client from freely and openly exploring his issues.

When you have fully mastered reflection of feelings move ahead to the next chapter and learn to combine reflection of *content* with reflection of *feelings*.

LEARNING SUMMARY

- Feelings are emotions, not thoughts. They are experienced at a gut level and not at a head level.

- Feelings are usually expressed by one word, for example, "sad", "happy", "lonely", and "bewildered".

- Reflecting feelings back to clients is helpful in promoting emotional release with consequent healing.

- Clients sometimes need permission to cry.

Examples of client statements for use by trainers in teaching reflection of feelings

1. "I don't know how I'm going to do it all. I have to go to work, pay the bills, look after the children, do the washing, and clean the house, all before Wednesday. I just can't do it!"
2. "I know he's got a gun and he could come round to the house at any time. The police say they can't do anything because he hasn't done anything yet. It'll be too late when they do come to help. I'll be dead."
3. "He's a good boy but he does get into trouble and I love him. I never know what he's going to get up to next. Every day I wonder who is going to come knocking at the door to tell me something terrible."
4. "We won. We won the big prize, the new car!"
5. "My brother died last week. I miss him dreadfully. I wish I hadn't criticised him so much recently because he was really a very good person."
6. "My mother treats me like dirt. She never praises me for anything. Colleen gets all the praise. All I get is black looks."

Table 12.2 Suggested solutions for Table 12.1

Line	Suggested solutions	Line	Suggested solutions
5	adored worshipped idolised	18	insecure
6	hopeful	21	exhausted
11	worried	24	nervous worried
14	amazed astonished	27	ecstatic
15	frightened scared	30	annoyed

13 Reflection of content and feeling

The skills which have been discussed so far are the most basic and important ones, because together they provide a foundation onto which other skills can be added. With experience you will find that you can quite often combine reflection of content with reflection of feelings. For example, the statement "You feel disappointed because your brother didn't do as he promised" is a statement that includes both feeling and content. The feeling is one of disappointment, the content is to do with the reasons for being disappointed—because the brother didn't do as he promised. So that the idea of combining reflection of feeling and content becomes clearer, let us look at a few examples. First, we will take another look at the examples given in Chapter 12, but this time the counsellor responses will include reflection of both feeling and content, whereas in Chapter 12 reflection of feeling alone was used. Notice that the responses are short and not wordy.

Examples of reflection of feeling and content

Example 1

CLIENT STATEMENT I keep expecting my mother to show more interest in me. Time and again I've asked her to come over to see me but she never does. Yesterday it was my birthday and she did come to visit me, but do you know she didn't even remember that it was my birthday. I just don't think she cares about me at all. (Said slowly in a flat tone of voice.)

COUNSELLOR RESPONSE "You're disappointed by your mother's behaviour" or "You feel hurt by your mother's apparent lack of caring".

Example 2

CLIENT STATEMENT First of all, my brother broke my electric drill. He didn't bother to tell me that he'd broken it, he just left it lying there. Then what do you think he did, he went and borrowed my motorbike without telling me. I feel like thumping him.

COUNSELLOR RESPONSE "You're very angry with your brother" or "You're furious with your brother".

Example 3

CLIENT STATEMENT I got a new job recently. It's quite different from the old one. The boss is nice to me, I've got a good office to work in, the whole atmosphere in the firm is really positive. I can't believe that I'm so lucky.

COUNSELLOR RESPONSE "You feel really happy with your new job" or "You're really happy with your new job".

Example 4

CLIENT STATEMENT Young people nowadays aren't like they used to be in my day, dressed smartly; they're dirty, they're rude, they don't stand for you in buses, I don't know what's become of the new generation!

COUNSELLOR RESPONSE "Young people disgust you" or "You feel disgusted by the younger generation's behaviour".

Example 5

CLIENT STATEMENT My boyfriend just rang me from his hotel overseas. He's a reporter and is in a real trouble spot. While I was talking to him on the phone I could hear angry voices in the background, and then there was an incredible crash, and the line went dead, and I don't know what's happened to him! (Said very quickly and breathlessly.)

COUNSELLOR RESPONSE "You sound really worried about what might have happened to your boyfriend".

Further examples of reflection of feeling and content

Here are some more client statements for you to practise with. In each case, invent a suitable counsellor response and write it down. Then compare your response with the one supplied at the end of this chapter.

Example 1

CLIENT STATEMENT I'm getting very worn out, whenever anything goes wrong I get blamed. I spend my time running around looking after other people's needs and in return I get no thanks and lots of criticism. It's just not fair. The more I do the less I'm appreciated.

Example 2

CLIENT STATEMENT You just wouldn't believe the dishwasher has broken down, the washing machine still hasn't been fixed, my husband ran the car into a post, my daughter's bike has a puncture, I just can't believe it, so much is going wrong. What's going to go wrong next? I just can't take any more.

Example 3

CLIENT STATEMENT I just can't understand my son and daughter. They always want to be together, but whenever they are together they fight. It doesn't seem to matter what I suggest they do when they're together, they start an argument. It's incessant, it never stops and now I'm starting to get like them, I'm starting to get angry and irritable too. Sometimes I'm so angry that I could knock their heads together.

Example 4

CLIENT STATEMENT I've done everything I can to get her back. I've given her presents, I've phoned her, I've written her letters, sent messages through her friends, I've said I'm sorry, and I've even offered to go and get counselling with her, but whatever I do I just can't get through to her and she just won't come back to me. I just can't live without her!

Example 5

CLIENT STATEMENT I can't understand why my landlord won't give me my bond back but he won't. I cleaned the flat, I left it in good condition, I know he doesn't like me and he just won't give me the bond back. I know I really ought to go and confront him and say to him that this isn't fair. It's not fair. I even got my friends to come round and help me clean up. I spent two days trying to make the place decent, and it was beautiful when I walked out, but he still won't give me the money back. I really ought to go and confront him, but he's a big man and he tends to be very angry at times and you never know—if there was an argument he might hit me!

Example 6

CLIENT STATEMENT I went next door to ask my neighbour if he would drive me over to my boyfriend's place because I'm worried about him. I know it's a long way, but I'm sure my neighbour could do it. All he said was, "No, I can't afford the petrol, and in any case I don't want to go out in this bad weather". I can't understand how he can be so callous because my boyfriend could be seriously ill for all I know. I just can't understand how my neighbour can sit and do nothing, and I'm sure that if it was one of his friends, someone he cared about, that he would go out tonight.

The use of short responses

As stated previously, it's desirable for a counsellor to keep his responses short so as not to intrude on the client's inner processes. The problem with using long statements is that they may take the client away from what he is currently experiencing and may bring him out of his own world and into the counsellor's world.

Deciding whether to reflect content or feeling or both

You have just been learning how to combine the skills of reflection of content and reflection of feelings. There are times when it is appropriate to use this combined type of response. However, at other times it will be more appropriate, in the interests of brevity, to use either reflection of content, or reflection of feeling, but not both. This is particularly true when using reflection of feeling. Sometimes reflecting the feeling alone, without mention of content, can be more powerful in helping the client to own a feeling that he may be trying to suppress. If a counsellor says "You're really hurting" the statement focusses on the client's pain rather than encouraging the client to escape from experiencing his pain by latching onto "content" words and moving into a cognitive rather than feeling level of experiencing. Whenever possible, help clients to experience their emotional feelings rather than to suppress feelings by working at a head or cognitive level. Experiencing feelings fully is often painful, but is cathartic and consequently therapeutically desirable.

The use of lead-in words when reflecting

Generally, it is sufficient to use the reflection statements as given in the previous examples in this chapter and in Chapters 11 and 12. However, sometimes it can be helpful to preface a reflection statement by using words such as those suggested below.

WHEN REFLECTING CONTENT

   "I've heard you say ... "

   "What I've heard you say is ... "

   "I get the impression that ... "

   "I'm getting the idea that ... "

WHEN REFLECTING FEELINGS OR CONTENT AND FEELINGS

   "If I'm hearing you correctly ... "

   "I'm sensing that you feel ... "

   "I get the impression that you feel ... "

These suggestions should be used sparingly, otherwise they are likely to sound repetitive and trite. Usually, a reflection such as "You're angry because ..." is sufficient.

Learning the skills

You have now learnt how to use the three basic skills of *minimal responding*, *reflection of content* and *reflection of feelings*. It is essential that these three skills should be practised until they are fully mastered before you proceed with learning any of the other micro-skills.

Initially, during the learning process, you are likely to feel awkward in using these skills and this awkwardness may get transmitted to the client. Keep practising until you can use the skills in a natural way which does not seem to be contrived or artificial. Once this has been achieved, the counselling interaction will flow smoothly and you will not feel pressured to think of "smart" responses. Instead your listening skills will be enhanced and you will feel more relaxed and spontaneous. Interestingly, if the skills are used competently, the client will not realise that you are primarily using reflection, but will feel as though you are listening and commenting in a sensible way on what is being said. An experienced counsellor is likely to use the three basic skills you have now learnt more frequently than any other skills, because they enable the client to explore his world fully in his own way without interference by the counsellor, but with the certain knowledge that the counsellor is actively listening to him.

Focussing on the counselling relationship

Remember that counselling is about walking alongside a person as he explores his world. Some people say that a counsellor should, metaphorically speaking, walk in the shoes of the other person. Certainly it is important that the counsellor attempts to see the world in the way the client sees the world. Thus at times, an experienced counsellor will almost get into the client's shoes, so that he can better understand what it feels like to be the client, and how it might be to look at the world from the client's viewpoint. By doing this a trusting relationship is developed which enables the client to risk exploring the most painful issues of his life, and so to move forward out of his confusion.

Suggested counsellor responses for further examples on reflection of feeling and content

EXAMPLE 1 "You feel resentful because other people don't appreciate your efforts."

EXAMPLE 2 "So many things have gone wrong that you're starting to feel pressured and unable to cope" or "You just can't cope with everything going wrong".

EXAMPLE 3 "The continual fighting between your son and daughter infuriates you."

EXAMPLE 4 "You're despairing because you can't get your wife to come back to you."

EXAMPLE 5 "Even though you believe the landlord is being unfair you're too scared to confront him."

EXAMPLE 6 "You're disgusted by your neighbour's unwillingness to help."

LEARNING SUMMARY

- Reflection of feeling and content can be combined into one statement.
- There are times when it is more effective to reflect back only feelings, or only content, and not both.
- Effective counsellors try to see the world as their client sees it.

Examples of client statements for use by trainers in teaching reflection of content and feelings

1. "My children are able to use computers without worrying. They learnt to use them at school. Unfortunately I haven't been able to keep up with the times and as a result, I don't think that my children respect me. I feel quite stupid."

2. "Every time my father comes to visit me I dread the time when he'll leave to go home because he lives such a long way away and he's so old now. He's going back this weekend and I can't stop thinking that maybe I'll never see him again."

3. "My son is driving me crazy. He never stops doing silly things. I have to watch him all the time. Yesterday he climbed onto the roof and then fell out of a tree. I'm starting to lose patience with him."

4. "I can't make sense of what Freda wants. Firstly, she asks me to go to visit her on Friday and then she tells me that if I do she'll feel overwhelmed. I just don't know what to do."

5. "Some very strange things are happening. A disreputable looking person keeps hanging around my house and I'm not sure but I think that some things have disappeared. I think I'll have to be careful to check that the house is kept locked."

6. "My partner has left and I can't track him down. I wish I could find him and tell him that I still love him and want him back. I know that I've hurt him badly by having the affair. Now it's me that's suffering."

14 Matching the client's language

The joining, listening and reflection skills covered in Chapters 10 to 13, together with the skill of summarising which is covered in Chapter 16, are Rogerian counselling skills developed by Carl Rogers. In this chapter, and in Chapter 17, we will consider skills which derive from Neuro-linguistic Programming as developed by Bandler and Grinder (see Chapter 3 for information about Rogerian counselling and NLP).

We all experience the world in different ways

You are unique because you are a human being. I am unique, I am a human being. Being unique is important to me—I'm not quite the same as you, and you're not quite the same as me. All of us in the world are a bit different from each other. The ways in which we do things are different, and most importantly, the ways in which we experience and think about the world are different. An important difference in the way individuals experience the world has to do with the senses we all use for maintaining contact with our environment.

As you know, there are a number of different senses that we use to experience our world. We can smell, taste, touch, see, and hear.

THE FEELING (OR KINAESTHETIC) MODE
By smelling, tasting and touching we make contact with things which are present in the environment surrounding us. Additionally, we have sensations within our bodies which are a response to our external environment. For example, when I am anxious, my body may tense up or I may get "butterflies in my stomach". When I am excited my adrenalin flows faster and my metabolism speeds up.

The senses of smelling, tasting and touching, together with our internal bodily sensations, link up with our emotional feelings. These sensations and feelings combine to contribute to our awareness of the world. Together, they make up what is generally referred to as the *feeling* or *kinaesthetic* mode of awareness.

THE SEEING AND HEARING MODES OF AWARENESS
We may also be aware of our world by using either the seeing mode or the hearing mode of awareness. By using either of these modes we experience the world in which we live.

THREE IMPORTANT MODES OF AWARENESS
Hence, we can describe three important ways in which we can experience the world by using our senses. These are:

1. the *feeling* or *kinaesthetic mode*

2. the *seeing* or *visual mode*
3. the *hearing* or *auditory mode*

Individual differences

We all have different abilities. Some of us are good at maths, others at languages, and some are good at doing things with their hands. During our lives most of us discover those things which we are good at and those things which we do not do so well. In the same way that we develop different practical and academic abilities during our lives, some of us learn to use particular senses more effectively than other senses. For example, there are people who are very good at detecting things that smell, and other people who have acute hearing and can hear the slightest sound. Some people are really observant and readily notice small details which others miss. When I learnt to be a scuba diver, the fellow who taught me was extremely observant and would frequently see things which I missed. He would see the heavily camouflaged and dangerous stone fish lurking among the rocks where I was probing, whereas I would fail to see it until it was pointed out to me.

USING DIFFERENT WAYS TO THINK

Not only do people experience the world differently, but they also think in different ways. Some people think predominantly by using visual imagery (the seeing mode), others think in the hearing mode by talking to themselves mentally, and others think in terms of their feelings and bodily sensations (feeling or kinaesthetic mode). There may be people who are equally versatile and can think easily in all or any of the three modes, but most people seem to rely more strongly on one mode than the others. What mode do you think in? Are you predominantly visual, auditory, or feeling (kinaesthetic)?

If you listen to someone talking, and listen carefully to the words being used, you are likely to get some clues as to which mode he generally uses when he is thinking. Let me give you a few examples. Some people use expressions like "I hear what you say", "It sounds as though you are saying", "It sounds as though", "Tell me what happened", or "That rings bells for me". People who use that sort of language are using the hearing mode of thinking.

There are other people of course who will say things like "I see what you mean", "I've got a clearer picture of the situation", or "It looks good". People who talk like that are using the seeing mode to think. The third category of people are people who predominantly think and experience the world by using feeling methods. They say things like "It feels good", "You touched a raw nerve there" or "I sense your discomfort".

Matching the client

Previously we've considered the value of matching the way in which the client behaves. We've talked about how it's helpful to sit in a similar way to the client, to talk at the same pace and with the same tone of voice as the client, and to match the client's breathing. Doing these things gives the client a feeling of connection with the counsellor, so that the client feels comfortable, safe and able to share openly. Another way in which a counsellor can join with a client is by using similar language to the client's. If a client is using predominantly "seeing" language, then you will need to use "seeing" language too, if you are to properly connect with him. Similarly, if a client is using "hearing" language, in order to join with that client properly, you will need to use hearing language yourself and of course the same is true when it comes to "kinaesthetic" or "feeling" language. It's really quite fun to try to learn the skill of matching the client's mode. When you are listening to people in general conversation, listen carefully to find out their preferred mode, and respond in the same mode. If you do this you may improve your rapport with them.

LEARNING TO MATCH THE CLIENT'S PREFERRED MODE

There is an enjoyable way of learning to recognise the type of language being used. If you wish you can use a practice session to play a game of "spot the mode". The game goes like this: One student, or player, talks about a problem, but continually changes the type of language that he is using, flipping from "hearing" to "seeing" and to "feeling" language in random sequence. While this is happening, other students hold up one of three cards on each of which is written "hearing" or "seeing" or "feeling". If the listening students are correctly following the one who is talking, then they will all hold up a "seeing" card whenever the speaker is using "seeing" language, and similarly they will hold up a "hearing" or a "feeling" card, at appropriate times, in order to match the language being used. For your practice now, here is a paragraph in which the mode continually changes. See if you can spot when the language changes from one mode to another.

Practice example of mode changes

“I remember the scene as I sat on the sand, which was cold and wet. As I sat there, I heard some seagulls squawking as they flew overhead casting shadows on the sand, and I could hear the waves crashing. On the horizon, I noticed a ship steaming along, and at the same time a young man's footsteps *thumped past me as he ran along the beach. I thought about what was going to happen later in the day and could picture the beautiful house which we were going to visit for tea. I imagined myself walking through the garden of the house and admiring the beautiful flowers that grew there. My body tingled with excitement in anticipation, and I told myself to be patient. 〝*

I wonder how many changes of mode you found in the above paragraph. According to my count there were nine. See the end of this chapter to find out how I arrived at this figure.

Practice examples of counsellor responses

The following are some examples of client statements and counsellor responses. In each case, notice that the response is in the correct mode, that is, either the hearing, feeling or seeing mode. Once again it is suggested that you cover up the given response and invent a response yourself. You can then compare your response with the one provided.

Example 1

CLIENT STATEMENT I went back there once more, but as before, the place gave me bad vibes. I had to leave because my stomach was churning and my hands were sweating.

COUNSELLOR RESPONSE You felt so uncomfortable that you left. (Feeling mode.)

Example 2

CLIENT STATEMENT In the past, my mother has frequently criticised my wife, and I have always listened to what she has said. Recently though, I've started to question what she's told me and I'm inclined to say that some of her statements about Monica may be wrong.

COUNSELLOR RESPONSE It sounds as though you've got doubts about the accuracy of what your mother tells you. (Hearing mode.)

Example 3

CLIENT STATEMENT She gave me a bunch of flowers and I was really touched by that. In fact, I feel quite different about our relationship now because the coldness we experienced before has been replaced by warmth.

COUNSELLOR RESPONSE Your feelings towards her have changed, and are now very pleasant. (Feeling mode.)

Example 4

CLIENT STATEMENT It seems to me that the writing's on the wall, there's nothing that I can do to save the situation, and I can see nothing but disaster from now on.

COUNSELLOR RESPONSE The outlook's a really bad one. (Seeing mode.)

Example 5

CLIENT STATEMENT It's as though there is a brick wall around him. It has no door, and no way in or out. When I look over the wall I see a very strange person.

COUNSELLOR RESPONSE You picture him as a strange man surrounded by a brick wall. (Seeing mode.)

Example 6

CLIENT STATEMENT When she spoke it was as though a bell was ringing in my head warning me not to prejudge what she was saying. Consequently I heard what she told me, responded sensibly, and then said to myself, "Well done, you've avoided another terrible argument".

COUNSELLOR RESPONSE You listened to your own internal warning system and the outcome sounds good. (Hearing mode.)

Matching the client's metaphors

Have you noticed how many people make use of metaphors in their everyday speech? In counselling clients may use statements such as the following:

1. "I can see myself being swept away by a river. I can't control my direction and I'm afraid that I'm going to drown."
2. "It's like being in a rock concert with the music turned up so loud that I can't think. The tune I want to hear is being drowned out by other people's music."
3. "I can't breath. I'm being suffocated, the stale air is poisoning me."

In example 1 above, the client uses the seeing mode to describe a metaphor of a river. In this case, it could be helpful for the counsellor to respond by using the same mode and metaphor. The counsellor might respond by using reflection to say, "You see the river as more powerful than yourself".

In example 2, the client uses the hearing mode, and the metaphor is about music. The counsellor might respond by saying, "The music is overwhelmingly loud". This would match both the client's mode and metaphor.

In example 3, the client uses the feeling mode and a breathing metaphor. The counsellor could match the client by using reflection to say, "You don't have the fresh air you need to breathe".

Modelling appropriate behaviour

In this chapter we have focussed on the usefulness of matching the client's mode of thinking and use of metaphor. In Chapter 10 we also considered the advantages of matching the client's non-verbal and verbal behaviour. However, there are times when it may not be sensible, appropriate, or useful, for a counsellor to match a client's non-verbal and/or verbal behaviour. For example, it is unlikely that it would be helpful for a counsellor to match angry or aggressive behaviour. In such situations it is generally more useful for a counsellor to remain calm and detached. By not getting caught up in the client's angry emotional experience, the counsellor may be able to model appropriate ways of dealing with aggressive encounters.

When a client uses expletives which are not acceptable to some, we have a more complicated issue. The counsellor's own values are almost certain to become involved. Some counsellors believe that expletives can be used appropriately at times, and that in such cases matching the client's language may be helpful in the joining process and may enable the client to continue to talk freely. Other counsellors are uncomfortable with this, either because they do not use such language themselves and need to be congruent, or because they think that it is inappropriate to use such language in a counselling situation. Clearly, you will need to make a personal decision for yourself in this regard.

Building on skills already learnt

In your practice sessions, continue to practise those skills you have already learnt: minimal responses, and reflection of content and feelings. In addition, practise matching the client's language by using the same mode and/or metaphors. If you do this, then the words you use will be more meaningful for him. Note that the ideas expressed in this chapter have their origins in Neuro-linguistic Programming. If these ideas strongly appeal to you then you may wish to study Neuro-linguistic Programming in depth once you have mastered basic counselling skills (see the suggestions below for further reading).

Modes used in practice example

I remember the scene as I sat on the sand,	Seeing
which was cold and wet. As I sat there,	Feeling (first change)
I heard some seagulls squawking as they	Hearing (second change)
flew overhead casting shadows on the sand,	Seeing (third change)
and I could hear the waves crashing.	Hearing (fourth change)
On the horizon, I noticed a ship steaming along,	Seeing (fifth change)
and at the same time a young man's footsteps thumped past me as he ran along the beach.	Hearing (sixth change)
I thought about what was going to happen later in the day and could picture the beautiful house which we were going to visit for tea. I imagined	Seeing (seventh change)

myself walking through the garden of the house
and admiring the beautiful flowers that grew there.

My body tingled with excitement in anticipation, Feeling (eighth change)

and I told myself to be patient. Hearing (ninth change)

LEARNING SUMMARY

- Three important modes of experiencing the world are the seeing, feeling, and hearing modes.

- An individual may predominantly use one of the three modes.

- Matching a client's predominant mode and any metaphor used can help in the joining process between client and counsellor.

FURTHER READING

Bandler, R. *Time for a Change*. Cupertino: Meta, 1993
Bandler, R., *Using Your Brain for a CHANGE—Neuro-linguistic Programming*. Moab: Real People Press, 1985

Examples of client statements for use by trainers in teaching matching language

1. "I really do need to complete the project in a hurry. I can hear the clock ticking by and know that if I delay any more the other members of the team will start to ear-bash me."
2. "I feel as though I'm flying by the seat of my pants and that gives me the shivers right down my spine. I'm not secure."
3. "I can visualise him now, doing nothing. All he does is to lie around getting in my way. I've half a mind to pick up his belongings and throw them out of the door. It would be interesting for me to watch his reaction."
4. "I can picture the scene. Me lying dead in a pool of blood and then Frank rushing home to protect me. It will be too late then. He will have missed the bus."
5. "I can sense when he's in a bad mood. He's like a time-bomb ready to go off. The atmosphere's tense and I'm scared in case I accidentally set off the detonator."
6. "I need to listen to my own ideas and not Mum's. What she says always sounds good but I always get taken to the cleaners. I'm going to tell myself to be careful from now on.

15 Asking questions

You may be surprised that the chapter on asking questions should come so late in this book, after you have already learnt several other skills. Well, surprisingly, it is not necessary to ask many questions at all in most counselling interviews. Certainly this is true for interviews concerned with counselling people for emotional problems. Most of the information the counsellor needs to know will emerge naturally without asking questions if the counsellor actively listens to the client, uses the skills which have already been learnt, and skilfully reflects back the content and feeling of what the client is saying.

Asking too many questions

It is very tempting for new counsellors to ask lots of questions. If you find yourself repeatedly asking questions, it's important for you to ask yourself what your goal is in asking these questions. If your goal is to stimulate the client into talking, then you may well be using the wrong approach. More often than not, simply reflecting back what has already been said will stimulate the client into further confidence sharing without the need for you to ask a question. If a counsellor asks too many questions the counselling session becomes more like an interrogation and the client is likely to be less open and less communicative. The counsellor then ends up controlling the direction in which the interview will go. This is, as a general rule, unfortunate, because it is desirable for the client to go in whatever direction her energy leads her. It is important for the client to fully explore the area in which her problem lies. Often a client won't zero in on her real problem until she has spent some time wandering around the general problem area. If the counsellor tries to find out what is really troubling her by asking questions the client may never move towards the most painful things that are causing trouble, but may in fact just go off at a tangent in a direction of the counsellor's choosing.

Another problem with excessive question asking is that the client will quickly learn to expect questions, and may wait for the counsellor to ask another question instead of thinking out for herself what is important. There is therefore a real danger in asking unnecessary

Interrogating is NOT counselling

questions and it is my view that question asking should be limited to those situations in which there is little alternative but to ask a question. When you do ask a question be clear about what it is that you hope to achieve by asking the question. Before looking at the goals that can be achieved through asking questions we need to think about the types of question we can ask.

Open and closed questions

There are two major categories into which questions fall. Some questions are called "open questions" and other questions are called "closed questions". Both types of question can be useful in the counselling process and it is necessary for you to fully understand the difference between the two types. Then it will become clear to you when it is appropriate to use which type.

CLOSED QUESTIONS

Closed questions are questions that lead to a specific answer. Usually the answer to a closed question is very short. It may be an answer like "Yes" or "No". Consider for example the closed question: "Did you come here by bus today?" Obviously the most probable answer is either "Yes" or "No". The client may choose to expand on the answer but is unlikely to do so. Closed questions such as "Do you love your wife?" and "Are you angry?" usually lead to the answer "Yes" or "No". If I ask the closed question "How many years have you lived in Queensland?" the answer might be "Twenty-four", and it is a specific answer.

There are times in a counselling session when you will need to ask closed questions because you require a specific answer to a very definite question. There are also other important reasons for asking closed questions as we shall see later. However, there is a problem with asking closed questions and I think that it will probably be apparent to you already. If you ask a closed question, it is possible that the client may continue to talk to you and to enlarge on the answer she has given, but it is not necessary for the client to do that. Moreover, you have limited the client in the sense that the sort of answer she can give, if she answers your question, is very restricted.

Lawyers in a court like to ask closed questions so that witnesses are restricted in the range of answers that can be given. Counsellors are not lawyers and generally the counsellor's intention is to free the client up so she can speak more openly.

OPEN QUESTIONS

The open question is very different in its effect from the closed question. It gives the client lots of scope, allows the client to explore any relevant area, and in fact encourages the client to freely divulge additional material. If I ask the closed question "Did you come here by bus?" the answer is likely to be "Yes" or "No". Contrast this with the open question "How did you travel here?" The client is freer to answer the open question by talking about the way she travelled and the answer is likely to be richer in information.

EXAMPLES OF OPEN AND CLOSED QUESTIONS

Examples to illustrate the difference between closed and open questions are presented below. In each case read the closed question and try to replace it by an equivalent open question yourself before reading the suggested alternative.

| Example 1 |

CLOSED QUESTION Do you feel angry?

OPEN QUESTION How do you feel?

| Example 2 |

CLOSED QUESTION How many children do you have?

OPEN QUESTION Tell me about your children.

| Example 3 |

CLOSED QUESTION Do you argue with your wife often?

OPEN QUESTION What is your relationship like with your wife?

| Example 4 |

CLOSED QUESTION Did you punish your son when he misbehaved?

OPEN QUESTION What did you do when your son misbehaved?

| Example 5 |

CLOSED QUESTION Do you love your husband?

OPEN QUESTION Can you tell me about your feelings towards your husband?

| Example 6 |

CLOSED QUESTION Is the atmosphere tense at home?

OPEN QUESTION What's the atmosphere like at home?

The closed questions above give the client little room to use her own imagination when giving an answer. The sort of answer she will give to a closed question will be direct and probably short. A closed question doesn't encourage the client to be creative and share new information with the counsellor, but tends to confine the client to a limited response.

The open question is quite different as you can see from the above examples. In each case, by asking an open question, the counsellor might get unexpected additional information. If you look at the open question "Tell me about your children", you will realise that the client could give a number of quite different answers. For example, the client might say "My children are beautiful and very happy" or "I have two sons and a daughter" or "My children

---

are all grown up and my husband and I live happily together on our own". It is clear from this example that by asking an open question the counsellor may get a variety of answers and may get an answer quite different to the one which she might have expected. This is an advantage because counsellors are not mind readers, and cannot know what the client is thinking unless the client verbalises her thoughts. Also, it is sensible for counsellors to use questions which will encourage the client to bring out those things which are of most interest to the client, rather than those things that are of most interest to the counsellor.

"Why" questions

There is one particular type of question that I sometimes ask but try to avoid asking. I try to avoid asking questions beginning with "Why". When I have asked "Why" questions, I've usually found that the client tends to look for an intellectually thought-out reason in reply and does not centre on what is happening internally. "Why" questions tend to generate answers that are "out there"—answers that don't seem to come from inside the client and often aren't convincing. They frequently fall into the category that I would call "excuses" or "rationalisations".

In comparison to "Why" questions, I find that questions beginning with "What", "How", and "When" are generally more useful. Open questions often begin with these words.

When to use closed questions

As explained previously, it is generally preferable to use open questions rather than closed questions. Exceptions are when helping a client to be more specific, or when specific information is required. In these latter cases closed questions are very appropriate. In order to make sense of the client's story a counsellor may need to know whether the client is married, whether she has children, and what the ages of the children are. If a counsellor needs to know this information, then it may be appropriate to ask directly by using closed questions.

Practice examples

Below are some more examples of closed questions. You may wish to practise framing open questions to replace them. Suggested open questions for each example are given at the end of this chapter.

1. Would you like fish for dinner tonight?
2. Do you like it when your husband praises you?
3. Was your mother a dominating person?
4. Did your father make you come to see me?
5. Did the change disrupt your life?

Goals when asking questions

There are three important goals which can be achieved through asking questions. These are:

1. to encourage the client to open up and disclose more
2. to help the client be more specific or concrete
3. to help the counsellor reach a clearer understanding of the client's situation

1. TO ENCOURAGE THE CLIENT TO OPEN UP AND DISCLOSE MORE
As we have discussed previously, it is clear that open questions are more effective in helping the client to open up, and disclose more. By using open questions the client is likely to talk about the things which are most important for her.

2. TO HELP THE CLIENT BE MORE SPECIFIC OR CONCRETE
The second goal is to help the client be more specific. Clients frequently make very general, vague statements, and this is unhelpful to both the client and the counsellor because it is impossible to think clearly about a problem if it is expressed in vague, woolly, non-specific language.

The counsellor's task is to help the client to clarify her thinking. For instance, if a client makes a vague statement like "That sort of thing always makes me annoyed", it may not be at all clear to either the client or the counsellor what is really meant by the words "that sort of thing". It is then appropriate for the counsellor to ask the client what she means when she says "that sort of thing". Similarly, a client might say "I just can't stand it any more." The word "it" is non-specific and to help the client to clear up the vagueness the counsellor might ask: "What is it that you can't stand any more?" Similarly, consider the client statement "I'm fed up with him". This is a very general statement and may need clarification, in which case the counsellor might well respond by saying: "Tell me in what ways you are fed up with him." When clients make generalisations, it is often useful for the counsellor to ask closed questions to help the client be more specific and to focus on the real issue.

3. TO HELP THE COUNSELLOR REACH A CLEARER UNDERSTANDING OF THE CLIENT'S SITUATION
The third goal in asking questions is to help the counsellor reach a clearer understanding of the client's situation. Sometimes a client omits important bits of information, and this makes her story difficult to understand.

Do you really need the information?

Requests for information should be made with caution. As a counsellor, before you ask for information, ask yourself whether you really need it. If you didn't have the information would you still be able to help the client? If the answer to that question is "yes", then asking a question is unnecessary, and the desire to ask a question probably stems from your own needs and/or curiosity. There is absolutely no justification for a counsellor seeking information in order to satisfy her own curiosity. To do so would be to pry unnecessarily into the client's affairs. Such prying merely intrudes into the counselling process and interrupts the proper flow of the counselling interaction.

In conclusion

In this chapter we have looked at the usefulness of closed and open questions and have discussed the differences between the two. Now is the time for you to practise using questions. There is a risk that through practising asking questions, you may quickly become reliant on using them excessively. If that was to happen it would be unfortunate because instead of the client feeling that you were travelling beside her as she explored her thoughts and feelings, she would feel more as though she was being interrogated. This would greatly diminish the quality of the counselling relationship and would inhibit the client from opening up freely. When a person is continually questioned, that person tends to withdraw rather than to open up.

Remember that paraphrasing and reflection of feelings are more likely to motivate the client to talk freely than asking questions. Because of this, I suggest that when you are practising asking questions you try to ask only one question in every three or four responses, with the other responses being reflection of content or feelings or minimal responses. There is no need to be rigid when doing this, because counselling needs to be a natural free flowing process rather conforming to rigid rules. However, if you use fewer questions than other responses in practice sessions, then your continued practice of the most important basic reflective responses will be ensured. Consequently, when you start counselling real clients you will be skilled in reflection of feelings and content, and will use questions only when reflection is not appropriate.

Suggested open questions to replace closed questions in practice examples

1. What would you like for dinner tonight?
2. How do you feel when your husband praises you?
3. What was your mother like? *or* How did your mother behave in her relationships with other people?
4. What brought you here?
5. How did the change affect your life?

LEARNING SUMMARY

- Dangers in asking too many questions:

  - The counselling session may become more like an interrogation.

  - The counsellor may deflect the client from the real issue by controlling the direction of the session.

- The client may stop exploring her own world and instead wait for the counsellor to ask more questions.

- Closed questions:

  - lead to a specific answer

  - confine the client to a limited response

  - help the client to be more precise

  - are useful in eliciting specific information

- Open questions encourage the client

  - to share new information

  - to speak freely and openly

  - to bring out those things that are of most importance

- Counsellors are not justified in asking questions merely to satisfy their own curiosity.

Examples of closed questions for use by trainers for conversion to open questions

Do you intend to arrive at 2 pm?
Are you disappointed?
Do you have two children?
Is your household always tense?
Will you achieve your goals by writing to him?
Did that happen on Thursday?

16 Summarising

Until now the skills we have discussed have been those designed to create a good counselling relationship and to encourage the client to open up, sharing with the counsellor the issues that are causing emotional distress. If we use the analogy of the counsellor walking alongside the client on a journey, then the skills we have described previously encourage the client to continue exploring. As he explores, the client moves in his own direction with the counsellor beside him.

What is summarising?

From time to time it is important for the client to stop and review the ground that has recently been traversed. This review is encouraged by using the skill of *summarising*. Summarising is rather like paraphrasing. When the counsellor paraphrases, what he does is to reflect back to the client whatever has been said in a single client statement. Similarly, when the counsellor summarises, what he does is to reflect back to the client what has been said in a number of client statements. The summary draws together the main points from the content, and may also take into account the feelings the client has described. A summary does not involve a complete re-run of the ground covered, but rather picks out the salient points, the important things that the client has been talking about, and presents them in such a way that he can get an overview of what he himself has been discussing. By doing this, the counsellor enables the client to absorb and to ponder what he has been sharing. Summarising clarifies what the client has been saying and puts it into an organised format so that the client is better able to see a clear picture of his situation.

Frequently when a client comes to counselling he is confused. It is as though he is walking through a forest and can see nothing clearly. He is lost in a confusing jungle of overgrowth and trees. By summarising, the counsellor assists him to see the trees more clearly and to find a path between them.

The following is a short transcript of part of a practice counselling session to illustrate the use of summarising.

Transcript to illustrate summarising

CLIENT You know ... [pause] ... I really believe in people taking responsibility for themselves ... [pause] ... and so I can't really understand why it is that I do so much worrying about my brothers.

COUNSELLOR You sound puzzled by your concern for your brothers. (Reflection of feeling and content.)

CLIENT Yes I am concerned. I'm not too sure what it's all about because I even seem to be worrying about them when I'm at work and yet I know that they are adults and are quite capable of looking after themselves.

COUNSELLOR Even though you know they're adults, you still worry. (Reflection of content and feeling.)

CLIENT Yes I do. Incessantly. I'm always thinking the worst, you know. That maybe Bill has had an accident in that crazy car which he will insist on driving around, and I'm afraid that as far as Sidney is concerned, he's just not in very good health and I'd hate anything to happen to either of them.

COUNSELLOR Even as you speak now you sound anxious. (Reflection of feeling.)

CLIENT Yes I am anxious, I'm really anxious … [pause]

COUNSELLOR As you experience that anxiety can you tell me more about it? (Open question.)

CLIENT Yes, yes I think I can, I'm just, uh-mm, becoming aware of some very painful memories that I have of my elder sister. (Said slowly and with hesitation.)

COUNSELLOR I get the impression that you're finding it difficult to talk about your memories. (Reflection of feeling.)

CLIENT Yes, it's really painful for me to remember what happened to her. I was really very fond of her and I hurt a great deal when I think about the way she finished her life. (Voice quivering.)

COUNSELLOR It distresses you to think about her death. (Reflection of feeling and content.)

CLIENT Yes it does. You see she killed herself. She took an overdose and it was too late when we found her.

COUNSELLOR I can almost feel your sadness. (Joining statement, bringing closeness between client and counsellor.)

CLIENT [Sobs] … yeah, it was very sad for me and it still is. I just wished I could have done something to have changed the way she saw her life.

COUNSELLOR You wish that you could have helped her. (Reflection of feeling and content.)

CLIENT Yes, I do. I would love to have been able to put my arms around her and to tell her that I really loved her. I couldn't have told her that her life was good because it wasn't, but I could have told her that she mattered to me.

COUNSELLOR You'd have liked to have told her how much you cared about her. (Reflection of content.)

CLIENT Yes I would, and that I guess would have made me feel a lot better even if she had still killed herself. I suppose it would have been much better for me if I could have told her how I felt when she was alive and now it's too late.

COUNSELLOR You're sad because you missed an opportunity. (Reflection of feeling and content.)

CLIENT Yes, I did, and I suppose I'm starting to realise something about the way I feel anxious when I think about my two brothers. You see, I would really like to be able to tell them how much I care about them, but somehow I just can't.

COUNSELLOR You've told me how you worry about your brothers and how your sister killed herself. It seems as though you're really sad because you weren't able to tell your sister that you really cared for her when she was alive and now you'd like to be able to tell your brothers that you care about them, but somehow you can't. (Summary.)

CLIENT You're right. That's what my problem is. I think what I need to do is to go and talk to them, and then maybe I'll stop worrying about them.

What the summary does

If you look at the above transcript you will see that in summarising, the counsellor tied together the elements of what the client had said during the previous statements. This enabled the client to put the whole package together and, as a result, to get some resolution for himself. The resolution was the client's own and as such was fitting for the client. It wasn't suggested by the counsellor.

When to summarise

Summarising is something which needs to be done from time to time during a counselling session so that the client is able to clarify his ideas and combine the various elements of what he is saying into an understandable form. In particular, towards the end of the counselling session it is often sensible for the counsellor to summarise the main issues that were dealt with during the session. By doing this, the counsellor ties together the thoughts, ideas and feelings that were expressed in the session, leaving the client feeling less confused and better able to deal with his life situation. This tying together enables the counsellor to move towards terminating the session as explained in Chapter 23.

LEARNING SUMMARY

- Summarising does the following:
  - picks out salient points;
  - draws these together; and
  - presents them to the client in a clear and precise way.

Transcript for use by trainers in teaching summarising

(Students can be asked to identify the types of counsellor responses used and to add a summary to complete the transcript.)

CLIENT My anxiety rises when I think about going to work. I almost start to panic ... I wonder how I am going to cope with another day at that place.

COUNSELLOR You're really worried. (Counselling skill used: _____)

CLIENT Worried? I feel as though I'm going crazy. I despair. The new boss is putting in place policies which infuriate me. They disadvantage our customers and are frankly disrespectful. She doesn't seem to understand the basics of modern commercial practice and if I comply with her wishes I will compromise my own standards. I just don't know what to do.

COUNSELLOR You are faced with a dilemma. (Counselling skill used: _____)

CLIENT Yes I am. If I continue to work there I either have to compromise my ideals or I will be in continual conflict with my boss. I'd like to leave, but the pay is excellent, and in the present economic climate good jobs in my line are difficult to find.

COUNSELLOR You're stuck in a frustrating situation because finding a new job wouldn't be easy. (Counselling skill used: _____)

CLIENT It wouldn't. There aren't many jobs being advertised right now. But I'll keep looking because I do want to leave and eventually a new opportunity is sure to turn up. I suppose in the meantime I'll have to make the best of the present situation. That's where my difficulty lies.

COUNSELLOR What ideas do you have about ways of responding to your current work situation? (Counselling skill used: _____)

CLIENT Well I suppose that I could avoid conflict by following the new policy but interpreting it fairly loosely whenever I can. Also, I could be clear with customers that I don't have any alternative but to follow company policy. That way, I would be making it clear that I wasn't being personally uncooperative. I'd need to be careful how I did that though, because I do have some loyalty towards the firm.

COUNSELLOR I am getting the impression that you believe that you could accept some compromise without too much difficulty. (Counselling skill used: _____)

CLIENT Yes, there are ways to alter the way I work without feeling personally compromised, particularly if I remember that I intend to leave as soon as I can ... mm ... Yes I know what to do.

COUNSELLOR SUMMARY

17 Reframing

Have you ever noticed how two people who observe the same event, such as a game of football, will give different descriptions of what happened? We all have individual perspectives, and the way in which I see things may well be different from the way in which you see things. Quite often clients have a very negative way of seeing the world. They interpret events as they see them, but often from a position of depression or of low self-esteem. The counsellor needs to listen very carefully to the client's description of the events or situation, and then try to look from the client's viewpoint and picture what the client has described. The client's picture, painted from his own perspective, will have a frame that is appropriate for the client with his own particular mood and viewpoint.

The process of reframing

Sometimes a skilful counsellor can change the way a client perceives events or situations by "reframing" the picture the client has described. The counsellor, metaphorically speaking, puts a new frame around the picture so that the picture looks different. The idea behind reframing is not to deny the way the client sees the world, but to present the client with an expanded view of the world. Thus, if the client wishes, he may choose to see things in a new way.

It would be quite useless to say to a client, "Things are not really as bad as you think; cheer up!", if the client really sees the world in a very negative way. However, it may be possible to describe what the client sees in such a way that the client has a broader vision of what has occurred and thus is able to be less negative.

Examples of reframing

Example 1

The client has explained that she seems to be unable to relax, because as soon as she turns her back her young son misbehaves and she has to chase after him and punish him. The counsellor has reflected back her feelings about this and now the client is calmer. At this point the counsellor decides to offer the client a reframe concerning the behaviour of her son.

COUNSELLOR REFRAME I get the impression that you are really important to your son and that he wants lots of attention from you.

By making this statement, the counsellor has reframed the son's behaviour in a positive way, so that the mother can feel important and needed. Maybe she will start to believe that her son is really crying out for more attention and will see his behaviour not as designed to annoy her, but as designed to attract her attention so that he can get more of her time. By reframing the child's behaviour in this way, there is a possibility that the mother may feel more positive towards her son and that this change in relationship could bring about a change in behaviour.

Example 2

The client has explained that he is continually getting angry with his daughter who will not study and attend to her school work but instead prefers to play around with what he describes as "layabouts". He explains how he can hardly cope with his anger and he is getting uptight and feeling very, very miserable. He blames his daughter heavily for what he sees as appalling behaviour.

COUNSELLOR REFRAME It seems as though you care so much about your daughter, you care so much about her turning out to be the sort of person that you want her to be, that you are prepared to completely sacrifice your own needs for a relaxed and enjoyable life, and are willing to make your own life a misery by putting a great deal of energy into trying to correct her behaviour.

This reframe allows the father to feel positive about himself instead of feeling negative about the way he is continually losing his temper. He may now be able to see himself as really caring about his daughter, and also may be able to see that he is putting his daughter's needs ahead of his own. He is reminded of his need to be relaxed and enjoy his life. The reframe might take some of the tension out of the situation by removing the focus from the daughter, and putting it onto the client himself.

Example 3

The client has separated from her husband against her will. Her husband is now pushing her away and hurting her badly by refusing to even talk to her or to see her at all. The client has shared her pain and suffering and the counsellor has reflected her feelings and allowed her to explore them fully. However the counsellor now reframes the husband's behaviour.

COUNSELLOR REFRAME You've described the way you see your husband pushing you away and not being prepared to talk to you, and that hurts you terribly. I am wondering if it is possible that maybe your husband can't cope with the emotional pressure of talking to you. I'm just wondering whether maybe what he is doing is really because of his own inadequacy, in not being able to face you. Maybe he feels guilty when he sees you, and it's easier for him to avoid seeing you altogether, rather than to tolerate his own pain. Do you think that's possible?

By tentatively putting up this alternative the client may see that there could be other reasons for her husband refusing to have anything to do with her, and that it may be that her husband is hurting and can't face the experience of seeing her. The counsellor's goal is to try to make it easier for the client to accept her husband's rejection.

Example 4

A senior executive has just described to the counsellor how terrified he is of having to stand up and address a large meeting of professionals the following week. The counsellor has reflected his feelings and allowed him, to some extent, to work through them. The counsellor then offers the following reframe.

COUNSELLOR REFRAME It seems to me that you have mixed feelings about giving the talk. At times I almost get the impression that you are looking forward to it, and yet you say that you are very anxious about it. I am wondering if it would be possible for you to think of your anxiety as blocked excitement. Sometimes anxiety is due to our stopping ourselves from being excited, and if we let go and allow ourselves to be enthusiastic and excited, then the excitement can overshadow the anxiety.

The counsellor here is using a useful reframe from Gestalt Therapy by reframing "anxiety" as "blocked excitement". Very often, holding our emotional selves in and putting restraints on ourselves prevents us from enjoying the exciting parts of our lives as we negatively reframe exciting events as anxious moments. A good example of this is the way a bride may prepare for her wedding. One way of thinking about going through the wedding ceremony and the reception is to say, "Wow, that's a really anxiety-producing situation". Another way of looking at it, a reframe, is to say, "Wow, this is going to be a really exciting day and it's going to be fun".

Example 5

The client explains how he is frequently being hurt by the boss who ignores him. The boss doesn't even look at him and she doesn't say "Hello" when she meets him in the morning. She walks straight past him.

COUNSELLOR REFRAME You've explained to me how your boss walks straight past you without noticing you, and I'm wondering if there is an alternative explanation for what's happening. Sure, it may be that she really does intend to snub you. On the other hand, is it possible that she gets terribly preoccupied and really isn't on this planet half the time?

In this reframe, the counsellor is presenting an alternative that may be partly true. It's quite likely that the boss is sometimes preoccupied, and that may be a partial explanation. By putting this possible explanation up as an alternative, some of the sting is taken out of the boss ignoring the client, and the client may then feel less uptight in his relationship with her.

Example 6

The client explained to the counsellor his feelings of inadequacy and failure. He knew that he was intellectually bright and that made him feel worse because he never completed any project he started. He would start enthusiastically and soon lose interest. He was deeply depressed by a long string of past "failures", things that he had started and then left half-finished.

COUNSELLOR REFRAME You seem to be a very intelligent person who is quite capable of completing any of the projects you have started. My guess is that you are excited by new projects because they present a challenge, and that you lose interest only when you believe that the challenge is easy for you to meet. Because you are highly intelligent you very quickly get bored and look for new stimulation.

This reframe enables the client to feel good about himself instead of perceiving himself as a failure. He is then left with the possibility that he can decide to do the boring thing and complete a project if he wishes, or can choose to continue looking for excitement and stimulation without feeling so guilty.

As you can see, reframing needs to be done carefully, sensitively and tentatively. If it is done in this way, it is likely to be accepted by the client but may be rejected if it does not fit. Sometimes though, the client may not think that your reframe fits his picture. However, by being offered an alternative way of viewing things he may be able to broaden his perspective with a resulting reduction in his hurt and pain.

Before reading the next chapter, practise reframing by using the following examples of client statements. If you are in a training group discuss and compare your reframes with those of other group members. Some suggested reframes for these examples are provided at the end of this chapter.

Practice examples for reframing

Example 1

CLIENT STATEMENT I can't believe something so terrible should happen. My husband has been granted custody of my children and I'm only allowed to see them on alternate weekends. He claims that I can't cope with them, and I feel like a total failure because in some ways he's right. They used to drive me crazy. But I love them and want to have a good relationship with them. Now I'll have so little contact with them, they'll hardly know me.

Example 2

CLIENT STATEMENT I crave for a long-term relationship with someone, and all I get is short relationship after short relationship. I just don't seem to be able to hold on to my lady-friends. They always criticise me for being so restless and for never relaxing, and none of them want to stay with me.

Example 3

CLIENT STATEMENT My father hates me, I'm sure. He picks on me for everything I do. All the time he follows me around and complains about my behaviour. He wants me to behave like a toffy-nosed snob instead of a normal human being. Not only that but he's always nagging me to study more!

Example 4

CLIENT STATEMENT I've got so much that I have to do in a day and I get so angry with myself because I keep making mistakes. Sure, I get lots done, but I keep forgetting things and mixing arrangements up. I'm hopeless. When will I learn?

Example 5

CLIENT STATEMENT I'm furious with my mother. She lets my sister, Annette, manipulate her with suicide threats and her refusal to eat properly. Mum rushes around attending to her every need. It's just not fair on Mum and I wish she'd stop doing it.

Example 6

CLIENT STATEMENT My son's unemployed again, and I resent having to support him financially. Why should I spend my money on a person who's mean and nasty to me? It would serve him right if I let him starve. What annoys me is that he knows that he can treat me badly and then twist me around his little finger and I will support him. I'm angry at myself for being so stupid as to be manipulated so easily.

Suggested reframes for practice examples

EXAMPLE 1 (This reframe would be used only after fully reflecting and working through the client's distress in the usual way.) Maybe when you do see your children now you'll be able to have some quality time with them, and will be able to recharge yourself and do something for yourself in the time when they are not with you.

EXAMPLE 2 You must be very attractive to the opposite sex to be able to build so many new relationships. By the sound of it, you have plenty of energy, and I wonder whether the woman friends you've had would have been able to satisfy you for very long.

EXAMPLE 3 I get the impression that your father wants you to be socially and educationally successful. Maybe he actually cares about you so much that he worries in case you fail in life.

EXAMPLE 4 People who do nothing never make mistakes. Making mistakes could be a sign that you are, to use your words, "getting lots done". You could feel good about that.

EXAMPLE 5 Your mother must care a great deal about Annette to choose to do what she does.

EXAMPLE 6 You must be a very caring person to choose to support your son, especially as you don't like his behaviour much.

LEARNING SUMMARY

- Reframing provides the client with an expanded picture of his world which may enable him to perceive his situation differently and more constructively.

- Reframing needs to be done sensitively and carefully.

- Reframes should be offered in such a way that clients may choose to accept or reject them.

FURTHER READING ON REFRAMING

Bandler, R. and Grinder, J., *Reframing—Neuro-linguistic Programming and the Transformation of Meaning.* Moab: Real People Press, 1982

Examples for use by trainers in teaching reframing

Example 1

CLIENT STATEMENT My teenage daughter is a great disappointment to me. I thought that when she reached this age that she and I would be good friends and would spend lots of time together. All she wants now is to do her own thing. I'm just irrelevant as far as she's concerned.

Example 2

CLIENT STATEMENT My husband interferes in everything I do. I just need to start doing something and he's there, taking over. I'm starting to think that I must be an incompetent idiot who isn't capable of doing anything for myself.

Example 3

CLIENT STATEMENT Don't sniff, stand up straight, don't be late, be polite, that's all I hear from Mum. She says she loves me but I don't think that she even likes me any more.

Example 4

CLIENT STATEMENT I don't know why the manager picks on me all the time. Whenever there is a difficult job to do or a difficult customer to deal with she always gives the work to me. She's obviously trying to make my life as difficult as possible.

Example 5

CLIENT STATEMENT I'm totally exhausted and realise I've been very stupid. In just a few months, I've completely redecorated my house, written several journal articles for publication while working full time in a very demanding job, driven 200 kilometres and back to see my dying brother most weekends, and organised a group project for the local community. I seem to be unable to stop working compulsively. I feel really depressed by my inability to relax and enjoy life.

18 Confrontation

What do you feel emotionally when you decide to confront someone? Many people feel apprehensive and worry about the outcome of confrontation.

What is it like for you when someone confronts you? Is it sometimes threatening? It may be.

Generally when we use the word "confrontation" we think in terms of opposing parties and of people disagreeing as they confront each other. In such a situation the person being confronted is likely to feel threatened and may become defensive, while the person doing the confronting is likely to feel anxiety.

Confrontation in counselling

Confrontation as a counselling skill is different from the generally perceived view of confrontation. The micro-skill of confrontation involves raising the awareness of the client by presenting to him information that in some way he is overlooking or failing to identify for himself. Correct use of this skill involves bringing into the client's awareness, in an acceptable way, information that may be unpalatable to him and which is either being avoided or is just not being noticed.

How do you help a child to swallow foul-tasting medicine? You can either force it down his throat, or use a more gentle persuasive approach. The problem with trying to force the medicine down is that the child may well vomit it up and your relationship with him will not be improved. Respecting the child's feelings is likely to have a more positive outcome than ignoring them. Similarly clients deserve a high degree of respect, and they usually don't like being told painful truths. Metaphorically speaking, the art of good confrontation is to help the client to swallow "bad medicine" voluntarily, so that he can incorporate it into his bodily system and digest it.

Confrontation is clearly a difficult skill to master and should not be attempted until the skills previously described in this book have become a natural part of your counselling style. The skills you have learnt already are often sufficient in themselves, making confrontation unnecessary.

Self-examination before confrontation

Before using confrontation look within yourself to examine your feelings, motives and goals. Ask yourself, "Do I want to confront because I am impatient and not prepared to allow the client to move at his own pace; do I want to confront because I just enjoy confrontation; am I wanting to use confrontation to put my own values onto the client; or am I feeling angry with the client and wanting to express my anger through confrontation?" If the answer to any of these questions is "Yes", then confrontation is inappropriate. Satisfying the counsellor's own needs is no justification for confrontation. Confrontation is most appropriately used after the use of other micro-skills has failed to sufficiently increase the client's awareness.

When to confront

There are a number of situations in which confrontation is appropriate. For example, confrontation is appropriate where:

1. the client is avoiding a basic issue that appears to be troubling him;
2. the client is failing to recognise his own self-destructive or self-defeating behaviour;
3. the client is failing to recognise possible serious consequences of his behaviour;
4. the client is out of touch with reality;
5. the client is making self-contradictory statements;
6. the client is excessively and inappropriately locked into talking about the past or the future and is unable to focus on the present;
7. the client is going around in circles by repeating the same story over and over like a cracked record;
8. the client's non-verbal behaviour does not match his verbal behaviour;
9. attention needs to be given to what is going on in the relationship between the client and counsellor, for example, where dependency is occurring, or where a client withdraws or shows anger or some other emotion towards the counsellor.

In situations such as these, the counsellor may confront the client by sharing with the client what he feels, notices or observes. Good confrontation usually includes elements of some or all of the following:

1. a reflection or brief summary of what the client has said, so that the client feels heard and understood
2. a statement of the counsellor's present feelings
3. a concrete statement of what the counsellor has noticed or observed, given without interpretation

In addition to the above, good confrontation is presented in such a way that the client can feel OK about himself rather than attacked or put down. These points are best explained by means of examples.

Examples to illustrate the use of confrontation

Example 1

The client had been referring obliquely to his concerns about his sexuality. He mentioned the sexual problem briefly several times and then immediately deflected away from it by talking about seemingly irrelevant trivia.

COUNSELLOR CONFRONTATION I'm puzzled because I've noticed that several times you've briefly mentioned your sexual problem, and then have started talking about something quite different.

COMMENT Notice how the counsellor first expressed his feelings by saying "I'm puzzled", and then gave a concrete statement of what he had noticed occurring. This response is minimally threatening as it merely feeds back to the client what the counsellor has observed, without judgment.

Example 2

An angry separated husband who had been denied custody of his children was threatening to burn down the matrimonial home when his wife and children were out. Even though he had been asked about possible consequences he failed to recognise the serious consequences of his threat. The counsellor had reflected back the client's anger and attitude towards his wife. This had reduced the client's anger level but he still felt excessively vindictive and admitted to this.

COUNSELLOR CONFRONTATION You are so furious with your wife that you want to hurt her by destroying the family home. I'm very concerned when I hear you threatening to do this because you would hurt your wife, your children, and yourself. Clearly, if you were to burn down the house your children would lose their home and possessions, and you might end up in jail.

COMMENT Notice how the counsellor first reflected back the feelings and content of the client's message, followed this by a statement of his own feelings, and completed the confrontation by giving a factual statement of likely consequences. This latter statement was not a statement of the counsellor's opinion, but was an accurate statement of the likely consequences.

There is also an ethical issue here. Where people or property could be injured or damaged the counsellor has a clear responsibility to take action to prevent this from occurring (see Chapter 7). You may wish to discuss the issue of confidentiality in a situation such as this with your training group or supervisor.

Example 3

The client had come to the counsellor as a result of a crisis in her current relationship with a longstanding close friend. The counsellor helped her to explore past events at length, as she chose to do that. It seemed to the counsellor that nothing further would be achieved by continuing to focus on the past. However, although the client said that she wanted to talk about her present crisis, she continually recounted past events.

COUNSELLOR CONFRONTATION I am puzzled. My impression is that you want to resolve your present crisis and yet you continually talk about past events.

Unfortunately, the past can't be changed but what you can change is what is happening in the present.

COMMENT The response started with a statement of the counsellor's feelings— "I'm puzzled"—followed by a reflection of the client's desire to talk about her present crisis, and then a concrete statement of what the counsellor had observed: "You continually talk about past events." In this example the counsellor adds another factual statement which might be useful for the client: "Unfortunately the past can't be changed, but what you can change is what is happening in the present".

Remember that it is appropriate for clients to deal with past events in a constructive way where those events are significantly influencing present thoughts and feelings. However, the suggested confrontation would be appropriate where a client was inappropriately and excessively using past history to avoid facing present problems.

Example 4

Here is an example of a counsellor response that addresses repetitive behaviour by a client, who kept repeating himself by going over and over the same ground.

COUNSELLOR CONFRONTATION I've noticed that we seem to be going round in circles, so I'll summarise what we've talked about . . . (the end of this statement is a summary).

COMMENT This example demonstrates how the client was confronted with his repetitive behaviour. The counsellor first told the client what he had noticed happening, and then gave a summary. By confronting in this way, a counsellor can increase the client's awareness of what is happening. With increased awareness he may be able move out of the rut in which he is stuck. However sometimes, even after confrontation, the client will persist in going around the track again and repeating the same details. It is here that stronger confrontation is needed and the counsellor might say "I'm starting to feel frustrated, because once again we are going around the same track".

Example 5

The client said "I feel really happy in my marriage", using a very depressed tone of voice and slumping down in her chair as she spoke.

COUNSELLOR CONFRONTATION I noticed that your voice sounded very flat and you slumped down in your chair when you said that you felt really happy in your marriage.

COMMENT Here the counsellor confronted by reflecting back what he observed without putting an interpretation on his observation. The client was then free to make her own interpretation of the feedback given.

In summary, confrontation increases the client's awareness by giving him information which he may have been unaware of himself. Confrontation is best done caringly, sparingly and skilfully!

LEARNING SUMMARY

- Confrontation involves bringing into the client's awareness information which:

  - may be unpalatable; or

  - may have been ignored or missed and needs to be considered by the client if the counselling is to be optimally helpful.

- Good confrontation often includes:

  - a summary, followed by a statement of the counsellor's feelings and a concrete statement given without interpretation.

- Good confrontation leaves the client feeling OK and not attacked.

Examples for use by trainers in teaching confrontation

Write suitable counsellor statements of confrontation for the following examples.

Example 1

The client tells the counsellor that he is very keen to receive counselling help but repeatedly arrives for appointments up to three-quarters of an hour late.

Example 2

The client has made it clear on several occasions that she is coming to counselling to address the post-traumatic effects of abuse during her childhood. However, each time she arrives for counselling she deflects away from talking about the abuse by introducing a range of other unrelated issues.

Example 3

The client admits to pushing and slapping his wife but minimises this behaviour and blames her for his behaviour, saying that she is provocative. He doesn't see that he needs to take responsibility for what he does.

Example 4

When the counsellor reflects back what she sees as angry non-verbal behaviour the client denies being angry but continues to look and sound angry and to make statements which suggest that she is angry.

Example 5

Although the client does not appear to be under any threat he is responding to others from a disempowered, victim, "poor me", position instead of being assertive in letting others know about his needs.

19 Challenging self-destructive beliefs

Every person is entitled to his own belief system, and has the right to choose what he will believe and what he won't. It is not the counsellor's role or right to try to change the client's beliefs, but it is a counsellor's responsibility to raise the client's awareness of his choices.

Sometimes clients have self-destructive beliefs or SDBs for short. There are two major categories of SDB. These are:

1. "should", "must", "ought" and "have to" beliefs
2. irrational beliefs

"Should", "must", "ought" and "have to"

Clients often make statements using the words "I should", "I must", "I ought", or "I have to". Sometimes the words are spoken with enthusiasm, firmness and meaning, and it is clear that the client feels good about doing whatever it is that he "should do", "must do", "ought to do", or thinks he "has to do" and that's OK. At other times the words are spoken in an unconvincing way, as though some other person is saying to the client "you should", or "you must", "you ought", or "you have to", and the client is reluctantly, uncomfortably and maybe resentfully accepting that message. When this occurs, the client is likely to feel confused and emotionally disturbed. If he does as the "should" message tells him, he may feel like a small boy reluctantly and miserably doing as he is told by others. He will not feel in control of his life, and will not recognise his behaviour as being of his own choosing. If, on the other hand, he disregards the "should" message, he may feel guilty, with consequent negative results for himself. The goal of counselling in such instances is to help the person to feel more comfortable with his decisions, so that when he makes a choice he does it willingly, and without feelings of either resentment or guilt. Provided underlying issues are correctly and fully addressed this goal is usually achievable.

WHERE DO SHOULD, MUST, OUGHT AND HAVE TO BELIEFS COME FROM?
As children we grow up in a world in which we have no experience. We do not know the difference between right and wrong, and we cannot distinguish good behaviour from bad behaviour. However, we learn, initially from our parents and close family, and then from others such as teachers, religious leaders, and friends. We learn from the people who care for us, from what they tell us verbally, and by watching and copying their behaviour. Gradually we absorb a system of values, attitudes, and beliefs. It is right and proper that we do so.

As we grow through childhood and adolescence there comes a time when we start to challenge and rebel against some of the beliefs we have absorbed from others. Interestingly though, many people, by the time they are young adults, hold onto most of the beliefs and values of their parents while having rejected some. As children it is clearly appropriate that we learn and absorb the beliefs of our parents and significant others. There is no other way for us to learn, because as children our experience is too limited for us to make mature judgments for ourselves. As adults, we do have that experience and it is appropriate for each of us to determine for ourselves which beliefs fit and make sense for us as individuals and which beliefs do not fit. We can then keep what fits and reject that which does not. We can replace what doesn't fit by something new which does.

BELIEFS THAT DON'T FIT

Sometimes when a client uses the words should, must or ought, he is stating a belief that has its origins in his childhood, and which he is holding on to, but which does not fit for him now. If he really accepted the belief as his own he would be more likely to say "I've decided", or "I want to", or "I choose to", rather than "I should", or "I must", or "I ought", or "I have to". Of course I am describing the general case and this is not always true. What is important is to encourage the client to own his choices as being morally right and fitting for him, rather than for him to attribute his decisions to an external moral code imposed on him by others or through childhood conditioning.

The problem with shoulds, musts, oughts, and have tos, is that often the words spoken are believed at a head or thinking level, but do not sit comfortably at a gut or feeling level. Where there is a mismatch between what is happening at a head level and what is being experienced at a gut level, the person will be confused and emotionally distressed. Human beings are holistic beings, so we cannot separate our emotional feelings, our bodily sensations, our thoughts and our spiritual experiences into discrete compartments. They all interrelate and must be in harmony with each other if we are to feel integrated and comfortable.

CHALLENGING BELIEFS

Sometimes a client will use an "I should" statement and then express reluctance to do what he has said he "should" do. In such a case I try to raise the client's awareness of what is happening within him and to help him to become more fully aware of his options. I explain to the client where many "I should" messages come from, and ask him where he thinks this particular "I should" message came from. I encourage him to check out whether the message sits comfortably with him. If it does, that is great! If it doesn't he can, if he chooses, challenge the "I should" message and maybe can replace it with something more fitting. Alternatively, he may decide that the message fits for him and accept it more willingly. A similar approach can be used when helping clients to challenge "ought", "must", and "have to" statements.

Irrational beliefs

As well as "should", "must", "ought", and "have to", SDBs include what Albert Ellis, the originator of Rational Emotive Therapy, refers to as irrational beliefs. Like "should", "must", "ought", and "have to", irrational beliefs are often absorbed from others during our childhood. Irrational beliefs often, but not always, include the words "should", "must", or "ought" or "I have to", but additionally they are intrinsically irrational. For example, to have the expectation that life will be fair and just is unrealistic. Life experience clearly demonstrates that life is often unfair and unjust. It is therefore irrational to assume that it will be fair and just. A more rational belief might be: "Unfortunately life is not always fair and just. If I can accept that, then I may be able to make sensible decisions to deal with those things which are unjust and unfair."

Although irrational beliefs are sometimes applied by the speaker to himself, they are also frequently applied to others in statements such as, "Other people should ...". Table 19.1 gives some examples of common irrational beliefs and rational alternatives. Notice how the irrational belief is certain to make the client feel bad whereas the rational alternative helps him to feel good. For other examples of irrational beliefs see Chapter 29.

Table 19.1 Comparison between rational and irrational beliefs

Irrational belief	Rational alternative
I must never make mistakes.	The only way not to make mistakes is to do nothing. I'm active, and all active people make mistakes.
Other people should not make mistakes.	No one's perfect. I can accept that other people will make mistakes.
Other people make me angry.	I make myself angry when I don't accept that other people don't live up to my expectations.
Other people should live up to my expectations.	Other people don't need to live up to my expectations.
My happiness depends on other people's behaviour and attitudes.	My happiness comes from within me and does not depend on others.
I must live up to other people's expectations.	I don't need to live up to other people's expectations to be OK.
I must win.	According to the law of averages most people only win 50 per cent of the time. I don't need to win to feel OK.

continued ...

Table 19.1 *continued*

Irrational belief	Rational alternative
Life should be fair and just.	Life is not fair and just.
Other people are bad if they do not have the same beliefs, attitudes and values as me.	All good people do not think the same or necessarily have the same beliefs, attitudes and values.
I must get my own way.	I do not need to get my own way to feel OK, and I can sometimes get satisfaction out of letting other people have their own way.
I need other people's approval to feel OK.	It's nice to get other people's approval, but I do not need their approval to feel OK.
I must always please other people.	It's unrealistic to expect that I can always please other people.
I must never get angry.	It's OK to be angry sometimes.
I should always be happy.	There is a time to be happy and a time to be sad.
I must not cry.	It's OK to cry.
I can't be happy if people misjudge me.	People sometimes will misjudge me. That's inevitable. But I know that I'm OK and that's what matters.

CHALLENGING IRRATIONAL BELIEFS

If a client verbalises an irrational belief, encourage him to question it by asking a question yourself. For example, you might ask, "Is it realistic to expect that life will be fair and just?" By doing this the client is very likely to challenge his own SDB, that life should be fair and just. If he does so, you may invite him to suggest a rational alternative.

You may wish to explain the difference between rational and irrational beliefs to your client and to point out that irrational beliefs are not only irrational but also inevitably make people feel bad. You can then encourage your client to write down a list of his irrational beliefs and replace them by rational alternatives. Remember that a client has the right to retain his irrational beliefs if he wishes. It is his choice, so do not attempt to persuade him to change, just raise his awareness of the consequences of irrational beliefs.

Care is needed

As when confronting, skill and care are needed when challenging SDBs. Ideally the challenge will come from the client rather than from you, the counsellor. However, it can be helpful for a client if you explain to him the nature, origin and effects of SDBs, so that he is able to recognise and challenge them.

Rational Emotive Behaviour Therapy

The ideas expressed in this chapter have their origin in Rational Emotive Therapy, although, in contrast to the approach described here, Rational Emotive Therapists are direct in their efforts to challenge and persuade their clients. If such an approach appeals to you then you may wish to learn more about Rational Emotive Therapy once you have mastered basic counselling skills.

LEARNING SUMMARY

- Self-destructive beliefs include "shoulds", "musts" and "oughts", and irrational beliefs.

- Most self-destructive beliefs come from messages absorbed during childhood.

- Self-destructive beliefs need to be challenged so that they can be replaced by constructive beliefs.

FURTHER READING

Dryden, W., *Brief Rational Emotive Behaviour Therapy*. London: Wiley, 1995
Ellis, A., *How to Keep People from Pushing Your Buttons*. New York: Carol, 1994
Ellis, A., *Better, Deeper, and More Enduring Brief Therapy: the Rational Emotive Behavior Therapy Approach*. New York: Bruner/Mazel, 1996
Walen, S. R., DiGiuseppe, R. and Dryden, W., *A Practitioner's Guide to Rational Emotive Therapy*, 2nd edn. Oxford: Oxford University Press, 1992

Examples of SDBs for use by trainers in teaching

Replace the SDBs below by rational beliefs:
1. Other people should always agree with me.
2. I should be able to expect that people will be reliable and trustworthy.
3. Other people should always respect me.

4. I should never be seen to make mistakes.
5. I need to be in control all the time or I will feel threatened.
6. Other people should care about my needs.
7. I need other people's approval to feel OK.
8. As a result of past trauma I can't enjoy life like other people.
9. I should do what other people want me to do.
10. People should never be impatient.
11. I will feel bad if other people reject me.
12. I must work hard all the time.
13. Things will sort themselves out if I just wait.
14. I must always help other people when they ask me to.
15. I must never refuse invitations.
16. Other people should appreciate what I do.

20 Normalising

Last week a person came to me in deep distress. "I think I'm going crazy", she said. "My head is buzzing with thoughts that flit in and out, I can't concentrate on anything for even a minute or two, and I'm getting nothing done in my daily life."

I was concerned. Was this person really going crazy? Did she need medication or specialist psychiatric help?

I listened to her story using the basic skills and processes of counselling as described in this book. As the counselling session proceeded she sobbed as she got in touch with her sadness and I began to understand. Once again she asked me, "Do you think I'm going crazy?" and this time I was able to say, "No, I don't think you are going crazy. If I had suffered the trauma you've just described I think that I would also feel the way you do". I continued: "I think that what is happening to you is inevitable and normal for someone who has had your recent experiences." I also said that maybe if she was finding the emotional pain too severe she could ask her doctor to consider prescribing medication. However, she chose not to do so, and I was pleased to notice that when she came back to see me this week she was slowly and naturally moving into a more comfortable emotional space.

The above is an example of the use of the skill called "normalising". I told the client that in my judgment what was happening to her was inevitable and normal. I noticed that she looked relieved and less tense as soon as I was able to tell her that I did not think that she was going crazy but saw her emotional distress as normal for the situation.

The skill of "normalising" is a particularly useful and powerful one if used correctly. Often a person's anxiety can be considerably reduced if she can recognise that her emotional state is normal and appropriate for the situation.

The example given above involved normalising a person's emotional response to trauma. However, the skill can also be used to normalise behaviour and relationship changes which occur as part of life's normal developmental crises.

The need for care

Clearly you need to be careful in using the skill of "normalising" because it would be irresponsible, unethical, and possibly dangerous to tell someone who was experiencing severe problems of a psychiatric nature that they were OK and did not need specialist treatment. If you are in doubt about a person's psychiatric condition, consult with your supervisor and refer the client to a professional who is competent to make a proper assessment.

Uses of normalising

Normalising can be used for the following:
1. to normalise emotional states;
2. to normalise changes in behaviours, roles and relationships due to developmental crises.

NORMALISING EMOTIONAL STATES

The goal in normalising a client's emotional state is to help the client to reduce anxiety by letting her know that her emotional response is a normal one. Time and again clients become frightened by their intense emotions in times of crisis. Fear of their highly charged emotional experience leads them to wonder whether they are going to fall apart completely and end up in a psychiatric ward. As we know, the reality is that this could happen to any one of us. A high percentage of the general population requires psychiatric help at some point in their lives so it is not realistic to deny a client's fear of what could happen. Instead, recognition of the fear with a response such as "You're frightened that you're going crazy" is sensible. However, if you think that the client's emotional response is appropriate for the situation, then it will probably be helpful if you tell the client that. If you are unsure about the need for more specialist help, give your client the option of seeking further assistance. You might say: "The emotional state you are experiencing and describing to me seems to me to be a normal response to your situation but if you are unsure about your ability to cope then you may want to look for more specialist help. What are your options in that regard?" It might then be possible for you to make suggestions with regard to referral for assessment or treatment. If in doubt consult your supervisor.

NORMALISING CHANGES IN BEHAVIOURS, ROLES AND RELATIONSHIPS DUE TO DEVELOPMENTAL CRISES

We all go through normal developmental stages in our lives. An example of a developmental stage is when a child takes its first few steps. Previously the child had been unable to walk and now her lifestyle is changed as she learns to walk. The time when those first few steps are taken involves anxious moments, so in some sense it is a crisis time. However, it is inevitable and normal for a child to learn to walk and for there to be associated anxiety.

There are many developmental stages in our lives. Some of these are listed in Chapter 28, entitled "Crisis intervention". These stages are generally inevitable and normal but usually involve anxiety. Unfortunately most people do not recognise the normal developmental processes and tend to respond to them inappropriately with panic and sometimes despair. Let me give you some examples.

Happily married couples frequently run into trouble when a second or third child comes on the scene. With the first child things are usually fine, because both partners are delighted and proud as new parents and lavish time and affection on the new member of the family. However, things naturally and inevitably change with subsequent children. Often, although not always in our contemporary society, it's the mother who has most responsibility for parenting young children and much of her energy is taken up in doing this. Consequently she does not have so much time or energy for her husband when the second or third child appears. She may feel resentful if she has temporarily given up her job with its associated social life and has interrupted her career. Her husband may feel resentful because his wife, due to the demands placed on her by the children, is no longer able to give him the attention and affection he previously enjoyed. Both partners may therefore be unhappy and may come to the conclusion that there is something terribly wrong with their relationship. However, this is a normal developmental crisis due to the changing nature of the family. It is to be expected and is almost inevitable.

It can be a great relief to the partners in such a situation if the nature of the developmental crisis is explained. A counsellor might say, "What is happening to you could almost have been predicted because you have reached this developmental stage in your family life".

Often, as a counsellor, I find that it is useful to use the word *inevitable* when I am "normalising" a client's situation even though using this word may result in an overstatement. For example, I might say to the couple we have been discussing, "It's *inevitable* that you would feel this way". By saying this, the couple are likely to feel relieved because if they believe that what is happening to them is inevitable, then they are likely to lose feelings of failure. Thus, they may be able to feel good about themselves. They may then realise that there is nothing fundamentally wrong with their marital relationship, but that there is a need for both of them to look for new ways to deal with this developmental crisis. Without self-blame, or blaming each other, they can then take action to rectify the situation.

Another common time for distress due to a developmental crisis is when children grow up to an age where they require very little parenting as they become more independent. This is a time when parents can feel a sense of worthlessness as one of their central life roles, that of "parent", is diminished. Some people find considerable satisfaction in life through parenting and when this role diminishes they feel empty and lost unless they can find satisfaction in other ways.

Once again, "normalising" the situation, by explaining to the client that what is happening is part of an inevitable and normal developmental stage in life, can help the client to feel better and to look for constructive ways in which to gain an increased sense of satisfaction.

I am sure that you can think of many examples yourself of times when behaviours, roles or relationships change due to normal developmental processes. It is often easier to recognise these for what they are when they happen to other people rather than to ourselves. This is why the skill of "normalising" is so useful because it brings emotional relief as it raises awareness of the inevitable and normal characteristics of a situation.

WARNING Normalising does not and must not involve minimising or devaluing the client's problem and pain. Normalising does not involve saying to the client,

"This situation is normal and inevitable, it's really no big deal, everybody has to go through the same process!" To do that would fail to address the client's genuine pain.

What normalising does do is to give the client a better understanding of her situation so that she understands why she is hurting, but in a way that enables her to deal more effectively with her pain and to move forward rather than to think that she is a failure and should somehow have been able to avoid the crisis. It is much better for her to be able to say, "I couldn't have avoided this crisis, it is a normal and inevitable crisis that couldn't be avoided. Now I can look for ways to respond to this crisis constructively".

LEARNING SUMMARY

- Normalising involves:

  - letting a client know that her emotional feelings are a normal response to her crisis; or

  - explaining to a client that she is experiencing an inevitable and normal developmental crisis that could not be avoided.

- Normalising needs to be carried out appropriately with attention to the possible need for onward referral if the client is at risk psychologically.

- Appropriate normalising does not minimise the client's problem or devalue her pain.

- Appropriate normalising may help the client to feel better and to respond more constructively to her situation.

Examples for use by trainers when teaching the skill of normalising

For each of the case descriptions below devise suitable counsellor normalising statements and explain how you would use that statement to help the client.

1. An elderly lady who had a successful career has recently retired. She is now bored with life, has no interests, and sees herself as a failure.
2. A man in his twenties who has previously enjoyed a single life has recently moved into a close live-in relationship with a friend. He is confused because he says that he loves his friend and wants to continue the relationship. However, he feels claustrophobic and unable to do the things which he would like to do for himself.
3. The father of a young child says that he and his partner (the child's mother) are having difficulty managing the child's behaviour and are arguing with each other about how to parent the child. It has emerged in the counselling

process that the father's own family of origin was very easy going and that physical punishment was never used. However, his partner's family of origin believed in the use of strict rules with physical punishment for disobedience.

4. A middle aged woman is unable to work or sleep and cannot understand "what is the matter with her". In counselling it transpires that there have been three deaths of near relatives in recent weeks. She herself worries about whether she has bowel cancer and is avoiding seeking medical advice.

5. In a time of very high unemployment a fifty year old, who was retrenched as a senior executive nine months ago, says that he has been unable to find employment. He is feels deeply depressed, has lost his motivation and feels a failure.

21 Exploring options

When a client comes to see a counsellor it is often because the client feels hopelessly stuck in an intolerable situation, in which she does not know what to do to ease her pain, and believes that there is no apparent solution to her problems. This hopeless feeling may lock the client into depression, anxiety and tension. Use of the reflective and other skills described previously enables the client to explore her issues and to clarify them. This process alone may be helpful in reducing her distress, and she may spontaneously move towards exploring options for herself and finding solutions for her problems. Sometimes however, the client does not move forward in this way and appears to reach an impasse, without properly exploring her options. An appropriate way for the counsellor to deal with this situation is to reflect the feeling of being "stuck" and then to ask the client what her options are.

Finding options

An open question such as, "You are obviously in a very uncomfortable situation. What do you see as your options?" can be useful in helping the client to identify options. By asking this question, rather than suggesting options, the counsellor encourages the client to take responsibility for solving her own problems. The client is then able to think about and suggest options for consideration. Some of these options she might immediately discard as impossible. However, be careful to remember all the options the client suggests, because an option that the client has ruled out initially may turn out to be the one she will eventually choose.

New counsellors often feel pressured into trying to find options for their clients. My experience is that, generally, it is not necessary to do this, and that it is far better if clients are able to come up with their own options. Of course there are times when for some reason a client fails to see an option that is obvious to the counsellor, and in such a case the counsellor may choose to tell the client about that option. However, when a counsellor does put forward an idea of her own, it's preferable that it should be put forward in a tentative way, so that the client sees it as nothing more than a possible suggestion and does not take it as advice.

Exploring options

When exploring options, let the client talk in a general way about the various alternatives and then summarise them clearly. Encourage the client to explore each idea individually and to talk about the positive and negative aspects of each option. There are some advantages in dealing with the most unlikely or least preferred options first. Thus, the client gets these out of the way, and this

leaves her with a smaller range of options, which makes it easier for her to move towards a decision.

Encourage the client not only to look carefully at the consequences, both negative and positive, of each option, but also to take into account her own gut feelings about the various alternatives that are available. Quite often a person's logical thinking will be pulling her in one direction whereas her gut feelings will be pulling her in a different direction. It is, for example, quite common to hear a client say: "That is what I really ought to do, that is what I should do, but I don't want to do that, it doesn't feel right for me." Obviously the client needs to feel very comfortable with the decision she makes, or she is unlikely to stay with it. Logical thinking alone does not provide sufficient grounds on which to choose an option. In fact, I believe that it's more important for the client to feel comfortable at a gut level with an option than for her to think that the option is the most sensible one. However, any option chosen obviously has to be the client's choice and may not be the choice the counsellor believes to be the most desirable, sensible or appropriate.

MAKING A CHOICE

Imagine that your client is in a dilemma and is unable to make a choice between two options, option A and option B. In order for the client to resolve her dilemma, help her to fully explore what it would feel like to have chosen option A, and to explore what the consequences of this choice would be. After this is completed encourage her to do a similar exploration for option B. This enables a clear comparison between the two options to be established.

One of the problems in making a choice between two alternatives is that whenever we make a choice, almost invariably there is a loss or cost involved. Let me give you an example. I'm writing this on a Saturday and don't have to work today unless I want to. It's a warm sunny day and I live near a sandy beach. I have two options. One option is to continue writing and the other option is to stop work and to go down to the beach for a swim, so I have a dilemma. In situations like this my usual response is to ask myself the question, "What should I do?" However, having written Chapter 19 on self-destructive beliefs, I prefer to replace the "should" question by the question, "What do I want to do?" By asking this question I can make a choice which is genuinely mine, is not excessively influenced by injunctions from the past, and fits with my current experience. I enjoy writing and quite enjoy what I am doing now, but it would also be enjoyable to go for a swim and maybe lie on the beach afterwards. Now this is not a heavy choice, but whichever choice I make will involve a loss. If I decide to keep on writing then I lose out on the exercise, the fresh air and the relaxed feeling of being down at the beach, but if I go down to the beach I'll have a different loss. I'll lose the satisfaction of continuing to do something creative—my writing—and I'll feel frustrated by not having made more progress with my writing when tomorrow comes. So, whether I continue to write or whether I go to the beach, I have to accept that there is a loss either way. If I choose one alternative I lose the other.

THE LOSS OR COST INVOLVED IN MAKING A CHOICE

One of the main blocks to making decisions occurs when people don't properly look at the loss or cost component involved. Frequently I discover that accepting the loss or cost associated with a decision is more difficult than choosing between the positive aspects of the alternative choices.

It can be very helpful to tell a client about the loss or cost component in decision making, and to explain this as applied to her particular dilemma. Ask the client: "If you choose option A, what are your losses going to be?" and "If you choose option B, what are your losses going to be?" Ask her whether she would be able to accept those losses. The choice is not just a choice between two positives, but also a choice that involves choosing between two losses and deciding which loss is acceptable, if either. By focussing on the loss or cost component as well as the positive component of options, clients are more readily able to make decisions and resolve their dilemmas.

THE EFFECT OF POLARITIES

Resolution of dilemmas is difficult for most people. Part of that difficulty is due to the polarities that exist within us. Let me go back to my previous example where I looked at the dilemma of continuing to write or going to the beach. Right now it is as though there are two parts of me. One part of me wants to go for a swim, and the other part of me wants to stay here and continue writing this book. I have found that it is very helpful for clients if I describe their dilemmas in terms of parts of themselves. Sometimes I say to a client: "Part of you wants to make choice A and another part of you wants to make choice B. These are both valid parts of you. They both exist in you at the same time." I ask the client to tell me about the part of her that wants option A and to explore that part fully, and then to tell me about the part of her that wants option B and to explore that fully. By doing this, I allow the client to integrate and own two opposite parts of herself and not to feel confused, but rather to accept that both are valid parts of herself (see Chapter 6 which dealt with parts of self). The client is then empowered to accept that choosing one of the options means letting go of the other option, and that involves a cost or the acceptance of a loss, the loss of the option that is not chosen.

THE MYTH OF THE "RIGHT" CHOICE

Many people have been taught as children that there is always a correct choice, and that in dilemmas the choice of one option is correct and the choice of the other is wrong. Confusion often arises from the unrealistic expectation that choice involves a decision between black and white, or between right and wrong. In reality, most human decisions involve deciding between shades of grey where both options have advantages or positive qualities and both have costs or disadvantages.

Remember, if I choose option A, I lose option B, and that loss is part of the cost of choosing option A. To resolve a dilemma, and choose one option, I have to let go of the other. The letting go is the hard part. Let your client know that and she may find it easier to reach a decision.

CREATIVE SOLUTIONS

At times dilemmas can be resolved by doing some creative thinking and introducing a new option so that the extent of any loss is reduced. If we use my personal example regarding whether I should continue writing or go to the beach, there is a third option. I could decide to continue writing for a while and then stop and go to the beach. This new option might provide me with a win–win solution!

Giving the client permission to stay stuck

Sometimes a client will stay stuck and will be unable to resolve a dilemma even though the issues are clearly understood. As a new counsellor, I often worried when a client was stuck and would sometimes prolong a counselling session unnecessarily in an effort to try to unstick the client and lead the client to a satisfying solution. I now realise that such counsellor behaviour is very inadvisable. It is much more helpful to reflect back to the client her stuckness, to say: "Look, it seems as though we've come to an impasse. There doesn't seem to be an easy solution, and today you seem to be stuck and don't know which way to go. Let's leave it there. Come back another time and we will talk together again." By saying this, the counsellor gives the client permission to remain stuck, reduces the pressure to make a quick decision, and lets the client know that she, the counsellor, still cares and is prepared to work with the client again. Sometimes the client will come back the next time saying "I've made a decision", because she was given permission to stay stuck and effectively given time to think through what was discussed in the previous session without pressure. At other times a client will remain stuck. Then the counsellor's goal is to assist her to come to terms with the consequences of being stuck in what may be a painful or uncomfortable situation. The counsellor does this by assisting the client to verbalise her feelings about being stuck, and then encouraging her to talk about how she will cope with her stuckness.

In the next chapter we will try to develop a deeper understanding of the process required to help clients deal with blocks to decision making. However, remember that it is OK to allow a client to remain "stuck". Often experiencing being stuck for a while is necessary before progress can be made.

LEARNING SUMMARY

- Ask your client for her options before suggesting additional ones.

- Tentatively suggest new options if important alternatives have been missed (are there any "win–win" options?)

- Summarise all the options clearly before discussing each in turn.

- Deal with the least desirable options first to exclude them.

- Examine the positive and negative aspects of each option, carefully considering likely consequences.

- There is a loss or cost involved in making any choice, and often accepting the inevitable loss is the hardest part of making a choice.

- Remember that most decisions are not choices between black and white but rather choices between shades of grey.

22 Facilitating action

By using the micro-skills described in the previous chapters an effective counsellor will most probably enable the client to move out of confusion and anxiety, and into a more comfortable emotional space. If that is achieved, then the client has clearly been helped by the counselling process in the short term, and for some clients that is sufficient. However, for many clients, their emotional distress is a consequence of entrenched life situations, and unless action is taken to change those life situations then emotional distress may well recur.

Some clients exhibit the "cracked record" syndrome. They go to see a counsellor again and again, with the same unresolved problem. The experienced counsellor needs to have the necessary skills to assist such clients to move forward by making specific and observable changes to their life situations.

Have you ever experienced resistance from a person when you have tried to persuade her to make useful life changes for herself? We human beings are rather like the proverbial donkey. The more someone pushes or pulls us, the more we tend to resist! If I am to enable a person to take action to change then I must resist the temptation to push for change and use a different strategy. The strategy needed was admirably described in Gestalt Therapy theory by Zinker (1978) and more recently by O'Leary (1992). A modified version of the *Gestalt awareness circle* is shown in Figure 22.1. An understanding of this circle enables counsellors to help clients to take action spontaneously after they have progressed through the necessary preliminary steps.

The Gestalt awareness circle

We will now look at the awareness circle (Figure 22.1) in some detail starting at the point of *arousal.*

Clients generally come for counselling when they are emotionally distressed—when they are at the *arousal* point on the *awareness circle*, with their emotions unpleasantly aroused. The counsellor's task is to enable the client to move around the circle towards *satisfaction* or *rest.* This is achieved by raising the client's *awareness.*

THE AROUSAL STAGE

In the *arousal* phase, the emotionally disturbed client is unable to focus clearly, and sees a confused picture of her world. It is as though she were looking at an overgrown forest, choked by too many trees and much undergrowth. She is unable to clearly see any one tree, but instead is overwhelmed by a blurred and confusing picture. In this state, the client's energy is depleted. She will be unable to see her options, and will therefore have little hope of taking any action to change her situation.

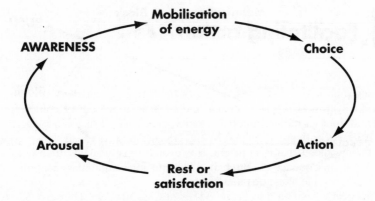

FIGURE 22.1 Gestalt awareness circle

RAISING AWARENESS TO MOBILISE ENERGY

If the client is to feel better, she needs to *mobilise her energy* so that she can work constructively to resolve her issues. The counsellor can facilitate this mobilisation of energy by raising the client's awareness of her inner experiences. As a trainee counsellor, if you have mastered the skills described in the previous chapters, then you have the tools required to do this. By using these micro-skills you will inevitably raise the client's awareness, and consequently will *mobilise her energy*.

As you progress in your training you will learn more advanced skills which will enhance your capabilities as a counsellor by speeding up the awareness process.

MOVING ROUND THE AWARENESS CIRCLE

Sometimes, once awareness is raised, the client will move with ease around the awareness circle. To use the previous analogy, the overgrown forest of trees will become a background against which the clear outline of one tree will emerge. The client's confusion will disappear and she will move naturally around the circle into making a *choice*, taking *action*, and coming into a state of *satisfaction* or *rest*.

In life, we do not stay in a state of rest, and if we did we would probably achieve nothing. What we do is to move around the awareness circle again and again.

BLOCKS TO PROGRESS AROUND THE CIRCLE

Unfortunately, most people don't move naturally and easily around the awareness circle but instead run into blocks as discussed in the previous chapter. Blocks often occur, as shown on the circle in Figure 22.2, before *choice* or *action*. If a client is blocked in either of these places, then it is tempting for the counsellor to focus on encouraging her to make a choice or to take action. Such counsellor

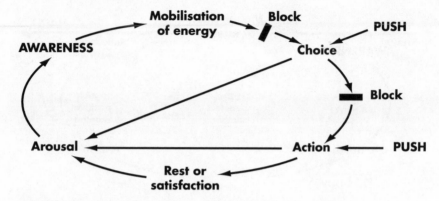

FIGURE 22.2 The effect of pushing for choice or action

behaviour is usually very unhelpful, creating greater difficulties for the client. Instead of achieving the counsellor's goal of helping the client to make a choice or to take action, pushing for choice or action usually returns the client to an even higher state of arousal (see the arrows in Figure 22.2).

If you want to help your client to make a choice or to take action, then a prerequisite is to enable the client to work through any block which might be impeding progress around the circle. The most common blocks which inhibit choice and action are identified in the simple dilemma model in Figure 22.3.

A client who makes decisions and takes action to change her life has to cope first with her own feelings, and then with other people's reactions. This is often difficult, particularly if the decisions or actions displease others. Also, if a client does something new, then she takes a risk; there may be unknown consequences, and these could be painful. It may be easier to go on living as now, with no changes and with known pain, rather than to take a risk and do something new and different with its unknown pain. Thus it is easy to understand how client choices and actions are often blocked by internal fears and anxieties including the following:

- inability to deal with own feelings;
- inability to cope with the reactions of others;
- fear of consequences;
- fear of a repetition of past bad experiences;
- the intrusion of inappropriate shoulds, musts and oughts;
- fear that something comfortable or rewarding will be lost;
- lack of skills to carry out the desired action.

DEALING WITH BLOCKS

Whenever a client is blocked and unable to make a choice or take action, resist the temptation to push the client into doing so, and instead return to the awareness point on the circle. Raise the client's awareness of her block and encourage her to explore how it feels to be blocked and unable to move

---

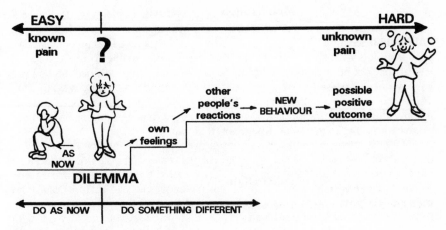

FIGURE 22.3 Dilemma model

forward. Encourage her to become aware of what she is experiencing internally. Ask her what messages she is getting from her body, from her emotional feelings, and from her thoughts, when she experiences her inability to decide or act. This may enable her to explore and to deal with the block, and thus free her to move around the circle to a more comfortable position. It is also possible that, by dealing with her block, she may discover that she has another more important issue which needs confronting.

Remember, the more you push a client to make a choice or to take action, the more blocked she is likely to become. If you want to help her to move on then you need to raise her awareness of the block.

Suitable questions to help clients explore blocks are as follows:

❝Tell me what you are experiencing emotionally as you think about making this decision (or taking this action)?❞

❝What are you aware of happening inside you when you think about making this choice (or taking action)?❞

For most clients, if you, the counsellor, use the micro-skills you have learnt to raise *awareness* and to work through blocks, then the client is likely to move spontaneously around the awareness circle, to make *choices* and to take the necessary *action* to achieve goals. However, for some clients this approach alone is not sufficient.

Clients who need additional help to take action

Some clients repeatedly use the counselling process to enable them to continue to exist in unsatisfactory life situations without change. Sometimes in the counselling process it appears as though they are replaying the same tape over and over again. When they do this they may well sink further into despair and hopelessness. Such clients need specific help in facilitating action, if they are to bring about meaningful changes to their lives. Also, there are some clients who, after deciding what they want to do, find themselves unable to move forward into action, not because of psychological blocks, but rather because they do not have the necessary skills or confidence to carry out the action they wish to take. These clients need additional help. The rest of this chapter deals with ways of helping clients who do not have the necessary confidence or personal resources to make and implement action plans on their own.

Clearly, it is not helpful for a counsellor to do the client's work. By doing that, the counsellor would reinforce the client's sense of helplessness, and lead the client to believe that she needed assistance each time new goals were to be targeted. What is helpful is for the client to learn how to organise, plan and execute decisions so that in the future she is able to do these things for herself. A good way of helping her to learn is to walk alongside her, and to work with her as she struggles with the issues involved in achieving one important goal. You can then, if you wish, explore with her the processes used in achieving her goal. Thus she may identify those processes which were most useful to her so that she can use them in achieving future goals.

Although every situation is different, there are some basic steps that are useful in enabling clients to take action to achieve goals. These steps are listed in the action plan below.

Action plan

1. Make psychological preparation.
2. Identify the goal.
3. Identify the first step towards goal achievement.
4. Concretise the first step towards goal achievement.
5. Decide how to carry out the first step.
6. Acquire the skills to carry out the first step.
7. Decide when to carry out the first step.
8. Carry out the first step.
9. Reward self for achieving the first step.
10. Reassess overall goal.

We will now look in detail at these steps in the order presented above. In order to make the exercise more meaningful consider the specific example of a father who has a dysfunctional relationship with his teenage son.

1. PSYCHOLOGICAL PREPARATION
This has been dealt with earlier in this chapter. The counsellor raises client awareness, to enable the client to work through blocks and to come to a decision.

2. IDENTIFYING THE GOAL
Imagine that the father in our example had come to the decision that he wanted to work on improving his relationship with his son. For many clients, identifying

such a goal would be sufficient to facilitate action, and the counsellor's work would be over. For other clients, further help would be needed.

3. IDENTIFYING THE FIRST STEP TOWARDS GOAL ACHIEVEMENT

For some clients, the goal of trying to improve a relationship with a son would be too broad and non-specific. It might not be clear how the goal could be achieved and consequently positive action would be unlikely to occur. Such a client may need to identify the first step towards achieving his goal. This first step needs to be realistically achievable, so that the client is likely to be rewarded by success rather than discouraged by failure.

The counsellor might ask: "How are you going to set about improving your relationship with your son?" Maybe the father would respond: "Well, I'd like to start by having a talk with him, but that's scary, because we haven't said anything pleasant to each other for some months."

Clearly at this point the counsellor would move the focus away from the contemplated action and return to raising awareness of the client's fear of talking with his son. If this were not done then the client would be likely to be blocked from action.

4. CONCRETISING THE FIRST STEP IN GOAL ACHIEVEMENT

Once the first step in goal achievement has been identified, it needs to be concretised, so that it is clear and specific rather than vague. For example, the statement "I'd like to have a talk with my son" is very general. The value of such a talk is likely to depend on what the purpose of the talk is, and on what the content of the conversation is likely to be. Questions by the counsellor, such as, "What do you want to say to your son?" and "What do you hope to achieve as a result of this talk?", might yield more specific information such as, "I want to tell him why I am so angry with him, so that I can get that garbage out of the way and can start relating to him in a positive way".

5. DECIDING HOW TO CARRY OUT THE FIRST STEP

This decision needs to take into account the likely consequences of the proposed action. For example, the statement in the paragraph above, "I want to tell him why I am so angry with him ..." suggests that the client intends to confront his son in a way likely to lead to further alienation rather than reconciliation. At this point the counsellor could usefully carry out some role-plays to allow the client to experience what it would be like to be the recipient of the intended message.

6. ACQUIRING THE SKILLS TO CARRY OUT THE FIRST STEP

The client may need to acquire new skills to be able to competently carry out the first step. In our current example the counsellor might coach the client in the use of "I" statements, and carry out further role-plays to determine the likely impact of client statements.

7. DECIDING WHEN TO CARRY OUT THE FIRST STEP

Sometimes when I have to carry out an unpleasant task I will delay doing what I have decided to do by using the excuse that the time is not right. Do you do that? I think that most people do, and delayed action often results in no action. I find that for me it is usually easier to carry out what I plan if I have made a clear decision about the proposed timing. I think that it's the same for many clients, and it's therefore useful to explore the issue of timing with them. This may result in more awareness raising—back to the awareness circle again!

8. CARRYING OUT THE FIRST STEP

Whether or not the client carries out the first step is unimportant. If he does, then he can feel good about that, and if he doesn't then there is a learning for him. He can once again get in touch with his inner experiences to discover what stopped him from carrying out the first step, and from that awareness a new decision can be made.

9. REWARDING SELF FOR CARRYING OUT THE FIRST STEP

Do you ever minimise your achievements? I sometimes do, but I am getting better at taking pride in what I am good at. Many clients fail to give themselves positive messages when they succeed in performing difficult tasks. As a counsellor, help your clients to feel good about themselves by maximising their achievements. A client who is properly rewarded for carrying out the first step is more likely to continue making positive decisions and carrying them out.

10. REASSESSING THE OVERALL GOAL

Often when the client has gone some way in one direction, he will realise that the goal he originally targeted is one which he no longer wants. That is clearly OK, but he will consequently need to reassess his overall goal.

In conclusion

In this chapter we have looked at the skills involved in facilitating action. Generally, if you use the previously learnt micro-skills and remember what you have discovered here about the *awareness circle*, you will be successful in helping clients to take appropriate action to bring about meaningful changes in their lives. Additionally, the action plan described above can be used when it is clear that the client is unable to move forward without more specific help.

LEARNING SUMMARY

- Pushing directly for choice or action is likely to fail and increase emotional distress.

- To maximise the possibility of choice or action raise awareness of blocks.

- A major client dilemma concerns the choice "to do as now" or "to do something different".

- Doing as now involves known pain.
- Doing something different involves unknown pain and outcomes. It's risky!
- Action plans are helpful for some clients.
- Action plans involve preparation for action, setting a specific goal, and having a reward for taking the first step.

FURTHER READING

Clarkson, P., *Gestalt Counselling in Action*. London: Sage, 1989

O'Leary, E., *Gestalt Therapy, Theory, Practice and Research*. London: Chapman & Hall, 1992

Zinker, J., *Creative Process in Gestalt Therapy*. New York: Vintage, 1978

23 Termination

It is often very hard for new counsellors to know when to terminate a counselling session or when to terminate a series of counselling sessions. In this chapter we will discuss the following aspects of termination:

1. the termination of an individual counselling session
2. the need for ongoing appointments
3. client and counsellor dependency
4. the termination of a series of counselling sessions
5. the termination of a telephone counselling call

The termination of an individual counselling session

Most counselling agencies and private practitioners schedule a particular length of time for each counselling session, and it is fairly common for this to be one hour. In my experience, this is a suitable time for most individual counselling sessions although a longer time may be required for marital or family counselling. Of course, there are exceptions. Sometimes it will be clear after a shorter time that an interview can be terminated because the client has resolved her issues and there is little point in sitting around chatting unnecessarily. At other times it may be apparent that a client is in a highly distressed emotional state at the end of a one-hour session and it may be necessary to continue the interview for longer.

WORK TO BE DONE BETWEEN SESSIONS

Between counselling sessions, the counsellor may need to make another appointment for the client who is leaving, to show the client out, and to write up notes on the interview. The counsellor may also need to debrief, to let go of any emotional consequences for herself which result from listening to the client's pain. If she is not able to do this then she will not be ready to meet a new client and is also setting herself up for burnout (see Chapter 34 entitled "Looking after yourself"). Debriefing can sometimes be achieved just by writing up case notes, or having a cup of tea, or by chatting informally with someone. However, in cases where the counselling session has been particularly stressful for the counsellor it may be necessary for her to talk through her issues with a supervisor or another counsellor. After debriefing the counsellor needs to prepare for the next client by reading case notes, if they are available.

Because of the counsellor's own needs and the work that is preferably done between appointments, I believe that it is wise for agencies to schedule in quarter of an hour between the end of a counselling session and the beginning of the next, particularly where counsellors are dealing with very distressed clients.

KEEPING THE COUNSELLING EXPERIENCE DYNAMIC

In my experience clients often deal with important issues in the first three-quarters of an hour of a counselling session, and then begin to lose energy. It is important that each counselling session is dynamic and that the client is working actively throughout the session. Once a client becomes used to sessions being of fixed length, she will tend to work comfortably within that time frame. During a one-hour interview a client will be likely to have raised important issues and to have explored them. The client then needs time in which to process the work done. It may therefore be appropriate to terminate the session at that point and to leave a few days, or maybe a week or two, before making another appointment, if that is needed.

CLIENT ANXIETY ABOUT TIME CONSTRAINTS

If the matter is raised, let the client know that you, the counsellor, are in control of the length of the counselling session. Frequently clients show anxiety by looking at a clock in the room, because they are worried about taking up too much of a counsellor's time. In such cases it is important for the counsellor to say that she will control the length of the session, and that the session will probably last about 60 minutes, or whatever is appropriate. If a client is told this, her anxiety regarding timekeeping is likely to be reduced.

PREPARING FOR THE END OF A SESSION

Where a counsellor is working within a set time frame, and knows that there is a time limit to the counselling session, the counsellor needs to prepare for terminating the session. This preparation should be commenced about 10 minutes before the end of the session. If the counselling session is to last 60 minutes, then after about 50 minutes the counsellor needs to assess the progress of the session. The counsellor can then decide how to use the remaining time in order to terminate in a way which is satisfactory for the client. It may be advisable for the counsellor to say to the client: "I am conscious of the need for us to finish the session in about 10 minutes time and it seems to me that you may wish to explore ... (a particular area) ... that we have been talking about." By giving the client some warning that the counselling session must end within a few minutes, the client is given an opportunity to deal with, or a least mention, any pressing unfinished business.

Closing the session

Near the finishing time, it is sometimes appropriate for the counsellor to provide a summary of the material discussed by the client during the session. Whenever possible it's useful to give the client some positive feedback, especially as clients usually come to see counsellors at times when their self-esteem is low. The counsellor might also add a statement regarding goals for the future and the possibility or probability of future counselling sessions being required.

The counsellor should take control of the termination of the session. She may need to be assertive, particularly with clients who want to linger on and chat rather than do useful work. In such a case, be direct and if necessary interrupt and say something like: "I realise that you would like to continue talking to me, but unfortunately that is not possible. We need to finish the session right now." Then stand up and lead the way firmly out of the room without stopping to linger, even if the client wishes to do so.

The need for ongoing appointments

Inexperienced counsellors are often apprehensive about asking clients to come back for further appointments. If you feel apprehensive about doing this, explore your feelings. You may be afraid that the client will not want to come back and will reject your offer of another appointment. If the client does do that, would it be a disaster? If you think that it would, then you need to discuss the issue with your supervisor. Remember that it is hard for clients to make appointments. It is much easier for them to cancel out. If you don't make another appointment for the client, then she is likely to assume that you don't think that it is necessary for her to come back. She may wonder whether you would consider it to be a nuisance if she were to do so. It is therefore important, if you do not make another appointment, that you say to your client: "I won't make another appointment for you now, because I am not sure that it's unnecessary for you to come back to see me as your issues seem to be reasonably well resolved. However, I would like you to know that if you decide later that it would be useful for you to come back, then you are welcome to ring up and make an appointment."

MAKING A CONTRACT FOR ONGOING APPOINTMENTS

For clients who need ongoing appointments, it may be desirable for the counsellor to spell out an ongoing contract. It may be sufficient to say, for example: "I think it would be useful for you to come back to see me again next week—would you like to do this?" Alternatively, it may be appropriate to say: "It seems to me that you have a number of issues which need to be resolved, and this is likely to take several counselling sessions. Would you like to come to see me on a weekly basis for the next three or four weeks and then review the situation?" In this way, the client can be made aware of the counsellor's willingness to continue seeing her.

Clients often feel insecure about the counselling relationship and are afraid that the counsellor will terminate the counselling process before important issues have been explored. It is therefore important to ensure that the client has some clear expectation regarding the possible duration of the counselling relationship.

Client and counsellor dependency

Sometimes it's desirable to terminate a series of counselling sessions sooner than the client would wish. This raises the issue of dependency. It's very easy, in fact probably inevitable, that dependency will occur in ongoing counselling relationships.

DEPENDENCY ON THE RELATIONSHIP

It is easy for clients to become dependent on counsellors for a number of reasons. Firstly, it is inevitable that a meaningful relationship will develop if the counsellor is genuine, warm and accepting. Of course, there are necessary and appropriate limits to the counselling relationship (see Chapter 7 regarding ethical issues). However, the quality of a counselling relationship is such that it is natural for some clients to wish that the counselling relationship could continue after its usefulness for legitimate counselling purposes has ended.

Clients tell counsellors their innermost secrets, whereas generally, from childhood, people learn to share such private material only with someone they love. There can be almost an expectation by the client, from previous life learnings, that intimate personal sharing will result in an ongoing relationship.

Some people who come to counsellors are very alone in the world, and do not have a close relative or friend with whom to share the problems and stressors which arise in their daily lives. There is good reason for such people to want to become dependent on the counselling relationship. We all have a need for some degree of closeness and affection, and the counselling relationship may provide this for the lonely, who may then become dependent on the relationship.

DEPENDENCY ON THE COUNSELLING PROCESS

After the initial traumas of a crisis have passed, it is often very comfortable for a client to be able to continue to discuss and work through less important life issues in the caring counselling environment. Most of us like comfort, but to continue to provide counselling to clients who no longer *need* it does them a disservice. It effectively interferes with the natural and desirable tendency of people to become self-sufficient. Effective counselling teaches clients how to work through most troubling issues on their own, and how to recognise when counselling help is really needed.

COUNSELLORS CAN BECOME DEPENDENT TOO

Dependency can occur in two directions. The client may become dependent on the counsellor, and equally the counsellor may become dependent on the client. Counsellors are not emotionless robots, but are human beings with emotions and needs. As described above and in Chapter 7, the counselling relationship often involves an unusual degree of intimate sharing, and by its very nature involves a degree of closeness. Consequently, it is easy to understand how a counsellor can get hooked into a dependency relationship. Clearly, a counsellor needs to stay vigilant to ensure that she does not encourage her clients to continue with counselling merely to satisfy her own needs.

It is inevitable that dependency issues will arise from time to time for counsellors. Sometimes counsellors will be unaware that such dependency is occurring. It is here that regular supervision is essential to help counsellors identify dependency issues and to reduce the likelihood of inappropriate transgression of professional boundaries (see Chapter 5).

THE TERMINATION OF A SERIES OF COUNSELLING SESSIONS

The decision about when to terminate a series of counselling sessions is often fairly clear, and will frequently be made by the client herself in discussion with the counsellor. However, there will be times when the decision is more difficult, particularly if either client or counsellor dependency is occurring. Counsellors therefore need to regularly review the progress that is being made in counselling sessions, and the goals that are being achieved, to ensure that counselling is continuing for the client's well-being, rather than for satisfying dependency needs. Where progress is not being made, and goals are not being achieved, it is unethical to encourage clients to continue.

CONFRONTING DEPENDENCY

If client dependency is identified, then the counsellor needs to bring the issue into the open, and to let the client know what she sees happening. This needs to be done with sensitivity, because it would be easy for a client to feel hurt and rejected as a consequence of inept confrontation regarding dependency. However, if the dependency is reframed positively, as a normal occurrence which involves both counsellor and client, then progress can be made towards termination.

Dealing with the loss of the relationship

With clients who are terminating a long counselling relationship, there will be some grief associated with the loss of that relationship. The client needs to be prepared, particularly where a long relationship has been established, for the feelings of loss that will occur when the relationship ends. In order to minimise this pain, it may be advisable for a counsellor to make one or two appointments at long intervals at the end of a series of counselling sessions. For example, when I have seen a client on a weekly basis for several weeks, I have often made the remaining appointments at fortnightly and monthly intervals.

With some clients it can be useful to have a follow-up session at the end of three months. A three-monthly follow-up session serves three purposes. First, it helps the client to adjust to the idea of being independent and not dependent on the counsellor; second, it enables the client to deal with the loss of the counselling relationship in a gentle way; and third, it enables the counsellor to review the progress that the client continues to make after regular counselling has ceased. Also, it sometimes happens that after a series of counselling sessions has been completed, a three-monthly follow-up session will reveal that there is a "loose end" that needs to be tied up before final termination.

Remember, termination of both single sessions and a series of sessions is often slightly painful. It is usually difficult to say "goodbye", and accept the loss of a meaningful relationship. A counsellor needs to be aware of this, both for the client and for herself. As discussed previously, it is important to address this issue openly and to help the client to adjust to termination. Termination needs to be done sensitively and caringly.

The termination of a telephone counselling call

Terminating a telephone counselling call is an art and if it is carried out expertly the caller will feel comfortable about hanging up, recognising that the call has come to a natural end. In order to achieve this result, the termination stage needs to be integrated with the total process of the call so that it occurs smoothly and is expected.

Generally, the termination process for a counselling call of average or longer length will follow a sequence of steps which prepare the caller for the end of the call. Naturally, each call is different and what is appropriate for one call will not fit another. Here are some commonly used steps which can be used when ending a call:

1. Decide when to finish a call.
2. Warn the caller that the time to finish is approaching.
3. Summarise the call.
4. Give the caller some positive feedback.
5. Take control.
6. Tell the caller that you are going to finish the call.
7. Invite the caller to phone back if appropriate.
8. Say "Goodbye" and hang up.

We will now discuss these steps in detail so that you can use them as a guide if you wish. However, remember that you are a unique individual and will need to develop your own way of ending calls.

DECIDE WHEN TO FINISH A CALL

As you know, there can be no standard rule about how long a telephone counselling call should be. However, I don't believe that it's useful to let calls continue after useful work has finished. If the call is losing energy, or not making constructive progress for the caller, then it is time to prepare for termination or alternatively to look for different strategies so that the call regains its usefulness. Generally, I find that it is not helpful to allow calls to continue for longer than one hour at the most, although there are naturally exceptions to the rule.

I think that it is worth mentally evaluating what is happening in a call if it is still continuing after about 45 minutes. A decision can then be made about how to influence the process of the call so that the remaining minutes are useful to the caller.

WARN THE CALLER THAT THE TIME TO FINISH IS APPROACHING

As with face-to-face counselling, it's a good idea to warn your client or caller, in advance, that the counselling session or call is to nearing its end. When you sense that it is appropriate, you may wish to say to the caller something like this: "I realise that we have been talking for a while now and hope that we have covered some useful ground together. I would like to finish our call within the next few minutes, and wonder whether there are some important things that you would like to say before we finish talking together." This statement gives the caller an opportunity to deal with anything pressing that has been omitted. The caller is also prepared for the impending closure. Notice that the statement is clear and owned by the counsellor: "I would like to finish our call." You may not be comfortable using this style and that is OK, because you are different from me. Personally, I like to let the caller know my expectations rather than be indirect. The message is then clear and the caller can deal with it in any way she thinks fit.

Having warned the caller that the call is nearing its end, the caller may take the opportunity to bring in new material. A judgment is then needed as to whether to deal with that material in the current call or whether to say to the caller something like: "You have now raised some important new issues and I think that they need to be considered carefully. Maybe you would like to phone back another time to talk through those issues. However, today I think that we should try to summarise those things that we have talked about and then finish our conversation."

SUMMARISE THE CALL AND GIVE POSITIVE FEEDBACK

If the caller doesn't raise new issues, then you, the counsellor, have the opportunity to move into summarising the content and possibly the process of the call. An example of a process statement included in a summary might be: "I notice that you seemed to be very distressed at the start of this call when you were discussing ... and I get the impression that you are now more confident of your ability to handle the situation."

Notice that in this statement the caller receives positive feedback. Wherever possible give your caller positive feedback because people in crisis often do not feel good about themselves and may not be getting positive feedback from others. Sometimes it is hard to think of something positive to say, but it is rare not to be able to find something if you join with your client effectively. Be careful, however, to ensure that the feedback you give is credible. Here are some examples of positive feedback.

"You seem to be a very clear thinker. You have been able to think through the issues and come to some decisions."

❝I have heard how you have struggled on your own against many difficulties. You strike me as a fighter; someone who doesn't give in easily. ❞

❝I think that you are remarkable to have done as well as you have when I take into account the negative messages you have received from your family. You must have a lot of internal strength. ❞

❝In spite of the personal setbacks you have suffered you have persisted in your efforts to do the best you can. You must be a very positive person. ❞

Notice that the positive comments may include things that the person has achieved, but more importantly praise the person and not just the person's actions: "You are a clear thinker", "You are a fighter", "You have a lot of internal strength", "You are a positive person", etc.

TAKE CONTROL

Having given your caller some positive feedback, it is now time for you to take control so that termination occurs. Terminating a telephone counselling call can often be quite difficult and is often more difficult than terminating a face-to-face counselling session. In the face-to-face session, as discussed previously, it's possible for the counsellor to stand up and to move out of the room, giving clear signals that the session is over. These non-verbal signals are not available to the telephone counsellor. Moreover, we human beings are conditioned to believe that it is bad manners to assertively break off a conversation, particularly if the other person would really like to continue.

Some clients love to talk and would happily keep you on the phone for hours. Others just do not know how to close off a conversation. With both types of clients it is important to be clear and assertive.

CLOSING THE CALL

Take control! Tell the caller that you intend to finish the call now and at the same time reassure her with regard to the possibility that she may want to phone back. It is very important to do this because some callers feel guilty about taking up a telephone counsellor's time and say things such as: "There must be other people with much more important problems who need your help." Such people need to be reassured that it is OK for them to ring up again.

Here are some suitable termination statements:

❝ Thank you for sharing your personal difficulties with me. I have appreciated the way you have trusted me enough to be able to share so much. Please feel welcome to phone back if you think that I can be of help. Goodbye. ❞

❝It has been good to talk with you about the issues which have been troubling you. I hope that you will feel free to call back another day. Goodbye. ❞

£ £I think that you were sensible to phone; everyone needs to talk about personal matters privately at times. Please call again when you need to. Goodbye. ♪♪

Notice that the statements are clear and end with "Goodbye".

Regular callers

Crisis telephone counselling agencies usually have some callers who phone in regularly, enjoy talking and do not want to finish their calls at an appropriate time. With these callers the telephone counsellor needs to be very firm in making a termination statement similar to one of the examples above. If the caller then tries to restart the conversation, the counsellor is, in my view, justified in saying: "I know that you would like to continue talking but I am going to hang up now because I really want to finish here. Goodbye." Then regardless of what the caller is saying the phone can be gently replaced on the hook. You may have noticed that in the example given the client is given a clear statement about the counsellor's intention before the hang-up occurs.

The three don'ts:

To terminate this chapter, here are three "don'ts". At the end of a face-to-face counselling session or telephone call:

DON'T ask the client a question.
DON'T reflect back content.
DON'T reflect back feelings.

If you do any of these things the session or call is certain to continue because the client or caller has an implied invitation to respond!

LEARNING SUMMARY

- Let the client know that you are in control of the length of the session.

- Warn the client when the session is coming to an end.

- Negotiate a contract with the client with regard to future appointments.

- Finish each session by summarising, outlining future goals if appropriate, and giving some positive feedback where possible.

- Take control when finishing a session.

- During a series of ongoing counselling sessions review progress and be aware of dependency.

- Deal with dependency by openly discussing it.

- If necessary deal with grief associated with closure of a series of sessions.

- Remember that terminating telephone calls may require considerable firmness.

- When terminating, don't ask questions or reflect content or feelings.

Part III

Combining skills in a counselling conversation

24 The process of a counselling session

Each counselling session is different from every other session. No two interventions are going to be the same. However, after counselling for a long time, most counsellors find that there is a common pattern, which can often be recognised, in the processes underlying their counselling sessions. The flow-chart in Figure 24.1 shows in diagrammatic form the processes that may evolve in a counselling session. Although this flow-chart is useful in creating an understanding of the counselling process, please be aware that the various stages described by the chart will often overlap each other, repeat themselves and occur in a different order from that shown. The flow-chart will be discussed in some detail in the following paragraphs under the headings shown on the right-hand side of the chart.

Preparation

The counselling process starts even before the client and counsellor meet. The client, on her way to a counselling session, will usually rehearse what she intends to say. She is likely to bring with her preconceived ideas about what's going to happen in the counselling session. She will have not only expectations, but probably considerable apprehension too. Coming to a counselling session can be quite difficult for a client because it is painful to talk about deep inner feelings, and it can be quite threatening to do this with a stranger.

THE COUNSELLOR'S OWN EXPERIENCE
The counsellor also brings her own expectations, agenda and personal feelings to the counselling session. Her expectations and agenda may be inappropriate for the client, and her personal feelings may intrude on the counselling process to the detriment of the client. The counsellor's own attitudes, beliefs and feelings are certain to influence what happens in the session. If she has personal problems of her own that are unresolved and pressing in on her, these are certain to affect her counselling. Obviously, it is very important for a counsellor

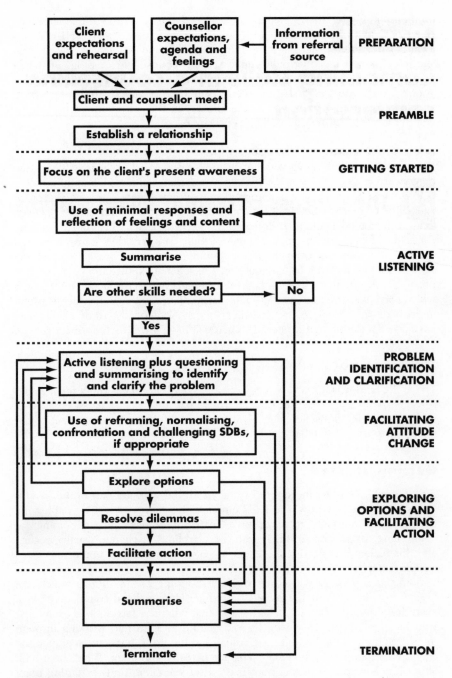

FIGURE 24.1 Process of a counselling session

Within the figure:

Client expectations and rehearsal	
Counsellor expectations, agenda and feelings	
Information from referral source	**PREPARATION**
Client and counsellor meet	
Establish a relationship	**PREAMBLE**
Focus on the client's present awareness	**GETTING STARTED**
Use of minimal responses and reflection of feelings and content	
Summarise	**ACTIVE LISTENING**
Are other skills needed?	No
Yes	
Active listening plus questioning and summarising to identify and clarify the problem	**PROBLEM IDENTIFICATION AND CLARIFICATION**
Use of reframing, normalising, confrontation and challenging SDBs, if appropriate	**FACILITATING ATTITUDE CHANGE**
Explore options	
Resolve dilemmas	**EXPLORING OPTIONS AND FACILITATING ACTION**
Facilitate action	
Summarise	
Terminate	**TERMINATION**

to try to minimise the intrusion of her own business into the counselling process. One of the best ways for a counsellor to achieve this is to become as aware as possible of the issues troubling her, and as aware as possible of what she is experiencing internally during each counselling session. If when counselling, you deliberately try to stay aware of what is happening within yourself, then you will be better able to deal appropriately with what is yours, and to separate that from what is the client's. In this way your own business will intrude less on the counselling process.

INFORMATION GAINED PRIOR TO COUNSELLING
Before a counsellor has met with her client, it is possible that she may have some preconceived ideas about her. Often the counsellor will have some information before the session starts. This information may have come from the person or agency who referred the client for counselling. As a new counsellor, I believed that such material often distorted my own understanding of the client. Consequently I went through a stage of trying not to listen to what referral sources told me, and of making an appointment and saying to the referral source: "I'll find it all out from the client." I have changed that approach because I have discovered that quite often a referral source will have factual information which may take time to come out in the counselling session, and which is useful in enabling me to understand the client better. Additionally, some clients may have an expectation that a referral source will have given me information.

The preamble

This is the joining stage where the client and counsellor meet and a relationship is established as discussed in Chapter 10, so that the client feels at ease. Also, at this time, the counsellor may be able to check out and adjust some of her initial ideas about the client.

Getting started

After the initial settling-in period, I usually start the working part of the session by asking the client how she feels emotionally, *right now*. This enables the client to get in touch with her own anxiety or tension about coming for counselling. By getting in touch with these feelings, a change usually occurs, and this makes it easier for the client to move on to talking about the issues troubling her.

Sometimes a client will come with a "shopping list" of things which she wishes to talk about, and may even produce lengthy handwritten notes. If a client has done this I try to make her feel that what she has done is useful and valuable preparation. However, I avoid getting trapped into working through the shopping list item by item, but instead use the list to generate energy in the client. For example, I might say: "This list is really important. When you think about it, what do you think about first?" Thus the client finds a starting point from which she can proceed naturally, in whatever direction her energy takes

---

her. More often than not the shopping list will become irrelevant as more important underlying issues emerge.

Unfortunately clients often perceive counsellors as "experts", with almost magical skills, who are capable of using clever psychological techniques to solve other people's problems. Consequently, there may need to be a re-education process, where you, the counsellor, spell out to the client exactly how you *do* see yourself. It may be necessary for you to say to the client: "Look, I don't see myself as an expert who can solve your problems for you. In fact, I believe that you will always know and understand yourself better than I will know and understand you. However, I hope that in this session you and I together can explore what's troubling you so that you can make some progress towards feeling more comfortable." Alternatively, you might say something like, "It would be great if I were a magician who could wave a wand over you to solve your problems. I can't do that, but I can offer you the opportunity to come here and explore your problems with me in a safe and confidential setting. Hopefully, by doing that, you will start to feel more comfortable."

Active listening

During the early parts of a session, as the client starts to talk about her issues, the counsellor is able to make use of minimal responses, and to reflect content and feelings. By doing this the client is encouraged to disclose what is troubling her, in her own way and at her own pace, and without unnecessary intrusion into that process by the counsellor. Consequently the client's story unfolds and the relationship between client and counsellor develops as the client feels valued by the counsellor's active listening.

RESPECTING THE CLIENT'S PACE
In the early stages of counselling it is common for clients to be unable to recognise and talk about their emotional feelings. Clients often want to talk about things "out there" rather than inside themselves. They want to talk about other people's behaviour, and about other people's fears. They want to focus on what happened in the past rather than on the present, and to focus on events, instead of on their own inner feelings. It is useful to encourage a client, in this situation, to focus on her inner feelings and thoughts, as they are, in the present, if she will. However, it is also important not to pressure her, but to allow her to move at her own pace. At first, allow your client to talk about the "out there" things, if it is too painful for her to focus on her own inner processes. With time, as she deals with the "out there" problems, and with the "out there" situations, she is likely to move slowly towards recognising and talking about her own feelings from the past. Past feelings will not be so threatening to her as present feelings. Later in the counselling process, she will move towards experiencing her present feelings. Move *slowly* towards helping the client to experience her own thoughts and feelings in the present. It is

important to do this sensitively because the client needs to be able to gradually approach the painful parts of her life, rather than to be pushed too quickly, and then to run away from looking at the issues that are troubling her. The counsellor who pushes too hard too early does the client a disservice, because the client may close the lid on her Pandora's box of uncomfortable feelings and thoughts, and not come back to another counselling session.

THE COUNSELLOR'S BEHAVIOUR
During the active listening phase, while keeping a check on her own inner experiences, the counsellor needs to focus her energy by concentrating as totally as she can on what is happening inside the counselling room. In particular she needs to fully attend to the client, to concentrate on listening to and observing the client, and to sense what the client is experiencing. This is not always easy and there will inevitably be occasions when a counsellor's attention does wander through an intrusion in the counselling environment, the presence of intrusive thoughts, over-tiredness, or for some other reason. If this does happen it may be best to be open and honest with the client and then to re-focus on the counselling process. Remember that no-one is perfect. If you are starting to become over-tired read Chapter 34 entitled "Looking after yourself".

Problem identification and clarification

At times, the counsellor will need to draw together the important parts of what the client has said, and to help the client to focus more clearly by summarising these. As the client's trust develops, the counsellor will be able to ask appropriate questions where necessary, in order to help the client move forward and identify her most pressing problem.

Facilitating attitude change

The skills of reframing, confrontation and challenging self-destructive beliefs can now be used, if appropriate, to encourage the client to choose more constructive attitudes and beliefs.

Exploring options and facilitating action

The counsellor may now be able to assist the client to move forward into exploring options, resolving dilemmas and planning for action. However, it is important to ensure, as stated previously, that the client does not feel pressured. Remember, as described in Chapters 21 and 22, to put energy into the raising of awareness rather than into pushing for choice or action. To encourage a client to make a choice prematurely will pressure her and will make it harder for her to reach a decision. If the client is not ready to make a choice, she must be allowed to feel that it is OK to be unable to make a decision, and to feel that it is OK for her to remain stuck for the present.

Termination

A good way to terminate a counselling session is to summarise the important awarenesses that have emerged during the session. Don't attempt to summarise everything covered in the session, as that is unnecessary and unhelpful. Just pick out what was important. Imagine that at the start of the session the client brought into the room an awkward bundle of thoughts and feelings. She dropped the bundle onto the floor and started to examine the contents one at a time. After examining each item, she retained some, threw some away and exchanged others. After that it was time to help her tie up the bundle into a neater, more manageable package. The idea of the summary is to help her do this, if that is what she is ready to do. However, the bundle belongs to the client, so it must be her decision about how and when she does her repackaging.

RESPECTING THE CLIENT'S PROCESS

Sometime a client will not be ready to tie up the package. Sometimes the client will be left in a very uncomfortable space, either feeling stuck, or fairly unhappy, or distressed about what she has discovered. New counsellors usually want clients to leave sessions feeling happy. It is important to remember that often it is useful for a client to be able to spend time mulling over what has been discussed in the counselling session. She can then process it on her own before coming back again if she needs to. Even so, it can be distressing to a new counsellor to find a client waiting for her in the waiting room before a session, looking composed, and then leaving the session with tears in her eyes. This will inevitably happen at times. Frequently, in a counselling session, the client moves into areas that she previously had not been prepared to openly explore. She allows herself to feel the pain of experiencing emotions that had been suppressed, and she leaves the counselling session exhausted and sad. However, allowing the client to do this can be therapeutic and the positive results of this process may be seen when the client returns for a subsequent session.

In conclusion

The process of a counselling session described in this chapter gives an overview of the process as it might occur. However, as a counsellor, do not attempt to follow this process, but rather let it emerge naturally. Do as described in Chapter 2: allow the client to go at her own pace, in her own direction, and to feel as though she is going on a journey with you, the counsellor, walking alongside. If you do this, the counselling process will occur naturally, smoothly and without great effort on your part. Most importantly, the client will be undergoing a process of growth which may enable her to lead a more fulfilling and less painful life.

LEARNING SUMMARY

- A typical process for a counselling session is described schematically in the Figure 24.1 "Process of a counselling session".

- Client and counsellor expectations, agenda and personal feelings will affect the helpfulness of a counselling intervention.

- The client's first impressions are important.

- Special relationship-building time is needed in the first session.

- Counsellors don't pretend to have magic wands!

- Initially clients often want to talk about "things out there", other people, and past events.

- When clients are ready, encourage them to move toward focussing on their own feelings and thoughts, as they are in the immediate present.

- When appropriate, move from active listening to problem identification and clarification, facilitating attitude change, exploring options, taking action, and termination.

FURTHER READING

Corey, G., *Theory and Practice of Counseling and Psychotherapy*, 5th edn. Pacific Grove: Brooks/Cole, 1996
Egan, G., *The Skilled Helper: a Problem Management Approach to Helping*. Pacific Grove: Brooks/Cole, 1994
Hackney, H., and Cormier, L. S., *The Professional Counselor: a Process Guide to Helping*. Boston: Allyn & Bacon, 1995

25 Using the "here and now" experience

I am sure you know people who are in the habit of continually complaining about their life situations, and who like to talk at length about the injustices of the world. They talk about things "out there", which are apparently out of their control and are the responsibility of others. Rather than saying, "What can I do to change this situation?", they use statements with words in them like "They should ...", and "They ought ...", and "It's disgraceful that they don't ...". Such people often go over the same ground again and again. It is almost inevitable that they will fail to move ahead, because no one can change a situation that is not within his own sphere of control.

Do you ever behave like the people I've just described? Do you ever grumble, moan and complain about "out there" things, things that are apparently other people's responsibility rather than yours? I do.

Taking personal responsibility

Notice how we started talking about other "people who complain" in this chapter and are now looking at ourselves. My guess is that you were more comfortable when the discussion was about others than you were when owning your own ability to grumble and complain. It's usually easier for us to distance ourselves from our own dysfunctional behaviour and to blame others for our problems. Unfortunately if I complain about things that other people are doing or not doing, or about external events or situations, then I am likely to get stuck in a rut of complaining, and to feel frustrated because I am powerless to bring about change. Conversely, if I focus on what I myself am doing, and on what is happening inside me, then I can, if I choose, take action to change what I am doing, or I can change my thinking so that I am better able to accept what is happening.

Focussing on the "here and now"

Similar logic to that just discussed applies to the present when compared with the past and future. I have no control over past events; they have already happened and I can't change them. Similarly, I have limited control over future events; they have not happened yet and I cannot be sure what the future will bring. Inappropriately focussing on the past and future is likely to lead me into unending philosophising, complaining and worrying, whereas focussing on the present allows me to make sensible choices for my own satisfaction.

The preceding discussion is not meant to imply that it is inappropriate and of no value for the client to talk about what other people are doing, to talk about situations beyond his control, or to talk about past or future events. It does imply that there is little point in the client doing these things unless he also focusses on what is happening inside him, at the present time, when he thinks about these situations or events. The focus in counselling needs to be on what is happening within the client at the moment in question, in the *here and now*, if the intervention is to be optimally therapeutic. The need to focus on the here and now is one of the central concepts of Gestalt Therapy (see O'Leary, 1992).

Imagine a situation where a client is really angry about the way his father treated him when he was a young child. He could talk about this past relationship time and again and make little progress. However, if the counsellor brings the focus onto what is happening within the client at the time when he talks about the past, then progress will be made. The counsellor might then tap into anger, resentment and bitterness that is present right now. As the counsellor listens to descriptions of past experiences, it is appropriate for him to ask the client how he feels as he talks about them. The counsellor might say: "Tell me how you feel emotionally *right now*, as you talk about those past events." By doing this, the counsellor brings the focus into the present, and brings current emotional feelings that are associated with the past traumas into the client's awareness. The client is then able to experience fully those feelings and deal with them appropriately. It is only by experiencing these emotional feelings fully that the client will be able either to reduce them or rid himself of them, or to discover ways of dealing with them constructively.

Helping the client to focus on the present

One way of bringing the client's focus into the present is to watch his non-verbal behaviour and to tell him what you notice. Alternatively, you might ask a question about what he is experiencing emotionally. For example, the client's eyes may become watery as he recounts some past event. Sensitively interrupting with the words, "I notice the tears starting to form in your eyes", or "Tell me what you are experiencing emotionally right now", is very likely to bring the client more fully in touch with his present internal experiences.

Give your client permission to take time, to stay with his feelings, and to experience them. In that way he is allowed to cry if he is hurting, is allowed to express his anger if he is angry, and is allowed to own whatever other emotion may be within him, and so to move forward into a more comfortable space.

Gradually the client will learn to allow himself to experience his feelings rather than to deny them. This learning, in the counselling situation, will hopefully extend into the client's daily life and enable him to be more responsive to his feelings generally. Thus he will be enabled to deal with his feelings as they arise rather than letting them build up to an intolerable level.

"Negative feelings"

A common cause of client distress is an inability to properly and appropriately express "negative" feelings towards others. For many people, for example, the expression of anger is repressed from childhood. Whenever small children get angry their parents tend to say: "Don't behave in that angry way. Don't throw a tantrum." As a result the child learns, incorrectly, that it isn't appropriate to express anger towards others even when an angry reaction is justified. Unfortunately blocked anger often leads to depression, anxiety or stress. What is worse, if we don't let other people know how we feel towards them, or how we feel about their behaviour, then we prevent ourselves from having fully functioning, open, and genuine relationships. Bringing issues out into the open and discussing them enables emotional feelings to be expressed, rather than suppressed with the pretence that they don't exist. The immediacy of the counselling relationship can be used to demonstrate how feelings can be shared in a constructive way which enhances rather than damages the relationship.

Modelling

In the immediacy of the counselling situation there is a real-life relationship between the client and counsellor. A skilled counsellor will naturally model adaptive and constructive ways of relating, and will also help the client to explore feelings that are generated by the counselling relationship. By learning to explore these feelings and bring them into the open, the client learns appropriate ways in which to deal with the feelings generated by his relationships with others, and hence is likely to improve the quality of his relationships generally.

Imagine that by carefully observing the non-verbal behaviour of a client, a counsellor suspects that the client is angry with him. The counsellor may have noticed, for example, an angry look flash across the client's face. However, because it is easy to misinterpret non-verbal behaviour it is important for the counsellor to check out whether in fact it was an angry look. The counsellor might say, "I've got the impression that you looked angry then", and as a result the client may become aware of his anger and may be willing to explore it more fully. In this way the client's feelings are brought into the open and the counsellor can respond appropriately and genuinely so that his relationship with the client is more fully authentic.

Feedback

If the counsellor is to be genuine in his relationship with the client, then he will need to share his own emotions about the relationship with the client at times when this is appropriate. For example, if a counsellor is annoyed by a client's behaviour towards him, it may be useful for him to say so, so that the client can learn how his behaviour is perceived. In this way the client can, if he chooses, change. Such change might significantly affect his life in a positive way, because it could be that the way in which he annoys the counsellor is similar to the way in which he annoys other people. Unfortunately, most people are too polite to give useful feedback to friends, even when their friends exhibit extremely destructive and maladaptive behaviours.

HOW TO GIVE FEEDBACK

In giving feedback, a counsellor might say to a client: "I feel irritated when you interrupt me." Thus, the client may discover that his tendency to interrupt is irritating, and he can, if he wishes, change that behaviour. Obviously, such feedback needs to be given in a way which is non-threatening and acceptable for the client.

When you give feedback, avoid starting your sentence with the word "you" but instead use "I". A typical feedback statement has the following structure: "I feel ... when ..." By starting with the words "I feel", the counsellor is owning and sharing his own feelings and this makes it easier for the client to hear what is being said. It also makes it less likely that the client will feel attacked and become defensive.

Notice again the example given: "I feel irritated when you interrupt me." The statement after the word "when" is a concrete statement of fact and not an interpretation. To say, for example, "I feel irritated when you interrupt me because you don't want to listen to what I'm saying" would involve an interpretation of the client's behaviour which might be incorrect. Be careful not to include interpretations in feedback statements. The following are some examples of appropriate and inappropriate feedback statements. See if you can decide which are appropriate and which are not, and then check your decision by reading the comments at the end of this chapter.

EXAMPLES OF APPROPRIATE AND INAPPROPRIATE FEEDBACK STATEMENTS

1. You keep coming late to appointments because you don't think it's worth coming for counselling.
2. I am puzzled when I notice that you continually come late for appointments.
3. You have put a barrier between us because you dislike me.
4. You are treating me like a father and I'm not your father.
5. I am uncomfortable because to me it feels as though you are relating to me like a son relates to his father.
6. Right now I have a shut-out feeling, as though there is a closed door between us.

From these examples and the comments provided at the end of the chapter you will have noticed that appropriate feedback involves the counsellor owning his own feelings in the relationship and sharing these together with a concrete statement of fact. Inappropriate feedback accuses, blames or interprets the client's behaviour and generally starts with the word "you".

Note that it is sometimes useful to teach clients how to use "I" statements themselves, instead of "you" statements. Teach them using the "I feel ... when ..." structure, as this is easy to understand. Stress the importance of making concrete factual statements and of not making interpretations.

Appropriately given feedback will leave a client feeling cared for and valued. Remember that a counsellor does not need to like a client's behaviour to be accepting of the client. It is not inconsistent to say, "I don't like it when you do that" and also to say, "I really care about you a great deal and accept you the way you are". I can accept someone the way he is without liking his behaviour. At a deeper level, I can love someone without liking all of his behaviour.

Transference and counter-transference

The immediacy of the counselling relationship often raises questions regarding what psychoanalysts call *transference* and *counter-transference*. Transference occurs when a client behaves toward a counsellor as though the counsellor were a significant person from the client's past, usually the client's mother or father. Naturally, it is quite possible for the counsellor to inadvertently fall into playing the role in which the client sees him. That is, if the client relates to the counsellor as though the counsellor were his father, the counsellor might start feeling and behaving like a father. Such behaviour, on the part of the counsellor, is called counter-transference. It is inevitable that transference and counter-transference will occur at times in the counselling relationship but, provided that this is recognised, brought into the open and discussed, it is not a problem. It would, however, be a problem if it were not brought out into the open, as it is not useful for the client to treat the counsellor as though he were someone from the past.

It may be that in some ways the counsellor is like the client's parent, but in other ways he is not, and it is important for the counsellor to make the distinction clear. This enables a genuine relationship between client and counsellor to be maintained instead of the relationship being inappropriately coloured by the client's past experiences with a significant other. When the counsellor realises that transference may be occurring, he might say: "I feel as though you are relating to me rather like a son relates to his father."

Where counter-transference is occurring, the relevant counsellor statement might be: "Right now I feel rather like a father to you." The counsellor needs to point out caringly that he is not the client's father or any other significant person from the client's past, and that he is himself—unique and different.

Sometimes a counsellor will not recognise when transference or counter-transference is occurring. It is here that supervision can play an important role in helping a counsellor to recognise what is happening and to explore appropriate ways of dealing with the issue.

Projection

Through the immediacy of the counselling relationship the client may learn something about his tendency to project characteristics of significant others from his past onto people in his life. Thus, he may be able to recognise when inappropriate projection onto others is damaging his relationships.

Whenever you notice what is happening in the relationship between you and your client, bring this into the open. If you sense that something unusual, different or important is happening in the relationship, then tell him what you are observing so that it can be fully discussed and explored. By exploring such material the client is able to learn more about himself, to realise what he does in relationships, and to become more in touch with his emotional experiences and thoughts. As a result, he may be able to move forward and to develop more fully as a person.

Resistance

New counsellors are troubled at times by a client's apparent lack of cooperation with the therapeutic process. This is called "resistance". A good example of resistance is provided by clients who come late for appointments or who miss appointments repeatedly. Of course, there may be good reasons for a client doing such things. It is well to be aware, though, that often the explanations given may be more in the nature of rationalisations or excuses than the real reason why the behaviour is occurring. For example, a client may be finding counselling very threatening and worrying, and may, for subconscious reasons, be postponing his involvement. It is important for the client to realise what is happening so that the real issue is addressed, and the client's fear is addressed. Once again, what the counsellor needs to do is to verbalise what he is noticing.

AN EXAMPLE OF RESISTANCE

As a trainer of counsellors, I have noticed that often trainee counsellors have come to supervision sessions and have said to me: "Unfortunately I haven't been able to make a videotape of a counselling session as promised." They have then given me a very convincing reason why it was quite impossible for them to make the videotape: "Oh, I couldn't find a blank cassette", or "The machine jammed when I put the cassette in", or "I put the cassette in and unfortunately I pushed the wrong button and it didn't record", or "Unfortunately somebody else borrowed the video before I did, as I had forgotten to book it". Of course, all of those "excuses" were valid. They were all genuine. The trainee counsellor was at no time lying but was being genuine and honest.

However, resistance was usually discovered when I said something like this: "I notice that for three weeks you have been unable to make a videotape, and have had perfectly good reasons. However, I am puzzled by this because you are a very capable person. I am wondering what happens emotionally inside you when you think about making a video." Saying this has enabled the trainee to explore more fully what was happening, and it has usually been discovered that it was threatening for the trainee to produce a video, and yes, if he had made a little more effort, it would have been possible to have produced the recording. It has never been necessary for me to say: "You must produce a video next week." Rather, just drawing attention to what I have observed has been sufficient to overcome the trainee's resistance.

DEALING WITH RESISTANCE

In the counselling process with clients, if you notice that a client is repeatedly late, or has missed several appointments in a row, draw the client's attention to what has happened. It may be necessary to say: "Yes, I have heard your reasons and I understand and believe them, but I am still left wondering whether at some other level something else is happening. I am puzzled that so often you should be late."

Resistance can, of course, take many forms. Sometimes resistance blocks a client from exploring a particularly painful area in his life, and as a counsellor you may feel frustrated by such avoidance. However, in my opinion, it is important to go with the resistance rather than try to burst through it. There are differences of opinion here, however, as some counsellors believe that actually smashing through the resistance is the way to go. I prefer the opposite approach, probably because I have an interest in Gestalt Therapy. I go with the resistance by drawing the client's attention to what is happening. I might say to a client: "I've noticed that you find it far too painful to discuss that particular area of your life so let's leave it alone altogether, let's just put it away, and not deal with it." The client is then able to experience his avoidance fully and usually something important will emerge spontaneously. If it does not, then I would ask the client what he was currently experiencing emotionally. As a result the client would be brought in touch with what it feels like to avoid exploring a painful area of his life and consequently might decide how to deal with his avoidance. Alternatively he might say: "I'm not prepared to explore that really painful area of my life. To do so would be like opening up Pandora's box. It's far too scary for me." He has a right to make that choice and to leave Pandora's box closed. If that is what he chooses I respect his wishes.

Uses of the "here and now" experience

In this chapter we have dealt with the ways in which the immediacy of the counselling relationship can be used to:

1. help the client to focus on his own behaviour, inner feelings and thoughts, in the present, rather than focussing on past behaviours, or on the behaviour of others over which he has no control;
2. help the client to learn to own and deal with his emotional feelings as they arise; this includes owning and dealing with so-called "negative" feelings towards others;
3. give the client constructive feedback, in an acceptable way, with regard to inappropriate behaviours that cause annoyance to the counsellor and may annoy others;
4. help the client to recognise and deal with the human tendency to project the characteristics of significant persons from his past onto others;
5. help the client to deal with his own resistance.

An effective counsellor will verbalise his observations of what is occurring in the immediacy of the counselling relationship so that client growth is promoted. Hopefully, what is learnt from the counselling experience will be carried into the client's everyday life.

Comments on examples of appropriate and inappropriate feedback statements

1. INAPPROPRIATE FEEDBACK The statement is threatening as it starts with the word "you". The words "because you don't think it's worth coming for counselling" are an unverified interpretation of the client's behaviour.

2. APPROPRIATE FEEDBACK The counsellor starts with an "I" statement which describes how he feels: "I am puzzled." He then gives a concrete statement of what he has observed: "You continually come late for appointments." The counsellor does not attempt to interpret the client's behaviour, but merely states what he observes.

3. INAPPROPRIATE FEEDBACK The statement is inappropriate because it consists of a "you" statement which could make the client feel attacked. Moreover, the counsellor is interpreting the client's behaviour. His statement, "You dislike me", is guesswork and could well be wrong.

4. INAPPROPRIATE FEEDBACK An inappropriate statement starting with "you" which could be received by the client as a put-down.

5. APPROPRIATE FEEDBACK This statement appropriately starts with the counsellor saying how he feels: "I am uncomfortable." Instead of accusing his client by using a "you" statement, the counsellor goes on to explain how the relationship feels for him. Compare this statement with example 4. It is very different.

6. APPROPRIATE FEEDBACK Notice how in this statement the counsellor describes how he feels rather than blaming the client for putting up a barrier. Compare this statement with example 3.

LEARNING SUMMARY

- Talking about the past and future, and about other people, is not constructive unless the client also focusses on his "here and now" experiences.

- Staying in the "here and now", and focussing on current experiences, emotional feelings, and thoughts is therapeutically useful.

- The immediacy of the counselling relationship can be a useful learning experience for the client.

- A counsellor can model adaptive behaviour and relationship skills and give feedback to the client.

- Appropriate feedback can start with "I feel ...", followed by a concrete non-interpretive statement.

- "Transference" is when the client treats the counsellor as though he were a parent (or significant other).

- "Counter-transference" is when the counsellor responds to the client's transference as though he were a parent (or significant other).

- Transference and counter-transference usually need to be brought into the open when they occur.

- "Resistance" may involve a client's apparent lack of cooperation with the therapeutic process or direct avoidance of painful issues.

- A good way to deal with resistance is to go with it and to raise the client's awareness of it.

FURTHER READING

Clarkson, P., *Gestalt Counselling in Action*. London: Sage, 1989

Kennedy, E. and Charles, S. C., *On Becoming a Counsellor*. New York: Continuum, 1990

O'Leary, E., *Gestalt Therapy, Theory, Practice and Research*. London: Chapman & Hall, 1992

26 Keeping records of counselling sessions

Many counsellors find the administrative and clerical duties associated with counselling a chore. However, it pays to keep detailed and up-to-date records on each counselling session. Ideally, report writing should be done immediately after the counselling session, while all the relevant information is fresh in the counsellor's mind, and before other inputs have had time to intrude.

In today's society we can either type records directly into a computer using appropriately formatted software, or keep handwritten records on printed forms or cards. Where records are computerised adequate security measures are required to protect client confidentiality. Similarly, handwritten records need to be kept in secure locations (see Chapter 7).

Identifying the client

Client records need to be clearly identified so that there can be no confusion, because in large agencies it is not unusual to find two clients with the same names. Identifiers might include:

1. client's family name (surname)
2. other names
3. date of birth (if known)
4. address
5. contact phone numbers

Where handwritten records are kept, it can be an advantage to label each page of the client record with the client's full name so that the possibility of pages being misplaced in the wrong file is reduced.

ADDITIONAL DEMOGRAPHIC INFORMATION ABOUT THE CLIENT
Commonly, when the information is available, records may include any of the following:

1. marital status
2. name of partner or spouse
3. names and ages of children
4. referral source

Notes about each counselling session

The notes for each counselling session may include:

1. date of the session;

2. factual information given by the client;
3. details of the client's problems, issues or dilemmas;
4. notes on the process that occurred during the session;
5. notes on the outcome of the counselling session;
6. notes on interventions used by the counsellor;
7. notes on any goals identified;
8. notes on any contract between client and counsellor;
9. notes on matters to be considered at subsequent sessions;
10. notes on the counsellor's own feelings relating to the client and the counselling process;
11. the counsellor's initials or signature.

The content of the notes will now be described in more detail under the headings listed above. However, although these headings are discussed individually, in practice, notes often flow together as the headings overlap. Handwritten notes should preferably be legible so that if a client transfers to another counsellor for some reason, notes can be easily read with the client's permission.

1. DATE OF SESSION
This heading is self-explanatory. When reviewing a client's progress over time, it's very useful to know the dates of counselling sessions.

2. FACTUAL INFORMATION GIVEN BY THE CLIENT
During a counselling session the client is likely to divulge factual information which may be useful in subsequent sessions. Sometimes small facts which may appear to be insignificant provide the key to unlock a closed door in the client's world, or could, if remembered, provide the counsellor with a clearer picture of the client's background. An example of information that might be included in a counsellor's notes could be:

> *"The client has been married for 13 years and during that time left her husband twice, once two years ago for a period of two weeks, and secondly six months ago for a longer unspecified period. She has considerable financial resources, lacks a social support system, had an affair some years ago and has kept this a secret from her husband."*

3. DETAILS OF THE CLIENT'S PROBLEMS, ISSUES OR DILEMMAS
Keep the record brief, so that it can be read quickly when required. An example of this part of the record would be:

> *"Mary suspects that her husband may be sexually involved with another woman, is afraid to ask her husband whether this is so, and is confused about her attitudes to him. She can't decide whether to pluck up courage and confront him, to leave him now, or to continue in an unsatisfactory relationship with him."*

4. NOTES ON THE PROCESS THAT OCCURRED DURING THE SESSION
The process is independent of the facts presented and of the client's issues, and is concerned with what occurred during the counselling session, particularly in the client/counsellor interaction. For example:

"The client initially had difficulty talking freely, but as the counselling relationship developed she was able to explore her confusion and to look at her options. Although she was unable to decide which option to pursue, she seemed pleased by her ability to see her situation more clearly."

5. NOTES ON THE OUTCOME OF THE COUNSELLING SESSION
The outcome could be that a decision was made, or that the client remained stuck, or that a dilemma was identified. Alternatively the outcome might be described in terms of the client's feelings at the end of the session. Examples of notes under this heading are:

"'She decided to confront her husband'; 'She left feeling sad and determined'; 'She said that she could now see things clearly'"

6. NOTES REGARDING INTERVENTIONS USED BY THE COUNSELLOR
Notes under this section are intended to remind the counsellor of particular interventions used. For example, the notes might say:

"'Taught relaxation'; 'Coached client in the use of assertive statements'; 'Discussed the anger control chart'"

7. NOTES REGARDING ANY GOALS IDENTIFIED
These may be goals for the client to achieve in the world outside, or for her to achieve in counselling, for example:

"'The client wants to learn to be more assertive'; 'She wants to use the counselling process to sort out her confusion and make a decision regarding her marriage'; 'She wants to experiment by taking risks'"

8. NOTES REGARDING ANY CONTRACT BETWEEN CLIENT AND COUNSELLOR
It is important to remember any agreements that are made with clients. These may be with regard to future counselling sessions, for example:

"'The client contracted to come for counselling at fortnightly intervals for three sessions and then review progress'; 'It was agreed that counselling sessions would be used to explore the client's relationships with people of the opposite sex'; 'I have contracted to teach the client relaxation during the next session'"

9. NOTES REGARDING MATTERS TO BE CONSIDERED AT SUBSEQUENT SESSIONS
Often during the last few minutes of a counselling session a client will bring up an important matter that is causing her pain and is difficult to talk about. If this

is noted on the card, then the counsellor can remind the client at the start of the next session, thus enabling the client to deal with the issue in question, if she wishes. Sometimes, as a counsellor, you will realise at the end of a session that aspects of the client's situation need further exploration. Make a note on the card as a reminder.

10. NOTES REGARDING THE COUNSELLOR'S OWN FEELINGS RELATING TO THE CLIENT AND THE COUNSELLING PROCESS

These are required to help the counsellor to avoid letting her feelings inappropriately interfere with the counselling process in future sessions. Such notes can be invaluable in the counsellor's own supervision and may be useful in helping her to improve her understanding of the counselling process. An example of such notes is:

> **"*I felt angry when the client continually blamed others and failed to accept responsibility for her own actions.*"**

11. THE COUNSELLOR'S INITIALS OR SIGNATURE

By initialling or signing case notes a counsellor takes responsibility for what is written in them. In many agencies counsellors work together with other counselling team members. In such agencies, over a period of time, more than one counsellor may see a particular client. Also, a client may come back to an agency for further counselling after a particular counsellor has left. In such situations it can be helpful to the client if the client's counselling history is available, subject to the normal constraints of confidentiality.

As stated previously, writing records of counselling sessions can be a chore. However, a counsellor who does this diligently will quickly become aware of the advantages. The effectiveness of future counselling sessions is likely to be improved if the counsellor reads the record card before meeting the client each time. By doing this the counsellor is able to "tune in" to the client right from the start of the interview and will not waste time on unnecessary repetition.

Clearly, records need to be detailed, accurate, and legible, if they are to be maximally useful. However, when writing records, be aware of the confidentiality issue (see Chapter 7) and of the possibility that the legal system may demand that such records be made available to a court. Also, bear in mind when writing cards that clients may later ask to read them. Clearly, clients have the right to read their own cards if they wish to do so.

LEARNING SUMMARY

- Ideally report writing is done immediately after a counselling session.
- Records need to include:
  - the date;

- factual information and details of the client's problems;
- notes on the process and outcome of the session;
- notes regarding interventions used, goals set, contracts made, and matters to be considered in the future; and
- notes regarding the counsellor's own feelings.

Part IV

Telephone counselling and crisis intervention

27 Telephone counselling

Let me ask you a question: "Do you think that it would be harder to be a telephone counsellor or a face-to-face counsellor?"

I feel certain that you will have to think hard about this question because the two types of counselling are in some ways similar but in other ways very different. Can you guess what the major differences are?

The nature of the contact between the counsellor and client is obviously quite different in telephone counselling when compared with face-to-face counselling.

Advantages of having visual contact

A telephone counsellor has much less information about the client than a face-to-face counsellor. The telephone counsellor can't see the caller and is consequently denied a wealth of information.

By contrast a face-to-face counsellor can directly observe the client. From this visual contact she may be able to make tentative judgments about the client's emotional state, coping ability, age, social status, cultural background and temperament. She is also able more easily to gauge the client's willingness to share and her comfort with the counselling relationship. From visual observation the face-to-face counsellor has the benefit of many subtle clues which are not available to the telephone counsellor. Most importantly, the counsellor is able to give and to receive non-verbal messages. This is much more difficult to do by phone. Have you ever tried to smile down a telephone line? It's not the easiest thing to do, is it? Have you ever wondered whether the person talking to you by phone was crying or not? In the face-to-face situation those telltale tears would leave you in no doubt.

Time to build a relationship

Another significant difference between the two types of counselling concerns the counsellor's ability to build a relationship with the client. The face-to-face counsellor has more time in which to build a relationship by using both verbal and non-verbal cues. Rarely does a client walk out of a counselling session during the first minute or two. But for the telephone counsellor the situation is quite different. If some level of trust isn't established early on in the call, the caller might well hang up, thereby terminating the counselling process!

In many ways then, telephone counselling is more difficult than face-to-face counselling. The telephone counsellor, "TC" for short, has to have good "fishing" skills. She needs to be able to engage her caller through a gradual process which is active but non-threatening, so that the caller feels safe enough in the relationship to begin and to continue talking.

Being prepared for a call

To be effective, a telephone counsellor needs to be ready to make the most of the first few moments of a call to engage the caller. The first minute or two of the call are often critical. A distressed caller in a highly emotional state will easily be frightened away, and is likely to hang up unless some immediate warmth and responsiveness comes through from the counsellor.

INFLUENCE OF THE COUNSELLOR'S OWN PROBLEMS

We counsellors are people with our own needs. If we are preoccupied by our own emotional problems and if our own unfinished business with other people is needing attention, then we are very unlikely to be ready to engage with a caller over the phone when the phone rings. It takes time to put aside our own stuff, and unless we have done that it will intrude.

Sometimes with face-to-face clients who are coming to a second or subsequent counselling session it's possible for a counsellor to let go of her own preoccupations by owning them openly and saying to the client something like: "I have just had a difficult few minutes and haven't yet distanced myself from that experience. I'm letting you know this so that I can put that experience to one side and give you my full attention without being distracted by intruding thoughts."

Sharing information like this can be useful in two ways. Firstly, it addresses the process occurring for the counsellor and will probably enable the counsellor to focus on the client without the problem of intruding thoughts. Secondly, there is good learning for the client as the counsellor models an appropriate way of displacing, or of putting to one side, troubling thoughts. Unfortunately this technique can't be used in telephone counselling unless the caller is well known to the counsellor. The telephone counsellor–client relationship is usually too fragile for such disclosure at the start of a call.

Preparing yourself for a call

As explained above, the telephone counsellor needs to be ready right from the start of the call to pay full attention to the caller and to the counselling process. The TC therefore needs to prepare herself adequately before the phone rings. If she is troubled by worrying or disturbing thoughts then she would be sensible to deal with these in some appropriate way. We are all different and the way in which I prepare myself may not work for other people. However, there are four common ways of preparing for a telephone counselling session. They are:

1. Talk through your own problems with your supervisor.
2. Own your intruding thoughts by telling a colleague that they exist.
3. Use relaxation, meditation or prayer, depending on your spiritual orientation.
4. Engage in physical exercise.

TALKING THROUGH YOUR OWN PROBLEMS WITH A SUPERVISOR
Owning the problems which are troubling you and talking them through with your supervisor is certainly the best approach. By doing this the problems are not just put to one side but are worked through. This is particularly useful, because if you just put your own problems to one side without working them through, then they are sure to re-emerge if the client's problems are in some way similar. Working through them first is clearly the ideal.

SHARING YOUR PROBLEMS WITH A COLLEAGUE
Unfortunately in practice, it is not always possible to talk through one's own problems prior to a telephone counselling session. It may, however, be possible to use a similar method to that described above for face-to-face coun- sellors, but instead of telling the client that you need to put aside some troubling thoughts you could tell a colleague. It might be sufficient to say to another TC: "I realise that I have brought with me some troubling thoughts about my family. I don't want to unburden them on to you because you may have needs of your own at this time, but I will talk them through with my supervisor later. Telling you that these thoughts exist helps me to put them to one side for the time being, so that I feel better prepared to answer the phone."

USE OF RELAXATION, MEDITATION OR PRAYER

The use of relaxation, meditation or prayer can be effective in helping counsellors to feel more prepared for a telephone counselling session. We are all unique individuals and so what suits one person will not be appropriate for another. While some counsellors find the use of structured relaxation exercises helpful, others have learnt techniques for meditating. People who have religious beliefs often find it useful to pray to ask for help in preparing them to receive calls.

USE OF EXERCISE

Engaging in physical exercise before a telephone counselling session can be helpful. People who enjoy exercising often find that they are able to feel good and to let go of troubling thoughts in this way. The alternatives are many and include jogging, playing golf, squash or tennis, and swimming.

The caller's perspective

Having dealt with the need for appropriate preparation by the counsellor, it is time to consider the caller's position. Callers are often anxious and uncertain about what to expect. The act of picking up a phone and dialling a stranger can be worrying for some people. Some callers, being anxious, may have made a few false starts before finally dialling your number. Consequently the first few words and the way in which you, the telephone counsellor, speak to them are crucial.

The initial contact

Most human beings tend to approach strangers with caution. We are wary and tentative in establishing relationships. Consequently if a TC were to pick up the phone at its first ring and to talk quickly, the caller may feel threatened and be frightened away. We human beings approach each other warily and in our natural caution we draw back when someone tries to meet us at a faster pace than is comfortable for ourselves. I wonder if you have ever felt taken aback when you have called someone and they have answered the phone before you have heard it ring?

We need to be careful to meet the caller at an appropriate pace, so remember to be calm and relaxed so that the process of joining occurs naturally. After two or three rings, pick up the phone and answer caringly in a way that is non-threatening. At Lifeline Centres, TCs often start by saying: "Hello, this is Lifeline. Can I help you?" The words are important and so is the tone and pace. The voice quality needs to be calming and inviting without being gushy.

RESPONDING TO "PRANK" CALLERS

Some callers, particularly children, may initially behave in a way which suggests that the call is a prank call (see later in this chapter regarding nuisance calls). However, we need to be careful not to respond inappropriately to such callers,

---

because their behaviour may be their way of attempting to access the counselling service and to test the counsellor's acceptance of them. It is important that all callers are treated with respect. By doing this it is sometimes possible to "turnaround" calls which initially appear to be pranks.

Continuing with the call

After the initial contact, the "fishing" gets seriously under way. Of course the caller–counsellor relationship is not one of catching someone on a hook, but there is a real similarity with fishing. Inappropriate responses or inappropriate timing will encourage the caller to hang up rather than to continue talking. The counsellor needs to be tentative, and to recognise and make allowance for the caller's hesitancy. She needs to explore cautiously what is safe for the caller and what is not. She has to listen intently and to use all her skills and judgment in an effort to build a comfortable non-threatening relationship so that the caller is empowered to talk freely. The counsellor has to maintain such a level of empathic understanding and warmth that the caller will become more at ease rather than be scared away. With some callers this is no problem, but with others, as explained before, the simple act of picking up the phone has in itself been a difficult step. Too much talking by the counsellor is sure to push the caller away, as is too much silence. Yes, telephone counselling is difficult! It involves knowing when to be verbally active, and when to draw back and to listen in silence. Judging the needs of the caller and responding empathically without intruding are what is required. A counsellor who is unable to do this is likely to lose calls.

Hang-ups

One of the advantages to the client of seeking telephone counselling rather than face-to-face counselling is that a caller can easily opt out at any time without embarrassment. Inevitably some callers who are not used to calling telephone counsellors are likely to hang up prematurely in their first attempts to engage in such a counselling process. Don't despair when a caller hangs up, because it is inevitable that this will happen from time to time. Even so, every experienced TC knows how demoralising it can be to lose a call. When it does happen remind yourself that the caller may have achieved a minor goal by learning that she can cope with picking up the phone, dialling the number and starting to talk. Having made what for her may have been a big step, she may then be able to phone back later to talk for longer.

Staying focussed

Telephone counselling often requires a high level of concentration with intense listening. Frequently distressed callers will talk quietly and consequently be difficult to hear. For new counsellors, there may seem to be too many things to attend to at the same time. The counsellor needs to listen to the spoken words, identify the emotions underlying them, understand and/or picture the caller's situation, attend to the process of the call, and make suitable responses. Telephone counselling certainly is very demanding of the counsellor but it can also be very satisfying for counsellors who sensibly and properly attend to their own personal needs (see Chapter 34).

Skills needed

The micro-skills described in Part II are all needed in telephone counselling just as they are in face-to-face counselling. On the macro scale, the process of a telephone counselling call will be very similar to the process of a face-to-face counselling session as described in Chapter 24. However, there are some differences at both the micro and macro level. Let us look at each of these in turn.

Use of micro-skills

In telephone counselling, all the micro-skills described in Part II are required. However, in using these skills special attention is required to compensate for the lack of visual and other non-verbal information. The caller can't see your face, your facial expression or your body posture. In our day-to-day communication, the words we say are moderated, amplified or changed in other ways, as a consequence of the non-verbal behaviour that accompanies the words. I may, for example, add emphasis to what I am saying by leaning forward as I say it. A caring expression may reassure my listener that what I am saying isn't meant to be hurtful to them although it may be confronting.

Telephone counsellors need to compensate for the lack of non-verbal cues by adding tone and expression to their voices over and above what would ordinarily be required in face-to-face contact. Additionally, whereas a face-to-face counsellor can listen in silence at times, it is important that in telephone counselling the counsellor should regularly give verbal cues that listening is still occurring. Obviously this shouldn't be overdone, but it is reassuring for a caller to hear minimal responses such as "ah-ha", "yes", "mm", etc., coming in response to her own statements. At times during personal telephone calls to friends or family, I have had to ask: "Are you still there?", because the other person has been listening silently. Have you ever had the same experience? Most people find it disconcerting when they get little or no response while talking to someone on the phone. Certainly, in the counselling situation the importance of the caller knowing that the counsellor is still there, and listening intently, can't be overemphasised.

Similarly, the TC can't see the caller and will sensibly need to check out with the caller information that would, in a face-to-face session, be obvious from the appearance of the client. Hence in a prolonged silence it may be appropriate to ask: "What is happening for you right now?" If you suspect that your caller is crying but are unsure, it may be worth waiting for a while and then saying in a quiet, caring tone of voice: "You sounded very sad as you spoke and I am wondering whether you are starting to cry."

Finishing a call

Finishing a call is difficult for many telephone counsellors. Generally, I believe that terminating telephone calls requires a higher level of skill and determination than terminating face-to-face sessions. See Chapter 23 with regard to the termination of telephone counselling calls.

A macro view: The overall process

The process of a telephone counselling call can often be described by the flow chart shown in Figure 24.1 in Chapter 24. Clearly each call is different from any other call, but it is important to recognise, and if necessary influence, the stages through which the call progresses. For example, a counsellor needs to recognise when it is sensible to move from the "active listening" stage into "problem identification and clarification", and when to explore options. To do these things a counsellor needs to trust her gut feelings, to be sensitive to the caller, and to be able to recognise whether the overall process of the call is meeting the caller's needs. It is here that experience and supervision are useful.

INFLUENCING THE PROCESS OF A CALL

While you are attending to the caller, take time to recognise where the call is heading and, if appropriate, make decisions with regard to the process. For example, it is not going to help a chronically depressed caller if you continue "active listening" for too long, particularly if you are reflecting feelings and negative thoughts. In fact you may well succeed in helping the caller further down into a trough of despair! Recognise the time to move on to "facilitating attitude change" or "exploring options" (see Figure 24.1).

It is important, as described in the earlier part of this book, to follow the direction the caller chooses and generally to meet the caller's agenda in preference to your own. However, these guidelines are not inflexible rules, and need to be seen in the context of the whole call, the caller's situation, the policies of the counselling agency, and also in the context of the counsellor's own goals for the counselling process.

In my view a caller is more likely to feel helped if some progress is made in the call towards an increased awareness such that there is a likelihood of adaptive change occurring for the caller. To achieve this, the TC may, at times, have to influence the direction and process of the call. Don't forget, however, that change usually occurs through increased awareness rather than through the counsellor's pushing for change (see Chapter 22 on facilitating action).

If a caller is repeatedly going through the same material, then it is appropriate to raise the caller's awareness of that process by directly confronting it. It will often be useful to tell the caller what you see happening in the call. For example, a counsellor might say to a chronically depressed client: "I notice that you seem to be sinking deeper into depression." Once the process has been identified, then the TC has the opportunity to move the call into a new stage. This might mean moving into the "problem identification and clarification" stage by asking: "Was there ever a time when you weren't so depressed?", followed up by: "What was different then?" or "So there was a time when you knew how to beat your depression" and "Is there anything that you could do now that would be similar to what you did before when you had some control over your depression?" I have used the example of depression because most telephone counselling centres receive a significant number of calls from chronically depressed people. Such people often need to have medical or psychiatric help and it is important to raise this as an option if it is not occurring (for further information on counselling depressed clients see Chapter 30).

You may be surprised that I am implying that telephone counsellors may need to pay more attention to control of the process of the counselling session than face-to-face counsellors. I think that this is true because telephone callers often do not feel constrained by time and when they become comfortable with a counsellor some callers are content to chat rather than focus their thoughts in order to use the interaction constructively. Also, telephone counsellors frequently only have a single interaction with a particular caller so there may be no possibility of ongoing work, as occurs in face-to-face counselling.

ADDRESSING EACH CALLER'S PERSONAL NEEDS

If we refer back to Figure 24.1 (the process of a counselling session), it is clear that for some callers it may be sufficient to move directly from the active listening stage to termination. For other callers, the other stages listed on the right-hand side of the chart are essential if the caller is to be helped. As each call progresses, a picture of the caller and her situation will emerge and you will need to make decisions about how best to help this caller. You may decide that it is sufficient for the call to stay mostly in the "active listening" stage with consequent cathartic release for the caller. However, for other calls it may be desirable for you to gently encourage the caller to move forward into subsequent stages that will enable fuller clarification of the problem, or may facilitate attitude change or the exploration of options.

To be a fully effective and responsible telephone counsellor you need to be able to assess what is most appropriate for each caller. Unlike face-to-face counselling, you may not get another opportunity to work with this caller so you will need to make the most of your opportunity. However, do not think that you have to achieve life-changing results in one call. If the caller finds it useful talking to you then she is likely to use a telephone counselling service again. Each call can be seen as one step in a flight of stairs up which the caller is moving one step at a time.

Solving the caller's problem

A FAIRY STORY

Once upon a time in the land of Great Tragedy and Despair there lived a wonderful person who became known as Super-TC. Super-TC was better than most TCs because his calls only lasted a few minutes. He was always able to give good advice and his callers usually politely thanked him for that. His approach was to identify the caller's problem swiftly and then to suggest a

---

solution. Sometimes, when Super-TC couldn't think of a solution himself, although that wasn't very often, he would refer the caller to someone else who might have a solution. Occasionally callers would make it clear that they wanted a longer counselling interaction. In these instances, Super-TC would say to the caller: "It's clear to me that you have a quite serious psychological condition, you need to make an appointment immediately to see either a face-to-face counsellor, or better still, a psychiatrist."

At times I think that we all behave like Super-TC. It is always tempting to provide a quick solution rather than to suffer the emotional pain of listening to someone else who is suffering. Of course there are times when it is appropriate and responsible to refer a caller to others. Generally however, before doing that, it is preferable to allow the caller to deal with her emotional issues in the here-and-now. Often, when I have done this, a referral has not been necessary.

Some TCs, who have trained specifically for working on the phone, believe that face-to-face counsellors are necessarily more competent than they are, with the consequence that they will refer to face-to-face counselling before helping the caller fully by using the normal counselling skills and processes. Unfortunately, we professional face-to-face counsellors, social workers, psychologists and psychiatrists vary in our competence. Yes, it is appropriate to refer on when you are out of your depth, and it is unethical and irresponsible not to do so. However, give your callers the opportunity to explore their pain fully with you on the phone if that is what they would like to do, in addition to giving them an onward referral if necessary. If you are unsure about what you are doing, then talk to your supervisor.

Unfortunately Super-TC disempowers his callers. By finding solutions for them they have their worst fears confirmed. The implied message they get is: "You are not capable of running your own life and making your own decisions. You need someone else to tell you what to do." There are times in our lives when we do need someone to tell us what to do, but usually human beings of normal intelligence prefer to make their own decisions, and can feel good about themselves if they are empowered through the counselling process to do so. If counselling has been really effective, an empowered client might think: "Counselling wasn't much help, the counsellor didn't tell me what to do, instead I made my own decision. I am an OK person and can run my own life."

Making notes during the call

It is not easy to give the caller your full attention and at the same time to pay attention to the process of the call so that you can facilitate appropriate changes in that process if necessary. A high degree of concentration is required and it is easy to become distracted and to forget important information. To avoid losing information, and to help me to more fully understand the caller's situation and thus to see the caller's picture more clearly, I find that it can be useful if I make notes during a call. I sometimes add sketches as the call proceeds and find that this helps me to focus on the caller more intently. However, I realise that this practice may not useful for you. It probably operates well for me because I tend to be fairly visual in my thinking.

If a caller is talking about family problems then I may draw the family tree in the form of a genogram. Figure 27.1 is a simple example of a genogram. You may find genograms useful too in helping you to more fully understand the caller's background.

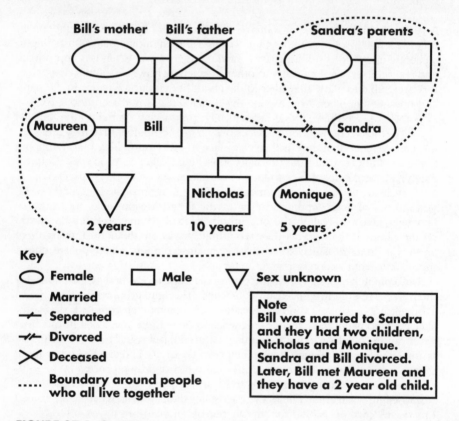

FIGURE 27.1 Genogram

Using your imagination

As a telephone counsellor you can't see your caller but you can, if you choose, imagine her. While she is talking, you can construct a visual picture and imagine yourself in the caller's position in her situation. If you do this you may be able to experience more fully what it is like to be the caller and consequently be able to respond with non-judgmental empathy.

Whenever I am starting to feel judgmental, I try to imagine myself as the client in the client's situation.

Advantages of telephone counselling

I have made the point previously that in my opinion telephone counselling is harder to do well than face-to-face counselling. It is, however, an extremely valuable form of counselling. Some people who would never come to a face-to-face counselling interview will use the phone. From the caller's perspective, telephone counselling offers the following advantages:

- It is safer for the caller because she can if she wishes protect her anonymity. This may help her to feel less concerned about the consequences of sharing private thoughts and emotions with a stranger.
- The caller knows that if she is feeling too threatened, then she can hang up. This is far easier than walking out of a counselling room.
- Telephone counselling is easily and immediately accessible (unless the line is engaged) with no waiting list. The caller just has to pick up a phone and dial.
- It is of low cost to the caller.

Setting boundaries

Because telephone counselling provides a safe environment for the client to share her deepest secrets, it also has some hazards. Some people who phone in are alone and have no close friends who can listen to them. Such people can be very vulnerable and may wish they had an understanding friend. Good counsellors are accepting, warm, empathic and non-judgmental with their clients. Lonely callers may build a very skewed picture of the person they are sharing with, perceiving the counsellor very positively. It is essential, therefore, to set clear boundaries so that the caller understands that the relationship is a phone relationship and cannot be extended beyond that. To do otherwise is to set up an expectation in the caller that, maybe, there could be the beginnings of a personal relationship. Remember that lonely, unhappy people are very needy and vulnerable. It is totally unethical to take advantage of them. Further, it is unrealistic to think that you could help them if you were to allow the relationship to change from a counselling relationship into a friendship. To do so would damage their ability to trust the counselling process as a safe one which they could use in the future.

Debriefing

Debriefing is a process used to enable counsellors to let go of the emotions which they inevitably experience as a consequence of listening to a distressed client.

If a counsellor said to you, "I'm an experienced telephone counsellor, I don't need to debrief because client calls don't trouble me", would you believe them?

All counsellors, however experienced, need to debrief, especially after particularly stressful counselling sessions. I work with experienced professional counsellors and we all make it a regular practice to debrief after difficult or emotional counselling sessions. If we were not to do so, the service we provide for our clients would inevitably become less effective and we would soon burn out.

Telephone counsellors are particularly vulnerable to the emotional after-effects of their counselling work. When people are in acute crisis, often the first thing they do is to reach for the telephone. Consequently telephone counsellors are frequently dealing with callers who are in extreme distress and/or panic. Sometimes telephone counselling will lead to crisis intervention (see Chapter 28).

Because of the inevitable crisis content of telephone counselling, TCs will often feel drained at the end of a shift on the phone. Callers' emotional pain inevitably triggers off personal emotional stress for counsellors. Telephone counsellors therefore need to be responsible by CARING FOR THEMSELVES. After a particularly stressful call, take a break before accepting another call, and if at all possible talk to your supervisor or another counsellor about the feelings you are experiencing. At the end of each counselling shift, debrief once again by talking to your supervisor or another counsellor for a few minutes. Debriefing need not be a long process but it is an important one.

Problem callers

No discussion of telephone counselling is complete unless it gives some consideration to what I will describe as "problem callers". These are callers who create special problems for telephone counsellors. They may have goals that are incompatible with those of the counselling service and consequently may want to use the service inappropriately. Some of them may want to satisfy particular needs which are not being met elsewhere. However, problem callers are people with genuine needs, so telephone counsellors need to be able to deal with calls from them in a constructive way which fully addresses their counselling needs.

Most problem callers fall into one of the following categories:

- nuisance callers
- regular callers
- chronically depressed callers
- sex callers

NUISANCE CALLERS
Inevitably there will be people who will call in to telephone counselling services with the aim of causing annoyance, or maybe of getting a laugh at the telephone counsellor's expense. Some of these will repeatedly ring up and then hang up, others will be openly abusive, and there will be those callers who make hoax calls. Sometimes angry or abusive callers will repeatedly knock the phone or slam it down. Such calls will naturally tend to make the counsellors receiving them feel frustrated and annoyed. Please remember that it is *normal* to be frustrated, annoyed, and possibly angered by such behaviour. Counsellors are human beings and we have our own legitimate emotions. Somehow though, we need to deal

with our frustration, annoyance and anger, so that we feel OK and are ready and able to deal appropriately with these calls and with subsequent calls.

The best way of dealing with emotions resulting from nuisance calls is to talk with someone about them. If this is not possible then you may be able to alter the messages you are giving yourself into more constructive ones. Can you think of the nuisance caller not just as an annoyance, but also as someone whose needs are not being fulfilled in a constructive way?

The reality is that any person who finds it necessary to harass a telephone counselling service most probably has an unsatisfactory or unfulfilled life. Could you be bothered to phone in to a counselling service just to be a nuisance? I couldn't.

Here are some suggestions as to why some people make nuisance calls:

- They may be angry and unable to express their anger in a constructive and adaptive way.
- They may be frustrated with life and not know how to deal with their frustration except by annoying others.
- They may be bored and lonely.
- They may be young people who want to bolster low self-esteem by "playing a joke" on a counsellor to impress friends.
- They may be young people "taking risks" or acting impulsively in a reasonably normal developmental way.
- They may be young people who are testing the service before deciding whether or not to talk about more serious issues.

All of these people have problems in their lives and are searching for something they cannot find. If you are able to think of nuisance callers as people dissatisfied with their lives and who are hurting inside, then you may be able to develop constructive strategies for dealing with them. I don't believe that there can be one correct response to such callers because they are all different. What I try to do is to decide what, if anything, can be achieved when dealing with such callers. I ask myself whether any of the following goals are realistic:

- To let the caller know that he is a valued individual.
- To encourage the caller to talk about his real issues.
- To let the caller know why it is that I believe that what he is doing is destructive.
- To let the caller know how I feel.
- To decrease the likelihood that the caller will repeat his nuisance-calling behaviour.
- To deal with the underlying issues that result in this unwanted behaviour.

Can you think of other suitable goals? If you are able to remember your goals then you may be able to deal with such callers constructively and effectively.

At all times, remember that it is not a part of your role as a telephone counsellor to be abused. You have a right to tell any abusive caller that you will not listen to abuse and to hang up if that is what you consider to be most appropriate. Of course, there are times when counsellors deliberately choose to listen to the abuse of an angry caller in order to allow such a caller to vent his anger and then to move on to dealing with constructive issues.

As a counsellor, although the choice about whether to hang up or not will be influenced by the policies of the agency in which you are working, it is ultimately your choice, and you have a right to hang up if that is what you choose to do.

REGULAR CALLERS

All telephone counselling agencies have problems with those callers who repeatedly call in over a long period of time. Some of these callers have genuine needs which can be appropriately met by counselling. However, many regular callers re-run the same story over and over again, like a cracked record. Others will use a variety of different names and stories, often with an underlying theme to their stories.

Regular callers can cause a considerable problem for telephone counselling agencies because they take up valuable time which could be used in working with other clients. Also, they tend to produce disillusionment and increased burnout in counsellors. Agencies that employ many counsellors have particular difficulty in dealing with regular callers because their counsellors are sure to find it difficult to recognise the regulars.

Although there are exceptions, I do not think that it is helpful to allow regular callers to talk at length. To do this shuts out other callers. Also, regular callers are more likely to dig themselves deeper into their regular caller's rut if they are permitted to talk for an extended length of time. Unfortunately some regular callers are very adept at manipulating counsellors because they are experienced clients. Here are a range of statements commonly made by regular callers with the goal of convincing the counsellor that she should continue to listen:

"You seem to really understand me."

"No one has ever been able to get close to me this way before."

"You are such a warm person that I feel so comfortable talking to you."

"I think I'll kill myself now."

"I just need to ask your opinion about one more thing."

"Other callers are much more important than me."

Many telephone counselling agencies have lists of regular callers giving details to assist counsellors in recognising the regulars, and also give guidelines for handling these calls. If these callers do not receive consistent responses from counsellors then their best interests are not served and additionally they may become a terrible nuisance. It's important to make clear decisions when handling such callers so that their real needs are met and they feel valued as people, but do not disrupt service to other callers.

Most agencies set time limits for calls from regular callers but terminating calls from some of them can be difficult. You may need to be very assertive (see the Chapter 23).

Regular callers can be frustrating and annoying at times, but I would like you to consider them from another perspective. Regular callers are often sad, unfulfilled people who would not call in if they were able to lead satisfying lives. Among them are the chronically sick, the mentally ill, people with disabilities, lonely people, people who are grieving heavily as a consequence of broken or lost relationships, the chronically depressed and people with significant past histories of abuse. They are all different from each other and unique as individuals. They each have their own personal needs and deserve to be treasured as other clients are treasured. They have a right to receive care and counselling. Let me give you some examples of regular callers I have known:

- I remember a case where some counsellors at a telephone counselling agency felt that they were wasting time listening to a particular old lady who phoned in several times each day. Then one day a relative phoned to say that the old lady was her mother and that she had died. She said that she was phoning to tell the counsellors how much her mother had valued the warmth and caring they had offered her during the last few weeks of her life.
- One day I met face-to-face with a seriously depressed regular caller who was boring TCs with his monotonous conversation. I was confronted by a sad, disfigured and disabled person who had no friends and was avoided by strangers. He had little chance, if any, of improving his lifestyle. He could hardly stand or walk, his speech was impaired, his conversation was uninspiring, he had barely enough income from his pension to survive. He lived alone. Almost his only human contact was by phone with the telephone counsellors who cared enough to listen.
- Once, to my surprise, a capable telephone counsellor who was well known to me, confided that before becoming a TC she had for a time been a regular caller herself during a very difficult period in her life. Thanks to the counselling process she had been enabled to deal with her problems and to climb out of her trough of despair. She was now helping others.

These examples are, I believe, not unusual. Regular callers are valuable people and require patient caring, although sometimes it is not easy to be either patient or caring when counselling them. It's easy to say: "Oh, she's a regular caller, and I really don't want to listen to her." It's harder to say: "This is a challenge, can I work with this problem caller in a way that will be satisfying for her and for me?"

If you are going to get satisfaction from helping a regular caller then you will need to be clear about your goals for each call. You will also need to be direct in telling the caller clearly what to expect from you. For example, you may say:

"Frank, I'm happy to talk with you for 15 minutes but then I would like to hang up so that other callers also have the opportunity to call in." By doing this you are up-front with your caller and can use the call caringly and constructively to achieve a goal. Here are some possible goals:

- To raise the client's awareness of the cracked record she plays.
- To help the client to recognise options.
- To empower the client to do something different, however small.
- To help the client to feel valued.
- To provide a listening ear for someone lonely.

Can you think of other goals?

Counselling goals listed in Chapter 30, entitled "Counselling the depressed client", may also be appropriate.

CHRONICALLY DEPRESSED CALLERS

A high percentage of regular callers fall into the chronically depressed category so I have decided to give them special mention. These people have very sad lives and call for a high level of caring from those who counsel them. Strategies for counselling them are in some ways the same as, but in some ways different from, those used in general counselling. Telephone counsellors therefore need to have appropriate strategies for working with such callers. These strategies are described in Chapter 30.

SEX CALLERS

Unfortunately, telephone counselling agencies are frequently troubled by callers who want to use counselling services to satisfy their sexual needs. In my experience almost all of these callers are male and generally they only want to talk with female counsellors. They will either recount a story with a high level of sexual content or may be direct in asking the counsellor if they may masturbate while talking.

It is probable that many of these callers are obsessed by sex and have little or no chance of building a satisfying relationship with a partner. For others, sex may be an escape from the reality of a very unsatisfactory life and they may believe that they have no options to enable them to change their lives. Many, if not all of these men, lack respect for women and have psychological problems with regard to them.

I can see no justification, regardless of circumstances, for male callers to attempt to use female counsellors for their own sexual gratification. For them to do this is sexual abuse and it can be dealt with as such.

However, counsellors need to be careful in assessing whether a caller is a nuisance "sex-caller" or not. There are callers who genuinely seek anonymous counselling help with regard to very personal sexual problems. Some of these would be too embarrassed to attend a face-to-face counselling session and may even be hesitant about talking to a telephone counsellor. Clearly they need counselling help, even if only a sensible referral to a clinic or sex-counselling service. Unfortunately, it's hard to separate these genuine callers from the abusers. If a genuine caller is treated as though he is a sexually abusive caller, then his trust in the counselling process may be seriously damaged. I wish I could tell you how to distinguish between the genuine and non-genuine caller. I can't. All you can do is to use your judgment and if you think that a caller is using you to fantasise sexually or to masturbate, then confront him!

By challenging the caller's attitudes which allow or encourage him to make sex calls and/or by raising the caller's concern about his behaviour, a counsellor may increase the possibility of the caller seeking help to stop the behaviour.

Obviously, sex callers have genuine psychological or life issues. If they did not, then they wouldn't attempt to use telephone counselling services in such a way. Consequently, a caring counsellor might choose either to deal with the caller firmly but caringly, or to be very abrupt and to hang up. Yes, it can be caring to give very direct messages about the consequences of inappropriate behaviour. If you are abrupt and hang up you do precisely that. Alternatively you may decide to be clear and explicit in telling the person how you feel about what he is doing, explaining that you intend to hang up, and in addition giving the caller an invitation to call back if he wants to talk about real-life issues rather than using you as a sex object. However, it pays to be cautious or you may find the same caller pretending to tell you about his "real-life issues" while continuing to masturbate. There are some counsellors who will tolerate this. That is their choice, and if they are able to achieve worthwhile goals then their caring is to be admired. They need to be careful, however, on two counts: firstly, that they are not implicitly encouraging inappropriate behaviour which may be detrimental to other counsellors and secondly, that they are not merely satisfying their own sexual or other needs. Here, supervision can be valuable in identifying the relevant issues.

Certainly, all counsellors need to be aware of their own personal rights and to know that they are fully justified in protecting themselves from abuse by refusing to listen.

TELEPHONE COUNSELLORS ARE SPECIAL PEOPLE!

LEARNING SUMMARY

- Telephone counselling is, in some ways, more difficult than face-to-face counselling because the counsellor has less non-verbal information.

- Telephone counsellors need to prepare themselves personally before taking a call.

- Skill in cautiously building a relationship is paramount or the caller may hang up.

- Hang-ups are inevitable and are not necessarily bad.

- All of the counselling micro-skills are important. However, minimal responses are particularly important in telephone counselling so that the caller knows that the counsellor is attending.

- The telephone counsellor needs to pay attention to the process of each call and if necessary will influence that process with the goal of increasing client awareness.

- Each call can be thought of as one step in a flight of stairs being climbed by the caller.

- Empower the caller to make her own decisions.

- Making notes and using the imagination helps to bring the client's situation into focus.

- Telephone counsellors need to set clear limits with regard to their relationships with clients.

- Telephone counsellors need to debrief after troubling calls or they will burn out.

- Nuisance callers, regular callers, chronically depressed callers, and sex callers cause problems for TCs and appropriate strategies are required for counselling each of these.

FURTHER READING

Hambly, G., *Telephone Counselling—A Resource for People Who Want to Counsel or Care Using the Telephone*. Melbourne: Joint Board of Christian Education, 1984

Rosenfield, M., *Counselling by Telephone*. London: Sage, 1997

Waters, J. and Finn, E., "Handling Client Crises Effectively on the Telephone". In Roberts, A. R. (ed.), *Crisis Intervention and Time-Limited Cognitive Treatment*. Thousand Oaks: Sage, 1995

28 Crisis intervention

In this chapter we will look at the following aspects of crisis intervention:

- the nature of crisis
- types of crisis
- the dangers and value of crisis
- the counsellor's personal response to client crisis
- appropriate counselling interventions
- practical responses to crisis
- post-traumatic stress

The nature of crisis

What comes into your thoughts when you think about the word "crisis"? Would you like to stop and think for a moment—to explore your own ideas about "crisis"?

My guess is that your thoughts focussed either on a disaster that affected other people or that you remembered a time when you were confronted by a traumatic experience of your own.

Here are some of the feelings that I experience and thoughts that come flooding into my mind when someone mentions the word "crisis":

- panic
- fear
- horror
- help
- I can't cope with this
- I don't know what to do
- I need to do something in a hurry
- if I don't act quickly there will be a bigger disaster, *and*
- more panic!

Are you rather like me or are you different?

Crisis situations are situations of high risk. In crisis something is happening or has happened to abruptly change the participant's perception of a safe and ordered world. It is as though the bottom brick in a column of bricks is being pulled away so that the whole column will collapse. However, there is another and very different perspective on crisis which we will consider later under the heading "The dangers and value of crisis". I wonder whether you can think of what it might be? First, however, let's think about the various types of crisis that people experience.

Types of crisis

There are several very different types of crisis. Although they are different, they also have similarities. They all raise the stress level of the person or people involved and call for a quick response in order to minimise practical, emotional and psychological damage.

Would you like to stop reading for a moment or two to see whether you can identify for yourself the different types of crisis that we experience?

Well, here are a few ideas of mine. We are all familiar with crises which fall into the following categories:

- natural disaster
- accidental
- medical
- emotional
- relationship
- developmental

These categories are not mutually exclusive or independent of each other, but they are useful in helping us to think about the similarities and differences of the various types of crisis. I will now discuss each of the categories listed in some detail.

NATURAL DISASTER

All of us who watch the evening TV news are very familiar with the practical type of crisis with physical and emotional consequences which occurs when a volcano erupts, or when there is a bush fire, a flood, an earthquake, or when lightning strikes. Sometimes the effects of natural disasters are lengthy. A drought can cause famine, and the effects may last for years unless there is an effective and timely response. Unfortunately, as with most crises, natural disasters usually occur with little or no warning.

ACCIDENTAL CRISES

These crises are inevitably a part of our daily lives. Examples are when a building catches fire, when two cars collide, or when a child falls down some stairs. In the worst accidental crises there is loss of life.

Obviously, these crises occur without warning with the consequence that those involved are not properly prepared and are often not able to make the most appropriate response. Such crises can be life threatening.

MEDICAL CRISES

Some medical crises fall into the "accidental" category. However, many do not. Medical crises occur when people have strokes, heart attacks, fits, asthma attacks, or any of the many medical conditions that afflict the human race. Similarly medical crises occur when people are incapacitated by illness. A migraine headache, for example, may prevent a person from doing those things necessary for the well-being of himself and others.

Other examples of medical crises are when a woman delivers a baby unexpectedly and there is no one around to help, or when there are complications with a birth. Similarly, a crisis occurs when a baby becomes sick or when there are problems with feeding a baby.

Medical crises are often very frightening because of high personal involvement at a physical, emotional and psychological level. As with accidental crisis, in the most severe cases there can be loss of life.

EMOTIONAL CRISES

An important and valuable human characteristic is our capacity to be emotional. If we were deprived of our emotions we would be automatons—mere machines. Unfortunately, at times the emotions we experience are painfully destructive and prevent us from functioning normally. Rage, sadness, depression and despair can all lead to states of crisis where the individual may be at risk.

RELATIONSHIP CRISES

Anyone who has worked for a telephone crisis-counselling service will tell you that relationships are a common factor underlying many crisis calls. Dysfunctional relationships, broken or lost relationships, and the absence of relationships are probably the most common causes of emotional crisis. However, I am separating "relationship crises" from other more general "emotional crises" because this is such an important sub-category.

Time and again people experience crisis when relationships are strained, break up, or are lost through death or unavoidable separation. Often, spouses feel devastated and as though their whole world has collapsed when they discover that their partner is having an extramarital affair. Similarly, those involved in having an affair usually experience a high degree of emotional pain.

Sometimes people experience profound disappointments due to the behaviour of those who are in close relationships with them. Parents are particularly vulnerable to such feelings. Time and again, parents have told me how disappointed and sometimes devastated they were when they learnt that their child was caught stealing or behaving in some other way contrary to their own expectations.

Unfortunately, too often in our present society relationship crises involve physical violence, usually with women and children as the victims. Counsellors are continually hearing about emotional, sexual and physical abuse occurring within families which should be places of safety and security.

DEVELOPMENTAL CRISES

There are some crises that none of us escape. These are the developmental crises that occur naturally and inevitably as we pass through the various developmental stages of our lives.

For most people the first developmental crisis is probably at the time of birth. However, for some there could well be earlier ones when, for example, sudden changes occur within a mother's body. From birth onwards the list of developmental crisis times is endless. Here are a few examples:

- When a child takes a first step
- The first day in child care
- Starting school
- The onset of puberty
- Starting work
- Leaving home
- Living with a partner
- Getting married
- Having a child
- Death in the family
- Separation
- Mid-life crisis
- Divorce
- Starting again with a new partner
- Retiring
- Growing old
- Dying

At each of these stages there is risk involved, a raised stress and anxiety level is inevitable, and there will probably be other emotional responses. Often, there is a need for appropriate decisions to be made with consequent action.

There is an inevitability about many developmental crises. They are often a natural and necessary part of growing up and getting older. However, each crisis can be threatening, calls for a response and marks the beginning of a new stage in life.

The dangers and value of crisis

Most crises spell danger. They are fraught with risk. They shake us up and interrupt the comfort of our lives. They call for responsive action and usually this needs to happen without delay. However, crises are not necessarily bad. Although they usually do have emotional consequences, there is another way of looking at crisis. A time of crisis is also a time of opportunity. The impact of a crisis is likely to produce an opportunity for change. A crisis can be the catalyst for the development of something new. It can be a time when we let go of what has been and start afresh.

Surprisingly, even from the most terrible tragedies something of value may possibly emerge. Saying this in no way diminishes the sadness and horror of tragedy, but it is worth remembering that given an appropriate response, something new and worthwhile may grow out of a tragedy. A person may grow stronger psychologically or spiritually, relationships may change for the better, or something in poor condition and of limited use may be replaced by something more useful. Unfortunately though, many people are permanently scarred by crises which they have experienced.

Sometimes, a good metaphor for crisis, which can be used with clients, is to describe the crisis experience as rather like going through a doorway from one space into another. If I imagine myself moving through a doorway I realise that

I am leaving behind those things in the room I'm leaving, I may be taking some things with me, and I am about to enter a new and different space where there are some unknowns. Consequently I may experience sadness and fear, and also possibly excitement, as I think of what lies ahead. If I wish I can focus on feeling apprehensive and threatened. Alternatively I may be able to give myself different messages so that I feel challenged and consequently energised.

Be warned, however, that it is usually not appropriate to be telling someone in crisis that something good may emerge! To do such a thing would usually be inappropriate and would not address the person's pain. However, be on the lookout for the positive opportunities present in a crisis so that, at the appropriate time, as the person moves out of crisis, these may be fully explored.

Additionally, in some instances it may be premature and inadvisable for far-reaching decisions to be made before the person concerned has had time to work through the trauma of a crisis.

The counsellor's personal response

I remember when I used to work as a crisis-line telephone counsellor. Sometimes, with a suicidal caller, or when a woman with children was trapped in domestic violence, I would feel my hair standing on end. My body would tense, my palms would be sweaty, and I would realise that I was gripping the phone as tightly as I could. It was then that I would recognise my panic.

Panic induces the frightened rabbit syndrome. The rabbit freezes. It can't move and is consequently unable to protect itself or its offspring. Are you a frightened rabbit at times? I am!

Rabbits can also run, and use their brains to avoid danger by changing direction.

The first step in dealing with panic is to recognise the physical symptoms that indicate the onset of panic. I would usually notice that my whole body was tense.

How do *you* recognise *your* panic? The way to do this is to learn to recognise the messages your body gives you. Then you can easily recognise your frightened rabbit mode and consequently be able to deal with it. Once you have recognised your panic, you are in a position to do something about it.

The first thing I do is to say to myself: "I'm panicking, and my panic is not helpful." Next, I consciously relax my body. I loosen the tight grip I have on the phone (if I'm working on the phone). I move my body into a more comfortable position, take a few deep breaths and at the same time let my body relax a little as I breathe out. I follow this by discarding those internal messages and self-destructive beliefs that contribute to panic, and replacing them by internal messages such as:

"I don't have a magic wand. "

"Nobody else has a magic wand. "

"There are limits to what I can do. "

If I stay calm I will be more likely to think sensibly.

The client is more likely to know the solution than I am.

Can I help the client to feel calmer and to have some degree of control so that she can use her resources most effectively?

What are the client's options?

What are my options?

What are the limits to what I am able to do?

Hopefully, I should then be able to attend to the client in an effective and caring way using appropriate counselling interventions.

Appropriate counselling interventions

What's appropriate at a counselling level will clearly depend very much on the nature of the crisis, and whether the counselling is face-to-face or by phone. For example, if a house is on fire and the client doesn't know what to do then it will not be appropriate to spend time reflecting feelings. Practical advice is urgently required! Give it.

Yes, we counsellors generally try to avoid giving advice and instead encourage our clients to make their own decisions. However, as with most rules, common sense is needed about when to apply the rule and when to do the opposite. Sometimes when quick action is needed we have to be very direct in order to avoid a disastrous consequence. Quick action does not mean acting in panic but means being carefully decisive and giving your client clear instructions.

If a counsellor is not to act in panic, then she must first stop panicking, if that is what she is doing. Then sensible decisions can be made with regard to the most satisfactory approach.

Similarly, if the client is panicking then she will be unlikely to respond effectively and act sensibly. Her panic needs to be addressed. A possible counselling response to a panicking client could be:

I'm catching the panic of this situation. Let's stop and think. Have you any idea what you could do right now?

What do you think of this response? It joins with the client, may enable her to recognise and deal with her panic, and addresses the need for action. It could be an appropriate response, depending on the situation. Can you suggest some other responses?

Throughout a crisis intervention, try to maintain a calmness so that your client is reassured. If you are able to do this then the client will feel more secure and will be more likely to believe that a satisfactory outcome will be achieved. She might then be able to match some of your calmness.

As the crisis intervention proceeds, the full range of counselling skills will probably be required. If you stay with the client, using the normal process of a counselling session as outlined in Chapter 24, then the client will feel supported and empowered to cope. She will be enabled to experience her feelings in the safety of the counselling relationship and should reach some sense of completeness by the end of the process. Yes, you may leave your client feeling intensely sad, drained, and possibly even devastated, but hopefully you will have managed to create a relationship of trust so that she felt supported through her crisis. If you did, then the client will feel able to come back to talk with you, or with another counsellor, in the following few days or weeks. It is during this time that she may well need counselling help as she copes with the emotional, psychological and practical after-effects of her crisis.

Although all the micro-skills are needed, it is worth remembering that the micro-skill called "normalising" (see Chapter 20) is particularly useful when dealing with developmental crises. Clients often feel relieved to know that what is happening to them is inevitable and normal, even if distressing and painful.

Sensibly, the counselling interventions used must take account of any practical options available to the client and counsellor, so we will now consider practical responses to crisis.

Practical responses to crisis

It is essential that counsellors involved in crisis intervention are clear about the range of practical responses available to them. Because crises usually come without warning, counsellors need to be prepared. As a counsellor you need to know what options you may have when confronted by a client in crisis. You need to have a clear idea of the boundaries within which you work so that you know what you can and can't do. The options available to you and the boundaries which constrain you will clearly depend on the policies and practices of the agency where you are working.

You, the counsellor, will need to know the answer to a number of questions including the following so that you are prepared for any client emergency:

- If a client phones you in crisis, are you able to go out to visit the client or not? If not, is there someone else on your counselling team who is able go? If so, what limitations do they have to their ability to intervene practically?
- Are you permitted, within the guidelines of your employing agency, to ask a client in crisis to come in to see you, or to see another counsellor? Under what circumstances can this be done?
- Can you supply or arrange for transport, accommodation, financial or material assistance, or any other service for your client?
- Does your agency's policy allow you to accompany your client and to assist her?
- Do you have a comprehensive list of resources available, so that if you can't provide the required help yourself, then you can let your client know who might be able to help?

- Are you permitted to call the police, ambulance, fire brigade or any other service? If so, do you need to have the client's permission in all cases or are there exceptions?
- Can you arrange for women and children in domestic violence to be accommodated in refuges or in other temporary accommodation if refuge accommodation is not available? If so, who will supply the transport? Will someone from your agency or another agency be available to accompany the clients or not?

Clearly, these are just some of the questions you may need to answer and there are countless more. Unfortunately, you probably won't think of some of them until a specific situation arises that is new to you. In training, it's useful to brainstorm and to try to think of every imaginable crisis so that you know exactly what is available, and exactly what you are, and are not, permitted and able to do.

CLIENT EXPECTATIONS
Clients sometimes have unrealistic expectations of counselling services. This is particularly so in the case of crisis telephone counselling services where some callers may expect that counsellors are at all times available to visit clients who would like such a visit. From the outset be clear with your client about the limits of your service so that false and/or unrealistic expectations do not develop. Can you say "No"? It's hard, isn't it? You may need to say to your client: "I'm sorry, but there is no one available to see you right now, but you are welcome to talk with me on the phone or to explore other options, if these exist."

PRACTICAL INTERVENTION
At an appropriate stage in the counselling process, you, the counsellor, may need to assess whether there is a need for practical intervention. For example, it might be advisable to call an ambulance, the police, the fire brigade, a medical practitioner or some other helper. Alternatively, for example, in a case of threatened suicide, it may be necessary to arrange for a crisis worker to meet urgently with the client.

In many agencies counsellors work under supervision. If you work in such an agency, then you may need to inform or get permission from your supervisor before being able to set in train an appropriate practical intervention. While doing this it is important to keep in touch with your client as much as is possible. A client who phones in is likely to feel anxious if left on "hold" for even a short time. Be careful to maintain as much continuity of contact with the client as possible and to keep the client fully informed of your actions. In particular, if you are putting a caller on "hold" tell the caller why you are doing that and let her know how long your absence is likely to be. If you take longer than expected then interrupt what you are doing, go back quickly to the phone and reassure your client.

Be cautious when considering whether it is necessary or not to intervene at a practical level. It is often tempting for a counsellor to take over responsibility from a client when this is not really necessary. Sometimes intervention by a counsellor is appropriate but at other times it is not.

Consider an example where a client needs an ambulance. In some cases, it may be advantageous for the client to call an ambulance herself. By doing this the ambulance personnel get a direct message from the client rather than one which might get altered in transmission. Also, it is empowering for a client to take action herself rather than to be left feeling that she is incapable of doing so. On the other hand, there may be some uncertainty about the ability of the client to perform the task satisfactorily herself, or she may be particularly vulnerable and in need of support. In such cases, the counsellor may sensibly decide, with the client's permission, to call the ambulance herself. Clearly, sensitive judgment is needed by counsellors in deciding when to intervene and when to encourage clients to take responsibility themselves for any necessary action. There can be no hard and fast rule.

GIVING SPECIFIC INSTRUCTIONS

At a time of crisis intervention a counsellor may need to be very directive and very direct in order to avoid an escalation of the crisis. This is particularly so in cases where the counsellor has professional knowledge that will be useful to the client. If we use childbirth as an example, a nursing sister, medical practitioner, paramedic, or other trained person may be able to provide crucial information which can be essential for the well-being of the mother and/or child. Such a person needs to be clear, concise, concrete and specific in giving directions to the client or helpers. Even so, it is imperative that the counsellor retains the full use of her listening and joining skills. It is at times like these that the person undergoing the crisis may have important information to give which could be overlooked unless full attention is given to her verbal and non-verbal communication.

As in counselling generally, it's desirable for you to stay in tune with your client's feelings, so that any intervention initiated is acceptable to the client. Exceptions to this are situations where you have a duty of care to the client or others. Clearly, counsellors have a duty of care in cases where clients are out of control of their own behaviour due to psychosis or drugs, or in cases where the safety of another person is at stake.

Post-traumatic stress

Unfortunately a counsellor's work does not necessarily finish when a crisis is over. It is now well documented that people often suffer from emotional and psychological after-effects as a result of severe crisis. These after-effects are generally referred to as post-traumatic stress.

Post-traumatic stress can occur in persons who directly experience a crisis, and in people who act as helpers at a time of crisis, such as emergency service personnel, police, ambulance personnel, medical and nursing staff, counsellors, and social workers. Additionally relatives and friends may also suffer post-traumatic effects.

Usually the first evidence of emotional trauma becomes apparent immediately after the crisis, or within a few days. Some people try to shrug off these post-traumatic effects, believing that time will heal all. Unfortunately, time often doesn't heal all, and it is common for those who have been personally involved in crisis, and those who have in some way helped them, to be seriously affected emotionally and psychologically some weeks or months after the event. Post-traumatic stress can best be minimised by those involved undergoing counselling within a few days of the conclusion of the crisis.

Because of the possibility of post-traumatic stress, it is sensible to follow up on clients who have been through a severe crisis. During the days and weeks following a crisis it can be advantageous if the people involved are offered counselling help. Without this, the risk of undesirable psychological effects showing up later may be increased.

As stated previously, counsellors may be affected themselves when they work with clients experiencing crisis. As a counsellor, don't forget your own needs. After counselling someone in crisis, talk to your supervisor or another counsellor about your own experience of the counselling process and the emotional feelings generated within you. Such talking through, or debriefing as it is called, needs to be accepted as necessary and normal after any crisis intervention work. It certainly is not a sign of weakness to engage in such debriefing. On the contrary it is a sign of maturity, good sense and personal strength.

LEARNING SUMMARY

- Crisis spells danger and opportunity.

- Crises occur naturally, accidentally, medically, developmentally, as a result of emotional and relationship problems, and in other ways.

- In crisis intervention counsellors need to deal with panic, be calm, use the full range of counselling skills, and sometimes give specific directions to the client.

- Counsellors need to know the limits of their ability to intervene practically. They need to be clear in communicating these limits to clients.

- Counsellors need to be prepared for crisis and to have ready access to information about available resources for practical help.

- There are times when it is appropriate to intervene practically on a client's behalf, and times when it is not.

- Appropriate action is required to deal with the possibility of post-traumatic stress in both the client and the counsellor.

FURTHER READING

Aguilera, D. C., *Crisis Intervention—Theory and Methodology*, 7th edn. St Louis: Mosby, 1994

Waters, J. and Finn, E., "Handling Client Crises Effectively on the Telephone". In Roberts, A. R. (ed.), *Crisis Intervention and Time-Limited Cognitive Treatment*. Thousand Oaks: Sage, 1995

Aguilera, D. C : „ Crisis Intervention-
Theory and Methodology "
        7th edn. St. Louis : Mosby, 1994
Waters, J. + Finn, E   „ Handling Client
    Crises Effectively on the Telephone "
(Crisis Interv. and Time -Limited Cognitive
Treatment), 1995

Part V

Dealing with particular problems

This section of the book deals with angry, depressed, suicidal and grieving clients. It is inevitable that before long a new counsellor will find that some clients who come for help fall into these categories. It is important to know your own limitations as a counsellor and to refer such clients to experienced and skilled therapists, after consultation with your supervisor, whenever appropriate. However, the problems dealt with in this part of the book are so common that it is important for new counsellors to have an understanding of useful ways in which to work with such clients.

29 Counselling the angry client

Counsellors frequently have to deal with angry clients. Bottled-up anger can be very destructive and also very dangerous because it may break out at some time or other and the client may do injury or damage to another person. Many counsellors, in the early stages of their counselling careers, become quite frightened when clients exhibit even moderate levels of anger. This chapter has been included to provide new counsellors with some practical ideas about how to deal with angry clients in cases where it is not considered necessary to refer them to more experienced counsellors.

Angry clients need to be able to dissipate their anger and then to change some of their thinking patterns and behaviours, if they are to feel better. We will discuss two different and complementary ways of helping clients to dissipate anger. One way is to encourage them to release their anger verbally in the safety of the counselling environment, and the other is to teach relaxation. We will also consider ways to help clients to think and behave differently, so that hopefully they can deal with anger more constructively in the future.

Helping clients recognise and express anger

Clients who are not dangerous or violent can be allowed to recognise and express anger verbally in the counselling room. However, if an inexperienced counsellor suspects that a client might have a potential for violence, the client should be referred to a suitably qualified and experienced therapist.

When a client starts to express anger use the normal reflective methods if you wish. However, if the level of anger starts to rise then it's sensible for you,

the counsellor, to take control and to ensure that the anger is directed away from yourself. As a counsellor, do not allow the client's anger to rise significantly while he is talking directly to you, or you may end up feeling tense yourself. Instead, protect yourself by using a method borrowed from Gestalt Therapy (if you want to learn more about Gestalt Therapy read Clarkson, 1989 or O'Leary, 1992 and if you like what you read enrol in a Gestalt Therapy training course). The method is as follows.

USE OF THE EMPTY CHAIR
Start by asking the client, "Who are you most angry with?" Next, place an empty chair facing the client and a metre or two away from him. Tell the client to imagine that sitting in the empty chair is the person who is the target of his anger. Say to the client something like: "I don't want to be the recipient of your anger, so I don't want you to tell me how angry you are; rather I'd like you to talk to the imaginary person who is sitting in that empty chair, about your angry feelings towards him." Preferably you should now stand beside your client and join him in facing the empty chair. You can then "coach" the client in his expression of anger towards the imagined person.

For example, if the client starts saying: "Well actually I'm very angry with Fred, because Fred has consistently offended me with his behaviour", then, as counsellor, you can say yourself: "*I'm* very angry with you, Fred, because you've consistently behaved badly." The client will then pick up the way in which he is expected to address the imagined person on the empty chair instead of talking to you, and he can then be encouraged to express his anger openly and fully. This method is useful for the client as it enables him to verbalise his anger, and avoids a situation where the counsellor becomes the recipient of the anger, because the counsellor is standing beside the client and joining with him. If this method appeals to you, then after completion of your basic counsellor training, you may wish to train as a gestalt therapist and learn other powerful techniques for enabling clients to release their anger.

Warning!

Remember that some clients have great difficulty in controlling inappropriately high levels of anger. Among these are people who perpetrate violence against spouses, others, children, and/or property. They must be referred to skilled psychotherapists and are not suitable clients for a new counsellor.

Helping the client to change thoughts and behaviours

Once counselling has been effective in enabling a client's high anger level to subside, the next stage is to teach him how to deal with his anger in the future. Give your client a copy of the chart shown in Figure 29.1 and discuss it with him.

Although the chart is fairly self-explanatory, it is useful to work through it step by step. The first step is for the client to learn to recognise physiological cues.

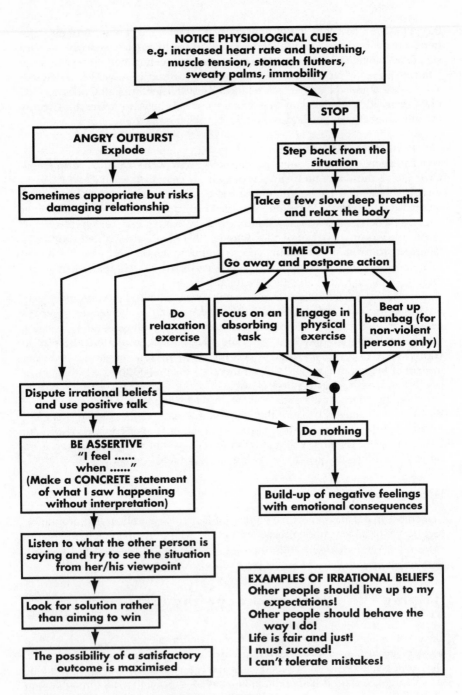

FIGURE 29.1 Anger control flow chart

When I start to get angry, things happen to my body. I might notice that my heart rate increases and that I breathe more rapidly. I might start to sweat, my muscles might tighten up, or I might have an uncomfortable feeling in my stomach. Some people freeze on the spot and feel their hair standing on end. We are all different and so each individual needs to identify for himself what happens to him physiologically when he starts to get angry. Once a client has learnt to recognise the physiological symptoms that occur as his anger starts to rise, he can use them as cues for appropriate action. He is then able to make a choice, either to allow an angry outburst to occur, or to stop and react differently. At times it may be better to allow controlled angry outbursts to occur, rather than to bottle up the emotion. Clearly, uncontrolled angry outbursts are dangerous, but letting off steam by continually having small controlled outbursts does enable anger to be dissipated. Unfortunately, people who continually behave angrily are certain to damage their relationships with others.

THOUGHT-STOPPING

The alternative to having an angry outburst is for the client to recognise the physiological cues that indicate a rise in anger and immediately to say "STOP" silently to himself. This is called thought-stopping. I knew a counsellor once who used to teach thought-stopping by getting his client to shut his eyes and imagine a scene that would make him angry. When the client was concentrating on that scene the counsellor would slam a book down on the desk and shout "STOP". The sudden impact would stop the client in his tracks. In fact, it would give the client such a fright that I do not use this method myself for fear of unpleasant consequences! However, this method did demonstrate effectively to the client that he could stop his thoughts instantly, and change their direction if he chose to do so.

Once a client has stopped letting his thoughts hook him into an angry outburst, he can make the choice to step back from the situation, to move back in his imagination by 10 metres, so that he is, in effect, looking at himself and his situation from a distant vantage point. He can then, if he chooses, take a few slow deep breaths and allow the muscles in his body to relax as they would when engaged in a relaxation exercise (see Chapter 33). As he takes those few slow deep breaths, each time he breathes out he can say silently to himself, "relax", and allow his body to relax.

Clearly, part of the process of helping clients to learn new ways of dealing with anger involves teaching relaxation. Clients can then use the method described. By learning how to relax and how to recognise their patterns of behaviour, some clients are able to lower the intensity of their emotional feelings in future times of crisis and hence are able to deal with their anger more appropriately (see Chapter 33).

TAKING TIME OUT

The next stage in the process of anger control involves several options as shown on the chart. The "time out" block shown gives the client time to cool off and reduce his anger level before deciding what action, if any, to take. The client may literally walk away from the situation and distance himself physically from it. In order to do this, he may need to negotiate with some significant person in his life, so that the person concerned allows him space when he asks for it.

After time out has been used to allow emotions to cool down, the emotional level may be further reduced by doing a relaxation exercise, by becoming fully absorbed in carrying out a task (such as putting full concentration into cooking a meal), or by engaging in physical exercise (like going jogging).

For people who are not violent, and not likely to become violent, another alternative is for them to dissipate their anger by beating up a beanbag, mattress or punching bag. This method can be very helpful for people who do not usually experience much anger, but are angry as a result of a short-term life crisis. However, a word of warning: physically releasing angry feelings in this way should never be recommended for clients who are likely to become violent with either people or property. These clients need to learn how to control their anger in other ways and should be referred to specialist counsellors and counselling programs. Teaching them to vent their anger by acting it out physically may be potentially dangerous because it could reinforce violent tendencies.

MAKING A DECISION
From this point in the anger control process, the options are either to do nothing further, or to move into the action described in the left-hand column on the anger control chart.

Sometimes doing nothing is satisfactory. It may be that as a result of "time out" followed by one of the anger-dissipating activities, the client will realise that he was overreacting and will feel OK. However, there is a danger in doing nothing at this stage as emotions may still be bottled up with a consequent increased likelihood of a future outburst.

CHALLENGING SELF-DESTRUCTIVE BELIEFS
If "action" is the preferred option, then the first step involves disputing irrational beliefs and using positive self-talk. We all at times, when angry, give ourselves messages that are destructive because they make us feel even more unhappy and angry. Such messages have been discussed in Chapter 19 and include statements such as: "Other people should live up to my expectations"; "Other people should behave the way I do"; "Life is fair and just"; "I must win"; "I must succeed"; "I can't tolerate mistakes". Statements like this are absurd. Why should other people live up to my expectations? Who said that other people should behave the way I do? I wouldn't like other people to tell me how to behave and it is not rational for me to expect them to live up to my expectations. Life is patently not fair or just. Some people have lots of luck, and other people just don't. It isn't necessary or likely that I will always win. If I win 50 per cent of the time that would be pretty fair, and even that might not happen. So I need to remember that it is not necessary for me to win, it is not necessary for me to succeed every time, and I can, if I wish, choose to tolerate other people's

mistakes. I can, if I choose, allow other people to behave in ways that are different from the ways in which I would behave myself.

Once I have put aside my irrational beliefs, I can replace them by positive ideas which will help me to feel better. For example, when someone fails to live up to my expectations I could say to myself: "He doesn't care enough about me to try to please me. I just don't matter to him." That would be irrational. It is equally likely that the person concerned is just a bit careless. A more positive self-statement would be: "Maybe that person is naturally careless. His behaviour may have nothing to do with the way he feels about me. For all I know he might think I'm a great guy. What's more, it's not important what he thinks about me, because I know that I'm OK."

Table 29.1 gives some specific examples of irrational self-statements which are likely to make a person feel angry, together with alternative self-statements which are more likely to have a positive outcome.

Once I have translated the negative, irrational messages that I am giving myself into positive messages, then I am in a situation where I can make other positive choices. I can do nothing, at least for the time being. That is a valid choice and it may be a sensible one. Sometimes it is better to let things cool off before taking action. However, it is important to be sure not to allow negative feelings to build up as a result of inaction. If negative feelings start to build up, then they need to be dealt with and that probably means confronting the person with whom I am annoyed. Where confrontation is the choice, it needs to be done in a way likely to lead to a positive outcome with a minimal risk of damage to the relationship.

BEING ASSERTIVE

Constructive confrontation requires assertive rather than aggressive behaviour. An assertive person has the goal of wanting to be heard, but not the goal of definitely getting all he wants. An aggressive person is determined to win at any cost and also is intent on hurting the other person. Assertion involves communicating as an equal. It involves respecting the rights of the other person, and demands that the other person's point of view must be respected. Consequently, two assertive people may well come to the conclusion that they have different opinions. They will, however, respect the right of each other to have a different opinion. It is sufficient for the assertive person to be heard rather than to win an argument by convincing the other person to change his mind. Sometimes I will not be heard and it is not rational of me to expect that the other person will necessarily be capable of hearing me. I can accept being misunderstood if I choose to do so.

One of the best ways to make assertive statements is to use "I feel ... when ..." statements as explained in Chapter 25. An example is "I feel frustrated when you interrupt me in the middle of a sentence." By using the "I feel" statement, the speaker is owning his feelings rather than blaming the other person, and consequently he is more likely to be heard. After the feeling statement follows a concrete statement about the behaviour that caused the feeling. As explained before, it needs to be an objective statement of behaviour, and not an

TABLE 29.1 Comparison of anger-producing irrational self-statements with positive self-statements

Irrational anger-producing self-statement	Equivalent positive self-statement
1. If I don't get him to give me what I want, I'll be humiliated and made to look like a loser.	It's not reasonable to expect that I can make anyone give me what I want. I can feel proud of my ability to ask for what I want and to accept that I may not get it.
2. People should not let me down. When they let me down, I know that they don't respect me enough to want to please me.	I am a worthwhile person. It's not realistic to expect other people to live up to my expectations. When they let me down, it says more about them than me.
3. I can't feel OK unless Bill agrees that I'm right.	I can't control the way Bill thinks. If he's illogical, that's his problem, and I'm not going to make it mine. I'm OK.
4. Mary's behaviour is ruining my life. Unless she starts to do things to please me, I'm going to get very angry.	If my happiness depends on other people's behaviour, I might never be happy. I can be happy if I accept other people, including Mary, the way they are and the way they behave.
5. I've been victimised and that just isn't fair. I've got to get even.	Life often isn't fair and it's unrealistic to expect that it always will be. I can get on with enjoying life, instead of harbouring disturbing thoughts of revenge.

(**Note:** For other examples of irrational beliefs see Chapter 19.)

interpretation of the facts. By contrast with an assertive statement, an aggressive statement would be one that began with the word "you", and implied blame. For example, I could say: "You are very rude because you deliberately try to annoy me by interrupting me." Such a statement implies blame, makes an unjustified interpretation, and is likely to lead to an argument.

Another good way of making an assertive statement is to make a request which might lead to some common agreement. For example, I might say, "Would you mind waiting until I've finished what I'm saying? If you do that, I'll feel heard and will be more receptive to what you have to say."

The goal of making assertive statements is to get a positive outcome. After making an assertive statement, the speaker needs to listen carefully to what the other person says in reply, with the intention of hearing and understanding his point of view, rather than with the intention of disputing what he says.

THE USE OF ROLE-PLAYING

A good way of helping a client to practise anger control is by role-playing in front of a video camera. By video recording and role-playing a real situation which recently made the client angry, the client is able to see how other people perceive him. The client can gain if he role-plays both himself and the other person. He will need to continually change position and role to do this. A review of the video recording enables the client to see how tempers become inflamed. The counsellor can then coach the client in the anger control methods described, and in particular can teach him how to make assertive rather than aggressive statements.

Remember that very angry clients may be dangerous. As a new counsellor you need to be conscious of the need to consult your supervisor and refer clients to other more experienced and qualified counsellors when necessary. Do not attempt to do what you are not properly trained to do yourself.

LEARNING SUMMARY

- Refer potentially violent clients to experienced professionals.

- Encourage clients to direct anger to an imagined appropriate target person on an empty chair.

- Encourage the client to verbalise his anger.

- Teach relaxation.

- Teach the client to use the process described by the "anger control flow chart" (Figure 29.1) starting with the recognition of physiological cues.

- Teach the client how to replace irrational beliefs by positive self-talk, how to be assertive, listen to others, and to look for solutions rather than to try to win.

FURTHER READING

Clarkson, P., *Gestalt Counselling in Action*. London: Sage, 1989
Feindler, E. L. and Ecton, R. B., *Adolescent Anger Control: Cognitive Behavioral Techniques*. New York: Pergamon, 1986

Goldstein, A. P. and Keller, H. R., *Aggressive Behaviour: Assessment and Intervention*. New York: Pergamon, 1987

O'Leary, E., *Gestalt Therapy, Theory, Practice and Research*. London: Chapman & Hall, 1992

30 Counselling the depressed client

When do you get depressed?

Why do you get depressed?

We all get depressed from time to time. Being depressed some of the time is a normal human condition and as counsellors we are sure to be working regularly with clients who are depressed. Depression only becomes a serious problem when it is either very deep or very prolonged. It is then dangerous and requires specialist treatment, so be aware of this and refer for appropriate professional help when necessary.

There can be many reasons for depression. Some people become depressed as a consequence of what they see as overwhelming pressure in their lives. Others are depressed as a direct result of sickness. People who are unable to meet their own expectations of themselves are usually depressed. Then there are those people whose depression is due to their inability to accept that other people do not live up to their expectations. There are people who are depressed because they are grieving as a consequence of loss, and my guess is that you can think of a range of other circumstances which are likely to produce depression.

It is also important to recognise that there may be organic reasons for depression. Problems with body chemistry, organic problems in the brain and other medical conditions can cause depression.

Use of the normal counselling processes

With many clients the normal counselling processes previously described will produce changes in emotional feelings and thought patterns so that depression lifts. Why then am I writing a special chapter on depression if the normal counselling processes are usually sufficient? I am doing this because for some people suffering from prolonged depression a heavy emphasis on the reflective counselling techniques described in the early chapters of this book will not be useful, and may even have a detrimental effect. This is particularly so in cases where the depression does not seem to be related to recent or specific causes.

Generally, when depression can be directly related to the client's personal life and can be attributed to specific life events, personal situations, or identifiable crises, it is appropriate to use the counselling techniques previously described. While doing this, it is useful to remember that depression can often be understood in terms of "blocked anger".

Depression as blocked anger

When a person suppresses or is unable to recognise anger towards someone else, it is quite likely that the person concerned will become depressed.

Can you imagine yourself being very angry with someone but being unable to express that anger? You might be unable to give vent to your anger for a variety of reasons. Maybe you care so much about the person who is the target of your anger that you do not want to hurt him by expressing your anger. Perhaps you recognise that really your anger is unjustified, although real. Possibly you have been taught not to blame others or not to express angry feelings. After all, how many times do parents say to children, "Don't be angry"? Sometimes we parents do this at times when it is appropriate for our children to be angry, and by doing so we encourage our children to block or suppress their legitimate feelings with inevitable negative consequences for themselves.

How are you going to feel if you suppress angry feelings? Probably frustrated. If you are not able to deal with your frustration by letting that anger out, then you are likely to experience feelings of helplessness and depression.

EXPLORING THE POSSIBILITY OF BLOCKED ANGER

During the counselling process it is therefore sensible to confront a depressed client with the possibility of anger existing below the surface of his depression. A variety of counsellor responses can be used for raising awareness of underlying anger. Below are some examples:

- "When you think about what has happened to you, who are you most angry with?"
- "If you weren't depressed, who would you be angry with?"
- "If instead of feeling depressed you felt angry, what would that anger be about?"

Sometimes, the client's response to one of these questions will be to deny that he is angry with anyone or anything, and this may be true. However, it may be that he is unable to get in touch with his anger, if it exists, or that for some reason he doesn't want to own it. If a counsellor suspects that anger is blocked then it may be useful to give the client a message that implies that it is OK to be angry in such a situation as his. A counsellor might say: "If I had experienced what you have experienced I think that I would feel very angry." This may enable the client to recognise and access anger. If it does, then the empty chair technique described in Chapter 29 can be used so that the client is allowed to express his anger verbally in the safety of the counselling environment. Be careful, however, to help your client to recognise appropriate and inappropriate ways of expressing anger.

Sometimes people who have learnt to disown angry feelings will tell you that they are not angry, but instead are just frustrated. There is a thin dividing line between frustration and anger. If a client is frustrated, the approach used for the expression of anger may be equally appropriate in dealing with the frustration.

Often when a depressed client expresses anger, there will be a change in his demeanour with depressed lethargy being replaced by an energised state in which the person becomes more active and looks more in control.

People suffering from depression due to the loss of a relationship are often angry with the person who has walked out of their lives. Appropriate expression of that anger in the therapeutic environment may enable them to deal with it in a constructive way. However, remember that some people have the potential to be dangerous to others (see Chapter 29). These people need to learn to control their anger and should be referred for appropriate professional help for the protection of others and yourself.

Clients who need referral

Counsellors need to be able to identify those clients who need referral for specialist counselling and for medical or psychiatric assessment and treatment. Included in this group are:

- people who are so depressed that they are a danger to themselves or others;
- people who are unable to function satisfactorily in their daily lives due to depression;
- people who have been depressed for long periods; and
- people who have no clearly identifiable cause for their depression.

If you are in doubt regarding referral to a suitable professional then I suggest that you talk with your supervisor.

Regardless of the need for referral in cases such as those described above, counsellors working in crisis counselling agencies will frequently become involved in counselling chronically depressed clients. Many of these may be either unwilling to seek specialist treatment or are engaged in long-term psychiatric treatment with little positive effect. I believe that it is appropriate for such people to talk to counsellors from time to time, provided that any other professionals involved are comfortable with that. Certainly, counselling by a skilled counsellor will, at the very least, enable the client to feel that someone cares enough to listen, and there may be other beneficial effects.

Counselling the chronically depressed

When counsellors are working with clients experiencing long-term depression, the effect of continually reflecting back depressed feelings is likely to do little more than to confirm to the client that he is hopelessly and chronically depressed and is beyond help. To do such a thing is clearly destructive! In dealing with such clients we therefore need to limit our use of reflection and to use a different emphasis in our counselling. This does not mean that we should discard our ideas about the counselling relationship or forget the basic micro-skills. We need all that has previously been learnt, but with a change in emphasis.

Refer to the "Process of a counselling session" chart (Figure 24.1, Chapter 24). The difference in dealing with chronically depressed clients is that we need to move forward more quickly and decisively from active listening and problem identification and clarification into the attitude change, options and action stages (see the right-hand side of the chart). The counsellor needs to be more active and confronting. Rather than accompanying the client on a journey down into his depression, invite the client to join you on a journey of exploration with some limited but positive goals.

Start off by attending carefully to the client and allow the counselling relationship to develop, using active listening as you would with any client. However, once you have reflected back the client's feelings of depression and believe that your client knows that he has been heard and understood, then do not continue to reflect that depression, although at times you may need to refer to it as something to be dealt with, rather like a piece of baggage that needs to be put away from time to time.

Counselling goals for the chronically depressed

When counselling someone who is chronically depressed make a decision about what are realistic counselling goals and what are unrealistic goals. As a new counsellor I believed that it should be possible, with skill, to help every person who is chronically depressed to feel better. Unfortunately I now believe this to be unrealistic. However, if counsellors choose suitable goals many people who are chronically depressed can be helped to enjoy a better quality of life. You might like to try to think of some realistic goals yourself before reading my suggestions as listed below.

- To help the client to identify what makes him feel better and what makes him feel worse.
- To help the client to recognise that he has some choice with regard to the here and now. For example, he could choose to do what makes him feel better or what makes him feel worse. He could choose to sit around and do nothing, or he could choose to do something active.
- To encourage the client to focus his mind on what he is actively doing instead of focussing on his depression.
- To enable the client to take action.
- To enable the client to make a decision to seek appropriate specialist or psychiatric help.
- To enable the client to come to a decision with regard to one of the practical problems in his life.
- To help the client to challenge a self-destructive belief which is making him feel worse.
- To help that client feel a sense of importance because you are listening to him. (Note that a depressed client will often deny that his counsellor cares because there is a clear limit to your caring. However, you do care enough to listen and you can tell your client that. Be specific though. A statement such as "I care about you" is likely to be challenged, whereas a statement such as "I care about you enough to want to listen to you" can't be sensibly challenged.)
- To be able to give the client a positive message about himself at the end of the counselling session. For example: "I'm impressed by the way you were

able to clearly identify what makes you feel better and what makes you feel worse."

If you decide that the goals described above might be too difficult to achieve, you could set an easier goal such as:

- My goal will be to listen to this person so that for a time he is not alone but will have my company. (In this case, you are really offering company rather than counselling so you may end up chatting together rather than using counselling skills.)

Even if the previous goals listed are not attainable, this last goal is definitely achievable and therefore realistic. If you decide to try to achieve one of the earlier goals mentioned, I suggest that you set one goal only because it will be hard for someone who is deeply depressed to find the motivation required to make choices and take action. The nature of depression leads to loss of motivation and consequent inactivity. Unfortunately inactivity reinforces depression which makes it hard for the person concerned to make changes.

Using a different approach

If you are to achieve a selected goal, once you have secured a warm and trusting relationship with the client by using active listening and problem identification, you will need to break the rules you have previously learnt. You will need to take control of the direction of the counselling intervention rather than walking alongside the client. You may also need to temporarily change your counselling style so that you are more confronting, but in a friendly, caring and non-threatening way. As explained, people who are chronically depressed lose their motivation and consequently find it hard to change. They find it hard to identify ways to reduce their pain. However, by confronting with care you may enable a client to explore options and take some positive action.

Encouraging action

It can be useful for a client to be able to recognise any behaviours and situations that make her feel less depressed. If she can discover what she needs to do or where she needs to go in order to feel less depressed, she may be able to escape from the intensity of her depression for a time. A good approach is to ask the client: "Was there ever a time when you weren't depressed?" Most people can identify some times in their lives when they enjoyed themselves. If you can find out when those times were for your client, then you may be able to help her discover some way of partially regaining some pleasant experiences.

Remember how difficult it will be for your client to think positively. When we are depressed we all tend to think negatively so don't be too optimistic yourself or you might set yourself up for failure. For example your client might say something like: "I was only happy while Judith was alive. She's dead now and so my life is meaningless." If this were to happen then you would need to use your ingenuity to try to discover what it was that Judith did, apart from being present, that helped your client to feel good. The question, "What sort of things did you do when Judith was around?" might lead to the answer, "We used to go for long walks in the bush". You could then explore whether, at the present time, a long walk in the bush would be more or less depressing than not going for a walk.

The question, "Would that be more or less depressing than doing what you are doing now?", is a smart way of avoiding a, "Yes but …", answer. Even so, you might get the answer: "Yes, but I would still be depressed". You can agree with your client: "Yes, you would still be depressed but would you be more depressed or less depressed?" Smile to yourself if you get the answer, "I'd be just the same, miserably depressed", and change to a less ambitious goal for the session, but do not give up. Remember that this person is in pain and deserves respect and help.

THE USE OF ACTIVITY
Research over many years has shown that generally people who suffer from depression tend to be less depressed when they are active. This is why occupational therapy is used in psychiatric settings to help the seriously depressed. Even a simple action such as going to have a shower or take a bath can be a useful activity which might temporarily ease the depressed feeling.

Setting time limits

There may be limited value in talking for lengthy periods with people who are chronically depressed. Short interventions tend to be more useful, particularly if they encourage the client to undertake some activity. To encourage activity remember to reward clients with praise when they do engage in meaningful activity, and when they succeed, for a time, in feeling less depressed.

Because depressed people are often bored and preoccupied with negative thoughts, they may wish to talk at length without purpose and to travel the same road, in their thoughts, over and over again. Because of these tendencies counsellors may need to use good termination skills. A useful way to terminate a counselling session is for the counsellor to be directive in suggesting that the client go to perform some task. For example, the counsellor may say: "I would like to finish our conversation now and suggest that you might like to go home and prepare a meal for yourself right away. Next time we meet I would like you to tell me whether you felt more or less depressed when you made and ate the meal." Once again, the suggestion is action oriented and includes the goal of identifying the usefulness of activity.

Debriefing

Counsellors who work with clients who are depressed, if they join empathically with their clients, will pick up negative and depressed feelings themselves. It is therefore important to debrief and to look after your own needs (see Chapter 34).

LEARNING SUMMARY

- Normal people suffer from depression.

- Sometimes depression results from "blocked anger".

- Depression calls for specialist treatment when it is either very deep or prolonged.

- For many depressed clients the normal counselling processes are recommended.

- For chronically depressed clients:

  - continual reflection of feelings can be counter-productive;

  - set goals for the session and take control of the counselling process;

  - be confronting;

  - encourage activity; and

  - keep counselling sessions short and energised.

FURTHER READING

Braiker, H. B., *Getting Up When You're Feeling Down*. New York: Pocket Books, 1988

Conroy, D. L., *Out of the Nightmare: Recovery from Depression and Suicidal Pain*. New York: Liberty, 1991

Gilbert, P., *Counselling for Depression*. London: Sage, 1992

Craig, K. D., *Anxiety and Depression in Adults and Children*. Thousand Oaks: Sage, 1995

31 Grief and loss counselling

A high proportion of client problems are concerned with relationships. Relationship problems fall into four major categories. These are:

1. dysfunctional relationships;
2. failure to form meaningful relationships;
3. lost relationships through death and separation;
4. negotiating the normal and/or developmental challenges and changes in relationships.

Loss associated with relationships

In each of the categories listed above issues of loss and grief may arise. In dysfunctional relationships there is a loss of expectation that these relationships will be functional and harmonious. People who are unable to form meaningful relationships may have to cope with the loss of their expectations. When couple relationships break up both people need to adjust to the loss of a partner. In the case of married couples there is also the loss of marital status and the loss of the expectation that marriage is for life. If children are involved, then each parent has a loss of support from his or her spouse in the day-to-day rearing of the children, and usually one parent has a significant loss of contact with the children and suffers a feeling that the parental role is greatly diminished.

When relationships are functioning normally new situations will arise from time to time and changes will naturally occur due to changes in roles and developmental stages of the relationship. There is therefore a need to confront the challenges incurred by change, and change often involves loss.

Other losses

Counsellors also hear about many other types of loss, for example the loss of a limb, loss of an internal part of the body, loss of mental functioning due to ageing or brain damage, loss of a job, loss of a home, or loss of self-respect.

Helping a person who is grieving

In order to be able to maximally help people who are grieving over a loss, counsellors need to understand the process of grieving. There are many books on loss and grief counselling. A selected list of these is provided at the end of this chapter for those who wish to do further reading on the subject.

When counselling somebody who has suffered a loss, or who is grieving, it is important to be able to reassure him that the feelings he is experiencing are normal for a person who is grieving, and that it is normal to take time to grieve.

One of the most important counselling interventions for me, as a client, occurred when a counsellor disclosed to me that it had taken him over two years to grieve over a lost relationship. By telling me that, he helped me to feel OK, instead of believing that I was going crazy because I could not push the thoughts about a similar loss out of my mind. This example demonstrates the usefulness of appropriate counsellor self-disclosure.

RESTRICTING COUNSELLOR SELF-DISCLOSURE

Although at times self-disclosure is appropriate, it should be used sparingly, and never solely to satisfy the counsellor's needs. Before self-disclosing, examine what is going on within yourself and make a decision about whether your motive is to satisfy your own needs or is genuinely to help the client. Where self-disclosure is used more than occasionally, its impact is lost, and the counsellor is certainly putting his needs before those of the client.

Disclosure of information about other counsellors or other people is unethical and should never occur in the counselling process. Additionally, it can be most unhelpful for telephone counsellors to self-disclose to regular callers (see Chapter 27) who may gather and distort information about a counselling team to the detriment of both the counselling process and the agency concerned.

COUNSELLING SKILLS TO USE

When a client is grieving, all the micro-skills discussed in Part II can be used in a counselling process as described in Part III to allow the client to verbalise thoughts and feelings, to experience rather than suppress pain, and to generally explore whatever is happening within himself as he experiences his loss. However, it is useful for a counsellor to have an understanding of the process of grieving. This understanding will enable a counsellor to recognise and appreciate the client's experience more fully so that an empathic counselling relationship can be established and maintained.

The stages of grief

People tend to go through a number of stages in the grieving process. For some people these stages follow a particular sequence, but for other people the stages overlap or occur in a different order. Everyone is unique and grieves in a uniquely personal way, so do not try to fit a predetermined grieving pattern onto your client. However, if you know what the commonly experienced stages in the grieving process are, then you will be better equipped to deal with the grieving person. You will be able to explain to your client that his experiences are not strange, or unusual, but are normal for someone who is grieving.

The most important stages of grief in the usual sequence are:

- shock
- denial
- emotional, psychological and physical symptoms

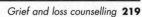

- depression
- guilt
- anger
- idealisation
- realism
- acceptance
- readjustment
- personal growth

If a person is unable to work through the stages of grief, then he is likely to be stuck in a trough of hopelessness and despair. He may become neurotically obsessed by his loss, and become deeply depressed and possibly suicidal. The following paragraphs explain the stages of grief in more detail.

SHOCK

Usually, the first stage of grief is shock. This may be particularly severe in cases of sudden loss, or where a person has not prepared himself adequately for an expected loss. The person almost seems to stop functioning, is numb, in a daze, and is incapable of doing anything constructive.

DENIAL

Along with shock, and following on from shock, comes denial. The grieving person can't believe that what is happening to him is really true.

The denial process can be prolonged for people who separate from a living partner. Very often a rejected partner will deny that the relationship is over, even though the other partner is clearly saying: "It's finished and I'm not ever going to come back to you." This is hard to deal with because the grieving person needs to have time to move through the denial stage. Perhaps the most useful approach is to reflect back the client's expectation that his partner may return, and to add to this concrete statements of fact that seem to indicate the opposite. The counsellor might say, for example: "I get the strong impression from you that you believe that your partner will come back to you. I also notice that she said to you that she would not do that, and that she has rejected all your approaches to her since she left. Do you think that it's possible that she may not come back?" This tentative statement and question enables the client to stay in denial if he needs to do that for a while longer, or to move forward. When the client is starting to accept the possibility that the loss may be permanent, it may then be useful to let him know that denial is a normal part of grieving. By doing this he can feel OK about his difficulty in not wanting to accept reality in its entirety.

People who are dying often grieve in anticipation of dying and such people sometimes have real problems with denial. When such a person is told that he is dying, he may try to convince himself that what his medical practitioner is telling him is not true. He may look for, and try, unorthodox methods to find a cure, and may start to bargain with God in an effort to get an extension on his life.

EMOTIONAL, PSYCHOLOGICAL AND PHYSICAL SYMPTOMS

Grieving people experience feelings of depression, despair, hopelessness and worthlessness. Very often they will exhibit symptoms such as insomnia, inability to concentrate, loss of appetite and physical ill-health. This is normal. There is little that the client can do but accept that such symptoms will pass with time as the painfulness of grief diminishes. Naturally if such symptoms are severe or persist, the client should consult with a medical practitioner.

GUILT

Guilt often occurs in the grieving person. A counsellor will frequently hear a client say how guilty he feels because he didn't tell the deceased how much he loved her, didn't tell her how much he cared for her, didn't apologise for something he had done wrong, or didn't make peace over an issue where there had been a disagreement. If your clients describe such feelings, allow them to fully explore them.

ANGER

Often after shock, denial, depression and guilt, anger follows. Remember though, that the stages often overlap, and sometimes a person will move forward from one stage and then go back to an earlier stage.

In the case of a person who is dying, anger may be directed at the medical practitioners involved. The client may feel that he hasn't had satisfactory medical treatment. Maybe he will believe that his illness was diagnosed too late and consequently that it's the doctor's fault that death is inevitable. Similarly, a person who has lost a loved one through illness may blame the medical practitioners who treated the deceased before his death. Additionally, a bereaved person may well experience anger towards the person who has died. He may feel that the deceased person "had no right to die" and has hurt him by leaving him alone to cope in the world. This may be especially so in cases where the deceased has committed suicide.

Often it is hard for a client to accept that he is capable of being angry towards somebody he loved and who has died. This is especially so for children who have lost a parent through death, and not had adequate counselling. They invariably feel guilty and confused by their anger and resentment towards the deceased parent. Without counselling, these feelings may endure for years.

People whose partners have rejected them often become very angry and, while being angry, desperately want to get back into the relationship. They inevitably make it hard for themselves to do this and probably spoil their chances of reconciliation because while saying, "I love you and I want to be back in a relationship with you", they may also be experiencing anger, and are likely to express it in some way. Thus they give mixed messages to their partner because they are simultaneously giving "please come back" messages and angry messages. The anger, of course, can easily be understood as part of the process of grieving.

Sometimes a person who has Christian beliefs and is grieving will feel angry with God, and will blame God for the loss that has occurred. For deeply religious people this may cause feelings of extreme guilt. When counselling such people a counsellor can explain that it is normal to experience anger in grief, and that God is quite capable of accepting, forgiving and loving someone who is angry with Him. When counselling clients who have faith in other religions similar issues may arise. Here it is important for the counsellor to gain sufficient understanding of the client's beliefs to be helpful.

IDEALISATION

Idealisation often follows the angry stage of grieving. It is very common for people who have suffered loss through death or separation to idealise the lost partner. The grieving person temporarily forgets any faults or negative characteristics of the deceased and remembers only an ideal person. He remembers everything positive that the deceased did and convinces himself that he loved her totally, and didn't have any negative feelings towards her. This is idealisation, and once again it is normal. It takes time for a person to move through idealisation and the counsellor needs to be careful not to try to move the client forward too quickly, but rather to let the grieving process occur naturally. When it is appropriate, ask tentatively whether the lost person had any bad points, any faults, or whether she sometimes made mistakes. Slowly the realisation will dawn that yes, there were opposite polarities in the deceased person. She was a real person, a human being with both strengths and weaknesses.

ACCEPTANCE, READJUSTMENT AND PERSONAL GROWTH

The client will hopefully, in time, come to terms with his grief and start to accept the reality of his loss. He will start to be more realistic about the person he has lost, and to accept his loss as a permanent reality. He is then free to move forward and to create a new life for himself as an individual. This may be rather scary for some clients, particularly for those who were heavily dependent on the lost relationship. Now the client needs to be active rather than passive, to try new experiences and thus to experience personal growth. New experiences, by their very nature, involve some degree of risk, and so may understandably cause the client to be apprehensive. Taking risks can be frightening and can also be exciting. Reframing "risk taking" as "exciting" may be helpful.

Allowing the grieving process to occur

Finally, do not try to calm or soothe the grieving person. Do not try to cheer him up or help him to contain his fears. Instead, help him to express his emotions freely, to cry if he wishes, and to grieve fully. It is only when grief endures for an excessively long period that it becomes maladaptive. In such cases, clearly professional help from an experienced counsellor, psychologist or psychiatrist is required. Once again, know the limits of your own competence, and refer clients on to others more qualified and experienced than yourself when appropriate.

LEARNING SUMMARY

- People grieve for lost expectations, relationships, bodily functions, jobs and losses of most kinds.

- Normal stages of grief include shock, denial, psychological and somatic symptoms, depression, guilt, anger, idealisation, realism, acceptance, readjustment, and personal growth.

- It's usually a mistake to try to calm or soothe a grieving person. Encouraging free expression of emotions is more therapeutic.

FURTHER READING

al Qadhi, S., *Managing Death and Bereavement: a Framework for Caring Organisations*. Bristol: Policy Press, 1996

Attig, T., *How We Grieve: Relearning the World*. Oxford: Oxford University Press, 1996

Bright, R., *Grief and Powerlessness: Helping People Regain Control of Their Lives*. London: Jessica Kingsley, 1996

Corr, C. A., Nabe, C. M. and Corr, D. M., *Death and Dying, Life and Living*. Pacific Grove: Brooks/Cole, 1997

Humphrey, G. M. and Zimpfer, D. G., *Counselling for Grief and Bereavement*. London: Sage, 1996

32 Counselling the suicidal client

My initial training as a counsellor was with a crisis telephone counselling agency. As a new telephone counsellor, my greatest fear was that I might get a call from a suicidal person. Later, I continued to be anxious when counselling suicidal clients and believe that for many counsellors such counselling is stressful. However, hotline counselling services frequently get calls from people who are contemplating suicide and sometimes such callers have already overdosed on prescribed pills before ringing for help.

Ethical issues

There are ethical issues involved when dealing with suicidal people, and before choosing strategies that are acceptable for you, you will need to clarify your own values with regard to suicide. As a counsellor, it is desirable that, if possible, you do not impose your own values on the client, that you be congruent and genuine, and that you do whatever is necessary to satisfy your own conscience. In addition, you need to be aware of any legal obligations and the legal implications of your actions. Remember that you have a duty of care for the client and that you need to respect the policies of the agency for which you work. If there are internal conflicts for you when dealing with suicidal clients, then you need to resolve these for both your own and the client's well-being.

Does a person have the right to take her own life if she chooses to do so? Your answer to this question may differ from mine, and our answers may differ from the client's. I suggest that you discuss this question in depth with your training group if you are in one, or with your supervisor, so that you have a clear idea of your own attitudes and beliefs regarding suicide and of your supervisor's expectations. You will then be better equipped to deal with the suicidal client.

Some counsellors believe that a person has the right to kill herself if, after careful consideration, she chooses to do so. Others strongly oppose this view and believe that firm intervention is justifiable and necessary to prevent suicide from occurring. Many counsellors believe that a person who is contemplating suicide may be temporarily emotionally disturbed and not capable of making a rational decision at that time. This belief is reinforced by experiences with clients who were suicidal and then later have thanked the counsellor, because they have found new meaning and satisfaction in their lives. Consequently, some counsellors see the need for firm intervention, involuntary hospitalisation, and subsequent psychiatric treatment where other options fail. Clearly, there are duty of care issues involved when making the relevant decisions. Whatever your view, suicide involves a one-way journey and suicidal clients need to be taken seriously. Remember that people who repeatedly make suicide attempts often succeed in killing themselves eventually. Their cry for help needs to be heard before it is too late.

Reasons for contemplating suicide

People who are considering suicide broadly fall into three categories although these overlap to some extent.

The first category comprises people whose quality of life is terrible, and who see little or no possibility for improvement. Included in this category are people who are chronically ill, in chronic pain, are seriously disabled, or are in extreme poverty with little possibility of changing their situations. Such people are often severely depressed and are seriously at risk of killing themselves because they can see little reason for living. This is particularly so if they are alone and do not have adequate social support systems.

The second category includes people who have experienced a recent trauma. These people are very much at risk around their time of crisis. Included in this category are people who have suffered losses such as those described in Chapter 31.

The third category comprises people who use suicidal talk or suicidal behaviour as a last resort in an attempt to get others to hear or respond to their pain. Sometimes their goal is to manipulate the behaviour of others. They are still genuinely at risk, but their motivation is different. They often have considerable ambivalence towards dying and may not really want to die. Some people in this category are openly manipulative and, for example, might say to a spouse who has left them: "Come back to me or I will kill myself."

Here is a summary of possible reasons why a person might contemplate or talk about the possibility of killing herself:

1. Because she despairs of her situation and is unable to see an alternative solution to her problems which seem to her to be unsolvable, intolerable and inescapable.
2. Because she is emotionally disturbed, is afraid that she may kill herself, and wants to be stopped.
3. To make a statement.
4. As a way of hurting others; an ultimate expression of anger.
5. To make a last-ditch effort to draw attention to her seemingly impossible situation, when other methods have failed.
6. To manipulate someone else by threatening suicide.
7. Because she has positively decided to kill herself, wants to do it, and wants other people to understand the reasons for her proposed action.
8. To be in contact with another human being, prior to, or while, dying.
9. To say "Goodbye", as preparation for death.

Assessment of risk of suicide

Any client who says that life is not worth living may be at some level of risk. However, many people who have no intention of killing themselves experience times when they despair and start to question the value of their lives. A difficulty for counsellors is the determination of the level of risk for a particular client. It is here that experience can be helpful in estimating level of risk, in deciding whether action needs to be taken or not, and in choosing the action to take if action is needed.

There are some factors which are commonly considered in the relevant literature to be useful in determining level of risk (see the further reading suggested at the end of this chapter). A number of risk factors will now be discussed.

GENDER AND ETHNICITY

Although women attempt suicide more often then men, males are associated with higher risk. This is because males are more often successful in completing suicide than females. In particular Aboriginal males are associated with high risk.

AGE

Suicide is more likely to occur in the young and old, with the risk being higher in people up to the age of 18 years and above 45.

INTENSE AND/OR FREQUENT THOUGHTS OF SUICIDE

Whenever a person thinks of suicide it is wise to assume that there is some level of risk. However, if the thoughts are persistent and/or strong with little ambivalence, risk is increased.

WARNING SIGNALS

People who commit suicide have often given out warning signals over a period of time. Unfortunately sometimes these are disregarded because they may have been given many times and be seen incorrectly as threats which will not be carried out.

HAVING A SUICIDE PLAN

If a realistic plan for committing suicide has been developed, then clearly the person has moved beyond vague thoughts that life is not worth living and there is a risk that the plan may be carried out.

CHOICE OF A LETHAL METHOD

Some methods of committing suicide are more likely to reach completion than others because they are quick and/or provide little opportunity for withdrawal if the person concerned has a change of mind as death approaches. Examples are when a person uses a gun or jumps off a high building.

AVAILABILITY OF METHOD

Risk is higher if the person already has the means to carry out the plan. For example if a person has a loaded gun, or enough pills to cause death, then the plan may be carried out.

DIFFICULTY OF RESCUE
Risk is increased in cases where it would be difficult for others to intervene and prevent the suicide attempt. Examples are where a person is in an isolated place or when the location is unknown or when someone has climbed a structure, making it difficult for others to follow.

BEING ALONE AND HAVING LACK OF SUPPORT
People who are alone, single, or separated, and believe that no one cares for them are vulnerable to depression and suicidal thoughts and action. It may also be easier for them to carry out a suicidal plan without interference.

PREVIOUS ATTEMPTS
Previous attempts are an indication of increased risk. This is particularly so if the attempts have been frequent, are recent, and have been serious.

A FRIEND OR FAMILY MEMBER HAS DIED OR SUICIDED
Risk of suicide is increased where a family member, close friend, colleague or peer, suicided. Additionally there may be risk where a loved one or pet has died.

LISTENING TO SONGS ABOUT DEATH
Some people, particularly the younger members of society, listen obsessively to songs about death, dying, and suicide. This increases risk.

DEPRESSION
People who are depressed, feel hopeless, helpless, or in despair are at risk. This is particularly so with severe depression where there may be symptoms such as loss of sleep, or an eating disturbance.

PSYCHIATRIC HISTORY
Psychiatric illness or history is another indication of increased risk.

LOSS OF RATIONAL THINKING
Loss of rational thinking can occur for a variety of reasons. People who have been traumatised, are under the influence of alcohol or drugs, are suffering from dementia, or have a psychiatric disorder may not be capable of thinking rationally. They therefore present increased risk and there are clear duties of care for the counsellor.

UNEXPLAINED IMPROVEMENT
Someone who has been exhibiting severely depressed feelings with suicidal thoughts and then suddenly changes to display a calmness and sense of satisfaction for no recognisable reason may be a very high risk. The person may have completed preparations for suicide and have a sense of relief at the thought of impending relief from ongoing pain. By misleading the counsellor into thinking that everything is now OK, they can effectively mislead the counsellor so that preventative action is not taken.

GIVING AWAY POSSESSIONS AND FINALISING AFFAIRS

Behaviours such as giving away personal possessions, making a new will or terminating a lease, may be indication that the person is preparing for suicide and at high risk.

MEDICAL PROBLEMS

Medical problems which severely interfere with quality of life, are painful or life threatening increase the risk of suicide. Chronic illness with little perceived hope of a cure or respite may increase a person's desire to terminate life. Here, there are both values and duty of care issues, as some people believe that euthanasia is morally justifiable while others disagree.

SUBSTANCE ABUSE

Excessive use of alcohol or drugs, both illegal and legally prescribed, raises the suicide risk. Certainly, alcohol or other substance abuse is associated with completed suicides.

RELATIONSHIP PROBLEMS

People who believe that they are locked in to highly dysfunctional relationships and cannot leave are at increased risk. Similarly, there may be risks for people whose relationships are breaking up, who are separating or separated, and for those who are going through the process of divorce. When relationships change through, for example remarriage, moving into a new step-family, having a new child in the family, or when children leave the family, there may be an increased risk. Additionally, some people worry excessively and start to despair when a family member is sick or not coping.

TRAUMA, LOSS, OR SIGNIFICANT LIFE CHANGING EVENTS

Suicidal ideation may occur as a consequence of significant traumas. For example, if a person's home or business is destroyed by fire, the trauma may push that person into deep depression and lead to suicidal thoughts and behaviour.

CHANGES IN LIFESTYLE AND/OR ROUTINE

Many people find it difficult to adjust to changes in their lifestyle or routine, so times of change can precipitate suicidal thoughts and increased risk. Examples are when a person changes job, school, or their place of residence. This may be particularly relevant when a person moves to a new locality and may lose access to long-term friends.

FINANCIAL PROBLEMS

Issues involving poverty, unemployment and financial difficulties, where the person concerned is depressed and feeling helpless to change the situation, lead to an increased risk. Important examples are bankruptcy and cases where a person loses a business or home.

TABLE 32.1 Assessment of suicide risk

Risk factors—tick boxes where risk is indicated

☐ Gender
☐ Age
☐ Ethnic background

☐ Intense and/or frequent
thoughts of suicide
☐ Warning signals given out over
a period of time
☐ Has a suicide plan
☐ Choice of a lethal method
☐ Availability of method
☐ Difficulty of rescue
☐ Is isolated or alone
☐ Lack of support

☐ Previous suicide attempts
☐ A friend, peer, colleague or
family member has suicided
☐ Listening obsessively to songs
about death, dying, or suicide
☐ Death of loved one, friend or pet

☐ Depression
☐ Psychiatric illness or history
☐ Loss of rational thinking

☐ Unexplained improvement
☐ Giving away possessions
☐ Finalising affairs

☐ Relationship highly dysfunctional
☐ Relationship break up,
separation, or divorce
☐ Relationship changes—
remarriage, new step-family,
addition of new child, children
leaving family
☐ Relationship worries—fear of
losing a family member or partner or that someone is not coping

☐ Medical problems

☐ Alcohol and/or drug abuse

☐ Significant life changing events
☐ Change in lifestyle and/or
routine
☐ Change in job, school or house
locality

☐ Financial problems
☐ Socioeconomic situation

☐ Trauma
☐ Abuse or perceived abuse—
emotional, physical, sexual or
social abuse in the past or
present

☐ Loss of employment or
employment opportunities
☐ Loss of business, home or
possessions
☐ Loss of self-esteem—feeling a
failure at work or
academically—or belief that
others have been let down
☐ Loss of role

☐ Other factors not listed

_____

_____

_____

_____

_____

_____

TRAUMA AND ABUSE

Traumatic events and the experience of abuse or perceived abuse, both in the past and present, may contribute to suicide risk. This includes emotional, physical, sexual, and social abuse.

LOSS

All losses of importance contribute to suicide risk. Examples include lose of job, employment opportunities, business, home, possession, loss of self-esteem and loss of role. People who experience failure either at work or academically or believe that they have failed others are likely to suffer loss of self-esteem.

The risk factors which have been discussed are included in Table 32.1. This table may be photocopied for personal use and used as an aid in identifying risk factors when counselling clients with suicidal ideation. However, it must be remembered that there is not a precise formula for assessing risk because we human beings are each unique possessing our own individual qualities. All talk of suicide needs to be taken seriously with appropriate help sought where necessary.

Counselling strategies

Perhaps the biggest problem for a new counsellor in dealing with suicidal clients is the counsellor's own anxiety. Sometimes new counsellors try to deflect clients away from suicidal talk rather than encouraging them to bring their self-destructive thoughts out into the open and deal with them appropriately. Unfortunately, such avoidance of the issue may increase the likelihood of a suicide attempt.

BRING SUICIDAL THOUGHTS INTO THE OPEN

Whenever you are counselling a depressed or anxious client, look for the smallest clues that might suggest that the client is contemplating suicide. Clients are often reluctant to say, "I would like to kill myself". They tend, instead, to be less specific and to make statements such as "I don't enjoy life any more", or "I'm fed up with living". In such cases, be direct, and ask your client: "Are you thinking of killing yourself?" In this way, suicidal thoughts are brought out into the open and can be dealt with appropriately. Remember that most people are at some times in their lives ambivalent about wanting to live and that many consider the possibility of committing suicide before rejecting it.

DEAL WITH YOUR OWN FEELINGS

You will be a very unusual person indeed if your hair doesn't stand on end the first time that a client tells you that she intends to kill herself. Allow yourself to experience your feelings and then you will be able to decide what to do about them. One thing that you can do is to give yourself new messages, after discarding the irrational messages that may be contributing to your tension. Table 32.2 presents some typical irrational and alternative rational self-statements for the situation.

Table 32.2 Comparison between irrational and rational self-statements for counsellors dealing with suicidal clients

Irrational self-statement	Rational self-statement
I am personally responsible if this client kills herself.	Sadly, in the long term, no one can stop this client from killing herself if she firmly decides to do that. Ultimately it will be her choice.
I should stay with the client until she no longer has suicidal thoughts.	It's impossible for me to watch over the client 24 hours a day. In the long term she has to be responsible for herself. However, if I wish, and am able, I can take steps to arrange appropriate psychiatric supervision.
I have the power to change this person's mind if I am skilful enough. OR I must persuade this client not to kill herself.	I don't have the power to change someone else's mind. The most I can do is to help her explore the issues involved, and then take any other action available to me.
I'm not as well qualified as other counsellors.	I am me, with my skills and limitations. If I am able to refer this client on to someone more qualified I will, and in the meantime I'll do my best.
If I am incompetent I will be to blame for this person's death.	It's unrealistic for me to expect to be a perfect counsellor in such a stressful situation. I cannot take responsibility for her decision. I can only do what I am capable of doing.
I must live up to the client's expectations.	I do not need to live up to the client's expectations.
I can't cope.	I can cope provided that I set realistic expectations for myself.

Challenge your irrational self-statements, and if your feelings of tension don't subside then share them with the client. For example, you might say: "I feel really uptight because I know that you are thinking of killing yourself. I guess it must be really scary for you too." By bringing these feelings into the open, trust can be created. A genuine and open sharing is now possible, and it is likely that the counsellor's tension will diminish.

COUNSELLING SKILLS

The micro-skills which have previously been learnt, together with an appropriate counselling relationship, are the basic tools for dealing with a suicidal client. Concentrate on building the relationship and when trust has been established address the question of responsibility. The way you do this will depend on you yourself and your own value system. For myself, after I have established a good working relationship with the client I will talk with her about the responsibility of her life being, in the last resort, her own. I will explain caringly how sad it is for me to know that she is thinking about killing herself and will point out that in the long term, even though I might like to stop her, if she is seriously determined to kill herself then I will be unable to prevent her from doing so, because I can't be beside her for 24 hours each day (even if she is hospitalised for a while, she will eventually be released). I will continue by telling her that I am concerned for her safety and well-being and that it is important for me to understand fully how and why she feels the way she does. I believe that by taking this approach my client will understand that she herself is responsible for her life and is likely to feel as though I am joining with her rather than pulling against her.

FOCUS ON THE CLIENT'S AMBIVALENCE

For me, the biggest lesson in counselling suicidal clients was to discover that if I stopped continually giving myself the message that I was responsible for the client's decision, and instead focussed on the client's ambivalence—"Should I kill myself or not?"—then there was the maximum possible chance of change occurring in the client's thinking. Most, if not all, suicidal clients have some degree of ambivalence towards dying. After all, if a client was 100 per cent convinced that she wanted to kill herself, she probably wouldn't be talking to a counsellor, she would just kill herself. I believe that exploring the client's ambivalence is the key to the successful counselling of people who are contemplating suicide.

EXPLORING THE CLIENT'S OPTIONS

As explained in Chapter 21, when a person chooses between two alternatives she loses one of the options and may also have to pay a price for the chosen option. By choosing suicide, a person loses life, contact with others and the opportunity to communicate with others about her pain. In addition she loses hope, if she had any, for a better future. The cost of dying is likely to include fear of the unknown, and for some religious people fear of being punished for killing themselves.

By joining with the client, she is free to explore the "I want to die" part of herself with me walking alongside her in her exploration, rather than pulling her away from fully exploring her negative thoughts. We will later move on together to look at the opposite part of her that still wants to continue living, or at least has reservations about wanting to die.

Make your client aware of her ambivalence. Help her to look at the consequences, costs and payoffs of dying and of living. Try, if you can, to avoid directly pressuring the client to stay alive and instead help her to explore the options as fully as possible. In this way she may be able to work through her pain, and feel sufficiently valued to reconsider her decision.

AN ALTERNATIVE APPROACH

An alternative approach is to try to openly persuade the client that living is the best option. This approach is not my personal preference because it sets up a struggle between the client who is saying "I want to die" and the counsellor who is saying "I want you to live". There is then heavy pressure on the counsellor to convince the client of the rightness of living, and this may be difficult as the counsellor and client are in opposition rather than joining together. Even so, this approach can be successful with some clients. There is no universal "right way" to go. Every client is unique and so is every counsellor. Choose an approach that seems right for you and your client. If you concentrate on establishing and maintaining a good relationship then you are optimising your chances of success.

DEALING WITH DEPRESSION AND ANGER

Suicidal clients are usually in deep depression, and depression, as explained in Chapter 30, is often due to repressed anger. Very often suicidal clients are turning anger, which could be appropriately directed at others, inward and towards themselves. It may be useful to ask the question: "Who are you angry with?" If the client replies by saying "myself", you can agree that that is obvious and consistent with wanting to suicide. You might say: "You are so angry with yourself that you want to punish yourself by killing yourself." This reframe of suicide as self-punishment rather than escape may be useful in some cases in helping to produce change. You could also ask: "After yourself, who are you most angry with?" Then, if you can help the client to verbalise her anger and direct it away from herself and onto some other person or persons, her depression and suicidal thoughts may moderate.

LOOKING FOR THE TRIGGER

Another way of entering the client's world is to find out what triggered off the suicidal thoughts *today*. Very often a single event is the trigger and this trigger can sometimes give important clues about the client's intentions. For example, is the client's intention partly to punish someone who has angered or hurt her? If so, there may be better ways of achieving this.

Recognise your limitations

Don't forget that it is unrealistic, unfortunately, to expect that the client will necessarily decide to stay alive. Although you may be able, if you choose, to take short-term measures to ensure that she stays alive, ultimately and in the long term, if she is determined to kill herself, she is likely to succeed. However, as counselling progresses you will need to decide, in consultation with your supervisor, whether direct action to prevent suicide is warranted and necessary. This decision is a heavy one and is certain to be influenced by your own values and those of the agency that employs you. There are some cases where the decision to intervene is clear. It would, for example, be unethical and irresponsible to allow someone who was psychologically disturbed due to a temporary psychiatric condition, or due to a sudden trauma, to kill herself without determined and positive action being taken to stop her.

A suicidal client is likely to need ongoing psychotherapy from a skilled professional, so be prepared to refer appropriately. The eventual well-being of such a client depends on her being able to make significant changes to her thinking and way of living, and this is unlikely to be achieved in one counselling session.

LEARNING SUMMARY

- People who make repeated suicide attempts often succeed in killing themselves.

- Suicidal people include those who are locked into miserable lives, those who have recently experienced trauma, and those who are wanting to manipulate others.

- When counselling suicidal clients it is important to deal with your own feelings as a counsellor and challenge any irrational beliefs you may have.

- When counselling suicidal clients focus on the counselling relationship using normal micro-skills:

  - find out what triggered the suicidal thoughts;

  - bring the client's anger into focus;

  - hook into the client's ambivalence if that can be useful;

  - explore the client's options and particularly the costs of dying;

  - use a more direct confrontationalist approach if you think that it is more likely to be effective;

  - decide what direct action is warranted and necessary to prevent suicide;

  - finally, refer to suitable professionals for ongoing help.

FURTHER READING

Appleby, M. and Condonis, M., *Suicide Prevention: What to Look for, What to Do, Where to Go*. Narellan, Australia: ROSE Education Training and Consultancy, 1990

Bongar, B. (ed.), *Suicide: Guidelines for Assessment, Management and Treatment*. Oxford: Oxford University Press, 1992

Donnelly, J. (ed.), *Suicide: Right or Wrong?* New York: Promethus, 1990

Scheidman, N., Farberow, N. and Litman, R., *The Psychology of Suicide*. New Jersey: Aronson, 1994

Fremouw, W. J., de Perczel, M. and Ellis, T. E., *Suicide Risk: Assessment and Response Guidelines*. New York: Pergamon, 1990

Jenkins, R., Griffiths, S., Wylie, I., Hawton, K., Morgan, G. and Tylee, A. (eds), *The Prevention of Suicide. A Conference Organised by the Department of Health, Faculty of Public Health Medicine, Royal College of General Practitioners, and the Royal College of Psychiatrists*. London: HMSO, 1994

Pritchard, C., *Suicide—the Ultimate Rejection? A Psycho-Social Study*. Buckingham: Open University Press, 1995

33 Teaching clients to relax

Some clients who are very tense and anxious find that counselling alone is insufficient help. Sometimes it's advisable to refer such clients to a medical practitioner or psychiatrist for assessment so that appropriate medication can be prescribed, if necessary. However, for many clients considerable benefit can be achieved through the use of relaxation techniques.

Most clients find it easy to learn relaxation, enjoy relaxing, and can be encouraged to use it regularly. However, there are a minority of clients who find relaxation techniques quite threatening. Instead of becoming relaxed during a relaxation exercise, these people experience increased tension and anxiety. For some, this can be severe. Be careful therefore to give your clients permission to stop the relaxation exercise if they find it is stressful rather than relaxing. With such clients it may be useful to explore the stressful experience, if this is not too threatening, because it may well be related to other stressful experiences in their present or past lives.

Preferably, a room used for relaxation will be quiet and will have subdued rather than glaring lighting. It will be protected, as far as possible, from external noises such as phones ringing and also from the intrusion of others. It is not helpful to have someone open a door and walk in while a client is trying to relax!

There are many different ways of teaching relaxation. The following relaxation exercise is one that I use. If you wish to use it, read the following instructions to your client using a quiet, slow, monotonous tone of voice. Pause between each statement for a few seconds.

Relaxation exercise

Lie on the floor with your head on a cushion, your hands beside you, and your legs straight.
Move around until you feel comfortable.
Close your eyes.
You will probably enjoy this exercise and find it pleasurable, but if at any time you are feeling uncomfortable and want to stop you may either choose to lie quietly and ignore my voice, or you may speak up and tell me that you want to discontinue the exercise.
Notice where your body touches the floor.
Move yourself so that you are more comfortable.
Be aware of your whole body from head to toe and stretch any part of you that is uncomfortable.
Let your body press down on the floor.
Notice the floor pressing up on you.
It's a good feeling.

You are in contact with the ground and the ground is in contact with you.
Notice your breathing.
Allow yourself to breathe comfortably and naturally.
(Longer pause.)
We are going to go through a series of exercises during which you will relax
various parts of your body starting from the tips of your toes and finishing
at the top of your head.
For each set of muscles, I will suggest that you tighten those muscles while
breathing in deeply, and then relax them as you breathe out.
Whenever you remember, say to yourself the word "relax" as you breathe out.
In between relaxing each set of muscles, focus on your breathing again.
Breathe naturally and say "relax" silently to yourself as you breathe out each
time. By doing this you will gradually become more relaxed. If any intruding
thoughts come into your mind, don't worry, just return to focussing on your
breathing again.
Notice your breathing now.
Each time you breathe out say "relax" silently to yourself.
(NOTE TO COUNSELLOR: Observe the client's body, and notice his breathing.
When he breathes out each time say the word "relax" quietly. Do this a few
times so that the client remembers to do it himself.)
Notice your body. If any parts of it are uncomfortable, stretch or move so that
you are more comfortable.
Focus on your breathing.
When you are ready, I will ask you, as you breathe in, to take a slow deep
breath and as you do this to clench your toes tightly and tighten up the
muscles in your feet.
(COUNSELLOR: Choose the time)
Breathe in deeply and tighten up the muscles in your feet.
Hold your breath and keep the muscles in your feet tight for a second or two.
Breathe out heavily and release the tension in your feet.
Continue breathing naturally and say "relax" to yourself each time you breathe
out.
(Wait for a while as the client continues to breathe naturally.)
Now tense your thigh and calf muscles as you breathe in deeply.
Hold your breath and keep your muscles tense.
Relax as you breathe out.
Breathe naturally and feel relaxed.
(Pause a while.)
Tense the muscles in your buttocks as you breathe in deeply.
Hold your breath and keep your muscles tensed.
Now breathe out and relax.
Breathe naturally and notice a feeling of relaxation flowing up your body from
your feet to your buttocks.
(Pause a while.)
Tense the muscles in your stomach as you breathe in deeply.
Hold your breath.
Relax.

Notice your breathing.
(Pause a while.)
Clench your fists as you breathe in.
Hold.
Relax.
(Pause a while.)
Now tense the muscles in your arms and stretch your fingers out as you breathe in.
Hold.
Relax.
Notice a relaxed feeling flow up from your feet through your calves, thighs, stomach, hands, arms and chest.
Let your body sink into the floor and feel supported by the floor.
Breathe naturally.
(Pause.)
Tighten your shoulder and neck muscles as you breathe in.
Hold.
Relax.
(Pause.)
Clench your teeth, screw up your face, close your eyes tightly, and feel your scalp tighten as you breathe in.
Hold.
Relax.
(Pause.)
Breathe naturally and notice the relaxed feeling moving up and encompassing your whole body.
Be aware of your breathing. Each time you breathe out feel yourself becoming more relaxed.
(Long pause.)
Soon it will be time to start getting in touch with your surroundings again. When you do this, allow yourself to feel good, to be wide awake and alert.
(Pause.)
Notice the floor. Move your fingers and feel it.
Wriggle slightly and when you are ready open your eyes.
Lie where you are and look around. Allow yourself to take in what you see, to feel good, and to be awake and alert.
When you are ready, roll over sideways and support yourself with one arm in a half-sitting position.
Sit up when the time is right for you.

The above relaxation exercise can be taught to a client in a counselling session, and he can then be encouraged to practise it regularly in his own time. However, warn your client about the dangers of being too relaxed. It is not advisable, for example, to drive a car in a very relaxed state. A certain amount of tension is useful so that the client's reactions to danger are fast. Therefore, do not go through the relaxation exercise with your client immediately before he is due to drive away!

Once a client has learnt to relax by muscle tensing and relaxing he will find it easier to relax when standing up and in a tense situation. Teach him to take a few deep breaths and each time he breathes in to tighten up his muscles and then relax as he breathes out. With practice he will probably find that he will be able to let himself relax as he breathes out naturally.

LEARNING SUMMARY

- Use a quiet, slow, monotonous tone of voice when teaching relaxation.

- Relaxation exercises can be threatening for some people.

- Make sure that the client understands that the exercise can be discontinued whenever he likes.

- Observe the client's body so that your instructions are correctly timed.

- Warn your client of the danger of being too relaxed when attention is required.

FURTHER READING

Madders, J., *Stress and Relaxation: Self-Help Techniques for Everyone*. London: Optim, 1993

Payne, R., *Relaxation Techniques: a Practical Handbook for Health Care Professionals*. Edinburgh, New York: Churchill Livingstone, 1995

Walker, C. E., *Learn to Relax: Proven Techniques for Reducing Stress, Tension and Anxiety for Peak Performance*. New York: Berkeley, 1991

Wilson, P., *Instant Calm: Over 100 Successful Techniques for Relaxing Mind and Body*. Ringwood: Penguin Australia, 1995

Part VI

The counsellor's own needs

34 Looking after yourself

A counsellor's own well-being is of paramount importance, because counsellors who are not feeling good are unlikely to be fully effective. Counselling can be draining, so counsellors need support; otherwise they are likely to find themselves emotionally depleted. If they are to feel good they must resolve their own personal issues satisfactorily while receiving the support they need. This can be done as described previously, through regular supervision from an experienced counsellor.

In recent years, it has become clear that all counsellors at times experience what is known as "burnout". Burnout is disabling, but if it is recognised in its early stages, then it is comparatively easy to take remedial action. Even experienced counsellors fail at times to recognise the onset of burnout and try to convince themselves that the symptoms they are experiencing are due to some other cause. It is difficult for many counsellors to admit to themselves, let alone to others, that they are burning out, even though there is now general acceptance that burnout is a common problem. The first step in dealing with burnout is to be aware of the symptoms.

Burnout symptoms

There is a wide range of symptoms that come under the general heading of burnout. These symptoms give an indication that the counsellor is becoming drained emotionally by the counselling work and is wanting to draw back. Counsellors may experience a feeling of being totally overworked and of having no control over their workload. They may perceive themselves as swimming against the tide and unable to keep their heads above water. This leads to feelings of hopelessness and helplessness.

PHYSICAL AND EMOTIONAL SYMPTOMS
Counsellors experiencing burnout are usually tired physically, emotionally and mentally. They start to feel that they can't face meeting another client. Typically, a counsellor may say to himself during a counselling session: "I really can't bear to be here. I wish the client would just go away." He may experience being

physically debilitated and find it hard to drag himself to work. His enthusiasm has evaporated and he may have physical symptoms such as headaches, stomach-aches, skin disorders, high blood pressure or back and neck pains. His susceptibility to viruses and other infections is increased.

NEGATIVE ATTITUDES

The burnt-out counsellor may develop strong negative attitudes towards clients. He may develop a cynical attitude to his clients and blame them for creating their own problems. He may even start to treat his clients in an impersonal way, as though they were objects and not human beings. Consequently, the counselling relationship will suffer and counselling becomes a chore, rather than an interesting, challenging and creative activity. The counsellor clearly no longer finds satisfaction in his work. Negative attitudes may also be experienced towards fellow workers, supervisors, other staff and the employing organisation.

DISILLUSIONMENT

Disillusionment with the counselling process is a major burnout symptom. Counsellors start to question the value of their work and begin to wonder if what they are doing is worthwhile. A burnt-out counsellor will often be unable to see any evidence of success in his work. He feels frustrated by his inability to bring about change in his clients and is dissatisfied with his job, believing that it involves giving and getting nothing in return. This leads to feelings of failure and low self-esteem. The demands of clients become too great and the counsellor may just want to withdraw from the helping situation. In the advanced stages of burnout, the counsellor starts taking days off sick, and may start frantically looking for a new job so that he can resign.

PERSONAL CONSEQUENCES

One of the sad consequences of burnout is that it is likely to affect the counsellor's personal life. As his self-esteem diminishes, his personal relationships may be put in jeopardy, and other people may become targets for feelings of anger, frustration, helplessness and hopelessness.

A major cause of burnout

What is the primary cause of burnout? Well, we can't be certain, and in any case all counsellors are different, but it seems likely that a major cause of burnout is the stress of the interpersonal counselling relationship. This is an unbalanced relationship, with the counsellor doing most of the giving and the client doing most of the receiving.

In the early chapters of this book, heavy emphasis was put on establishing an empathic relationship, and on the need to join with the client. It is essential that, as a counsellor, you learn to do this effectively, because *empathy* is one of the essential ingredients of successful counselling. However, *being empathic can be hazardous to a counsellor's health!* That is, unless proper precautions are taken.

Clients are often in a highly emotional state, and if a counsellor listens with empathy and effectively joins with an emotional client, then the counsellor himself is likely to be infected by the client's emotional state. Emotions, like viruses, are catching, which is probably why people who aren't counsellors try to calm their friends down when they are emotional. After all, who wants to be emotionally distressed? In contrast to most friends, counsellors encourage people to experience and express their emotions fully. Empathic counsellors are certain to experience, at some level, emotions similar to those of their clients. Clearly, no counsellor can afford to be emotionally distressed for a significant part of his working day, because to allow this to happen would be certain to result in burnout. Counsellors who are working mainly with emotionally disturbed clients are therefore very much at risk and need to take special precautions to avoid burnout.

PROTECTING YOURSELF

With experience, you will learn how to walk beside a client with empathy and also how to protect yourself from the excesses of emotional pain by at times moving back for a while, grounding yourself, and then joining more fully with the client again. Certainly, if you are to protect yourself from burnout, you will need to learn how to do this. I will describe the technique I use for myself, and then you will need to experiment for yourself, to find out what works best for you.

In a counselling session, when I notice that I am starting to experience a client's emotional pain *excessively*, I immediately set about grounding myself. This grounding process takes only a second or two to happen, but will take longer to describe.

USING AN IMAGINARY SPACE-BUBBLE

I imagine myself to be encapsulated by a plastic space-bubble which separates me from outside emotions, but enables me to observe them, and allows me to respond to them appropriately. I then slow down my breathing, and relax my body, so that my troubled emotional state is replaced by tranquillity. In my imagination, I float, in the space-bubble, upwards and backwards to a position several metres behind and above my body. It is as though the part of me in the bubble is able to observe both the client and the physical me, which is still sitting in my counselling chair. I am still able to concentrate fully, but am more detached and less involved. In this position, I can make sensible decisions with regard to the counselling process. However, I can in a split second travel back in my imagination to my counselling chair, to give empathic attention and empathic responses to the client. Clearly I have a powerful imagination, and have trained myself to relax quickly, when necessary. You will need to experiment for yourself, to devise an effective way in which you can protect yourself from emotional damage due to excessive exposure to client pain.

Despite the above discussion, there will inevitably be times when, as a counsellor, you *are* affected by the emotional traumas of your clients. Personally, I don't think that it is helpful to let a client know that I have been emotionally affected by what he has told me. Most clients are caring people who do not like to upset others. Consequently, if a client thinks that I have been emotionally disturbed by what I have heard, then he may be less likely to tell me about other disturbing information. Counsellors therefore need to control the expression of their own emotions appropriately, so that the clients feel able to talk freely.

RECHARGING

If you are left in an emotionally disturbed state after a counselling session, talk to your supervisor about your feelings as soon as possible. Remember; the counselling relationship is substantially a one-way relationship, in which the counsellor is the giver and the client is the taker. Such a relationship will inevitably drain the counsellor of emotional energy. Clearly, unless a counsellor recharges himself, he will experience the symptoms of burnout as he becomes drained.

Other factors which lead to burnout

THE DANGERS OF OVER-INVOLVEMENT

It is important to be aware of the dangers of over-involvement with clients and their issues. We all have different personalities and differing capabilities for coping with emotionally stressful situations. Some counsellors get over-involved with their clients and take their client's problems home with them, whereas other people are more philosophical and are less affected by their counselling work. I have trained myself so that when I leave my place of work, I will allow myself to think about client material only until I reach a particular set of traffic lights. Once I have passed these lights, I give myself the option of going back to my place of work to think about clients, or of forgetting them and continuing my journey. I invariably continue my journey.

SUICIDAL CLIENTS

Experienced counsellors who deal with suicidal or violent clients have an extremely stressful time and are particularly prone to burnout. A counsellor who has a high case-load of suicidal clients has little option but to accept that, even with the use of properly accountable practices, eventually one of his clients may succeed in killing himself. This knowledge creates anxiety in the counsellor and increases the likelihood of burnout. Remember that it is not appropriate to blame yourself for what you are unable to prevent. Protect yourself, as a new counsellor, by ensuring that such clients are referred for appropriate professional help.

ISOLATION

Being isolated and working alone puts a counsellor at increased risk of burnout, because of a lack of peer support during the working day. After all, if I'm being drained of my energy, I need to be able to get some back by interacting with others who can meet with me in more equal two-way relationships.

PERSONAL STRESS

A stressful personal life may make a counsellor more susceptible to burnout because of diminished emotional resources.

Combating burnout

As stated before, many counsellors are afraid to admit to themselves, let alone to other people, that they are starting to experience burnout symptoms, because they feel that it would be an admission of failure. This is understandable for many reasons. Firstly, we have all learnt from childhood to appear to be strong enough to cope with our load whatever that may be. That learning is based on a myth that human beings are inexhaustible, which is obviously not true. Secondly, new counsellors invariably start counselling with very high ideals and unrealistically high expectations of what they will be able to achieve.

HAVING REALISTIC EXPECTATIONS

My own experience as a counsellor is that usually the outcomes of counselling interventions give me satisfaction. However, there are times when a client does not seem to be helped by the counselling process and when this does happen, it would be easy for me to become disillusioned. At times like this I remind myself of the need for me to look at the overall picture. Outcomes with clients are often different from what the counsellor would prefer, and it is therefore necessary to have realistic expectations in order to avoid disillusionment. The idealism of the new counsellor can easily be eroded and lead to later dissatisfaction if unrealistic expectations are not fulfilled.

Giving with no expectation of return, caring for people unconditionally, and being dedicated to counselling work are all attitudes that are implicitly absorbed as part of most counsellor training programs. These attitudes conflict strongly with feelings that may be experienced during burnout. It is therefore not surprising that counsellors find it difficult to own burnout feelings.

ACCEPTING THAT BURNOUT IS NORMAL

It is strongly recommended that counsellor training programs always include education for trainee counsellors about the inevitability of burnout occurring, at times, even in the most dedicated counsellor. If counsellors realise that burnout feelings do occur in normal, competent, capable and caring counsellors, then they will be able to start accepting their own burnout feelings and to share those feelings with their peers and other professionals.

Burnout comes in cycles and it is helpful to expect these cycles to occur. It is healthy to say: "Ah-ha, I'm starting to recognise some of the symptoms of burnout." By making that simple statement, a counsellor is able to admit truthfully what is happening and is then empowered to take the necessary action to deal with the problem.

Most counsellors start their job with some feelings of nervousness, but very soon this is followed by enthusiasm and excitement. However, it doesn't take long for other feelings to set in. These may be feelings of stagnation and apathy, or even of frustration and annoyance. In other words, the counsellor's initial enthusiasm and excitement will, from time to time, be replaced by feelings associated with burnout. In the same way, by using sensible burnout management techniques, the initial enthusiasm about counselling can be re-experienced.

ACTIVELY DEALING WITH BURNOUT

Quite often people look for a new job or resign as a result of burnout. That is one way of dealing with it, but it is not necessary to do that if you recognise the symptoms early enough and do something positive to deal with them. Experiencing burnout is not a disaster if it is recognised and dealt with effectively. For a counsellor, dealing with burnout can be compared to a car owner servicing a car. The car needs to be serviced regularly or the car will not function well. Similarly, as a counsellor take steps to continually look after your own needs. If you become aware of burnout feelings, take the appropriate action to recharge yourself, to regain your enthusiasm and the excitement you experienced at the beginning of your counselling career. This can be done time and again, so you can work as a counsellor for a lifetime if you choose by recharging yourself and starting afresh from time to time.

Here are some suggestions for dealing with burnout.

1. Recognise and own the symptoms.
2. Talk with someone about your feelings.
3. Re-schedule your work.
4. Cut down on your workload.
5. Take a holiday.
6. Use relaxation or meditation.
7. Use positive self-talk.
8. Lower your expectations of yourself.
9. Lower your expectations of your clients.
10. Lower your expectations of your peers.
11. Lower your expectations of your employer.
12. Allow yourself to enjoy life and have a sense of humour.
13. Use thought-stopping to stop worrying about clients when not at work.
14. Use your religious or other belief system for support.
15. Care for yourself as a person by doing some nice things for yourself.

Some of these ideas will now be discussed further. First, it is interesting to note that simply admitting that you are experiencing burnout will affect your behaviour and enable you to cope better. Talking with your supervisor or someone else may also be helpful, as by doing this you may more easily be able to clarify your options with regard to suitable methods of intervention.

It can be helpful to re-schedule your work so that you have a feeling of being in control. You may need to be assertive with your boss if he doesn't understand your need for a reduced workload. Reducing your workload may not be sufficient initially, and you may need to take a few days off, to have a holiday, or to take some days off sick. Help yourself to feel more relaxed, more in control and fitter. Build into your lifestyle proper times for rest, recreation, exercise, light-hearted relief and relaxation. Doing relaxation exercises or meditating can be helpful. Use positive self-talk to replace negative self-statements and challenge the negative self-statements you make about others. This involves changing your expectations of yourself, your clients and your peers.

A useful way to deal with burnout is to take a less serious view of life, to allow yourself to have a sense of humour, and to be less intense in your work. Be carefree and have fun. Most important, do not take client problems home. If you do catch yourself doing this, practise thought-stopping. The first step in thought-stopping is to recognise that you are thinking about client problems when you should be relaxing. Then recognise your choice, to continue thinking about these problems or to focus your attention on something in your present environment. This may involve doing something physical or it may involve concentrating on something specific such as listening to music. Focus all your energy and attention on the here and now to block out the intruding thoughts. Sometimes you may find that the intruding thoughts recur and that you catch yourself saying: "If I don't think about this client problem now, then I will never deal with it and that will be bad for the client." If such a thought comes into your mind, then fix a time at your place of work when you will deal with that issue, and say to yourself: "OK, at 10 o'clock tomorrow morning, I will devote half an hour to thinking about that problem, but right now I will get on with doing and thinking about things that are pleasant for me."

Many counsellors find strength in their religious beliefs and gain through prayer and meditation. They find that by doing this they receive an inner strength that enables them to be more effective in their work. Similarly, people with other philosophical belief systems can use their philosophy of life as an aid in combating burnout.

If you care for yourself, and take appropriate action to attend to your own needs by leading a less pressured and more balanced life, then your burnout symptoms are likely fade and you will be able to regain your energy and enthusiasm. However, if you are like most counsellors, you will have an ongoing struggle with burnout which will come and go. There will always be times when you will give too much of yourself, and then need to redress the balance so that your own needs for recharging are adequately met.

Gaining satisfaction from counselling

If you are pro-active in caring for yourself then you will be more able to care for others. You will be likely to get satisfaction from counselling and to enjoy being a counsellor. I hope that you, the reader, will gain as much personal fulfilment from counselling as I have. I wish you all the best for your work.

LEARNING SUMMARY

- All counsellors need regular supervision because:

  - counselling can be emotionally draining for the counsellor

  - counsellors need a way to resolve their own issues and without supervision they are more likely to burn out.

- Burnout includes the following symptoms:

  - feelings of disillusionment, being emotionally and physically drained, somatic symptoms, and negative attitudes to clients.

- Burnout comes in cycles and with self-awareness and adequate supervision recharging can occur.

- Methods for dealing with burnout include:

  - recognising the symptoms and talking with someone about them;

  - changing your workload or schedule;

  - taking a break;

  - using relaxation, meditation, or positive self-talk;

  - lowering your expectations;

  - taking life less seriously and having a sense of humour;

  - using thought-stopping; and

  - using your religious or other belief system for support.

FURTHER READING

Carter, R., *Helping Yourself Help Others: the Caregivers Handbook*. New York: Times Books, 1994

Grosh, W. N. and Olsen, D. C., "Prevention: Avoiding Burnout". In Sussman, M. B. (ed.), *A Perilous Calling: the Hazards of Psychotherapy Practice*. New York: Wiley, 1995

Schaufeli, W. B., Maslach, C. and Marek, T. (eds), *Professional Burnout: Recent Developments in Theory and Research*. Washington: Taylor & Francis, 1993

Index